THE PROBLEM OF CATHOLICISM

THE LIBRARY OF HISTORY AND DOCTRINE

The aim of this international Library is to enable scholars to answer questions about the development of the Christian tradition which are important for an understanding of Christianity today

THE PROBLEM OF
CATHOLICISM

VITTORIO SUBILIA

TRANSLATED BY
REGINALD KISSACK

Philadelphia
The Westminster Press

To the
Faculty of Protestant Theology, Paris
in token of gratitude
for the conferment of their Doctorate,
Honoris Causa

© SCM Press Ltd 1964
Translated from the Italian
Il Problema del Cattolicesimo
(Libreria Editrice Claudiana, Turin, 1962)

Library of Congress Catalog Card No. 64-12392

PRINTED IN GREAT BRITAIN
Published by The Westminster Press Philadelphia, Pennsylvania 19107

CONTENTS

ITALIAN PUBLISHER'S NOTE

WHETHER it be in the relations between states or groupings of states, between races or between cultures, one of the ideas that has found the deepest response in our age is that of encounter, of dialogue, of peaceable and constructive contact. Is this merely a psychological reaction to the weariness and tension left by two world wars, so close to each other in time, and to the rationale of fear of what could be the consequences for all humanity of the advent of new technical power? Or are we to trace this anxious universalism to sources more profound and less contingent? It is the symptom of an urge to rectify age-long trends that have made for division, and to carry humanity to the creation of a new unity that transcends all precedents in history?

Among the Christian Churches no external motive forces have inspired movements to unity, as witnesses the fact that ecumenism has preceded in point of time these other general movements of the spirit, even if it is equally true that the Ecumenical Movement travels in a track parallel to that of the spirit of the age, and that this both shapes its orbit and gives it momentum. In this bid for ecumenism the fundamental issue is the disagreement between Catholic and Protestant, and up to now this has never been squarely confronted.

Our book is offered as an attempt to understand the religious and theological bases of this disaccord, and to trace out at least faintly their consequences for civilization. It is written by a scholar who has lived intimately with all the intense feelings of ecumenism, yet, in the present climate of reconciliation and hope, it may seem to strike a discordant note. It would however be a grave error of judgment to write it off as a voice from an age of inter-Christian relationships now past and gone. If its language is sometimes severe, let the reader not put this down to any animosity of polemic or to any smug sense of confessional complacency, but rather to the anguish—one could even say the impatience—that the thoughts of faithfulness and of unity create in those who realize how difficult, how impossible, it is for Christians to fulfil their calling in human history.

ENGLISH TRANSLATOR'S NOTE

OF THE many possible positions for viewing Roman Catholicism, that of the Italian Protestant must be unique, and one point of interest about this book is that it is the most thorough study which has yet come from the Waldensian community in Italy. This particular Protestant is a theologian honoured by doctorates in many countries. He is Dean of the *Facolta Teologica Valdese* of Rome, which stands a bare half-mile from the Vatican and is a recognized point of contact for Roman Catholic scholars who seek authentic knowledge of Protestantism. Professor Subilia's study of the present phase of Roman Catholicism possesses an intrinsic value which is self-evident. Here is the authority of a sensitive non-Catholic Christian writing of a situation in which he is historically involved, and of a scholar uniquely fitted to record, analyse and document it from the day-to-day writings of speeches of the Catholic protagonists. The pearls of insight and wisdom (if one may so put it) that accumulate around the conscience of the Reformed scholar, included like a grain of sand inside the oyster of Catholic Rome, are likely indeed to be of great price.

In his own words, Professor Subilia offers the book 'as an attempt to understand the religious and theological bases of the Catholic-Protestant disaccord, and to trace out (at least faintly) their consequences for civilization'.

The first chapter deals with Rome's present, and seemingly novel, ecumenical outlook, and traces the emergence of this new mood in the speeches and writings of Pope John XXIII and the Curia. He analyses very closely the psychology of this new 'integrationist' (as opposed to the old 'integrist') line. Next, he sets the ideas of that small band of *avant garde* Catholic thinkers (Küng, Congar, Daniélou, etc.) which underlie the new look at Rome in the context of Catholic action and dogma, as it has shown itself developing in history. He reviews the issues under the heads which he believes will prove to be the significant lines of Roman Catholic thought: dogma and its possibilities of evolution, the Scriptural foundation of the Faith, the doctrine of Justification, Mariology,

the reassessment of the place of Episcopacy, the Laity and the extent
to which the Roman Church is capable of reform.

This last point has the third chapter to itself, and in it the author
minutely examines the points in its structure where Rome seems to
be considering change. A strong body in Roman Catholicism today
admits that its 'Western' overweight, its psychological attitude to
non-Catholics, its use of Latin, and its straitjacket of Thomist
concepts, need revision. In 1963 two widely noticed books by able
American journalists, Xavier Rynne and Robert Kaiser, have
informed the public about this spirit of self-criticism, so prominent
in the first session of the Second Vatican Council. But Dr Subilia
finds no evidence of any operation being contemplated that might
cut deep enough to alter Catholicism's self-understanding. The
most adventurous Roman Catholic ecumenists deliberately stop
short of this, eschewing what they regard as 'compromise in
dogma'. This is indeed the real problem of Catholicism, and in
chapters 4 and 5 Professor Subilia proceeds to analyse the issues.
He traces the growth of the idea of Catholicism back through
Augustine to the margins of the New Testament. Then he applies a
shrewd ecclesiological analysis to this faulty self-understanding
as it works out in the Roman Church's claims to possess *in toto* the
Christly offices of Prophet, Priest and King. The author casts a no
less devastating look at contemporary Protestantism, and finishes
with a challenge to both Catholic and Protestant alike. Only an overpowering sense of God in his Triune fulness, and an ecclesiology
that reflects this faithfully and completely, can resolve what is a
problem for both Catholic and Protestant.

Professor Subilia's thesis is, in his own words, this: 'Every
ecclesiology based on the assumption that the Church has been once
and for all made over by God to man takes account only of the
Christological element in the Godhead. An ecclesiology based on so
one-sided a theology gives rise to the institutional type of Church,
with a disproportionate stress on the element of succession as the
ground of the divine right of hierarchy and teaching, of priesthood
and sacrament. Then the Church conceives of herself as an extension of the Incarnation, and elevates herself into an institution where
truth is deposited, outside of which there is no salvation. She loses
her sense of reference to God, the Lord of election, who, though he
communicates himself, never annuls his mystery. Though he
humbles himself he never abdicates from being the Most High, and

though he takes the form of an obedient servant, he never gives up his sovereignty, nor suspends his constant command.'

The work was first published in Italian on the eve of the Second Vatican Council, with a note by the Italian publisher which is retained in this translation. It was hailed by Catholic reviewers as being one of the most realistic studies of the subject from a Protestant pen, and a much needed counterweight to over-facile and sentimental Protestant ecumenism. The author was an observer at the first session of the Council, and on reading the proofs of this English translation said that nothing had yet happened to make him want to change a word. The English translation, which I made while Methodist Minister in Rome, is now sent out with the prayer that it may be useful in the Catholic–Protestant dialogue in the Pontificate of Pope Paul VI.

REGINALD KISSACK

I

Roman Catholicism and Ecumenism

1. *New Attitudes in Roman Catholicism*[1]

AT the core of our study is the problem put in a nutshell by a great English Modernist: 'We can never be sure exactly what Catholicism is.'[2] For that matter the statement has its other side, for Catholics feel like confusion in assessing Protestantism and its contradictory aspects. However, the fact remains that in its relations with other Confessions the Catholicism of today appears different from that of yesterday, quite apart from variations within itself at the same time. There is no need to go back to the days when men were condemned for heresy; it is enough to recall the Encyclicals *'Satis Cognitum'* of Leo XIII, 1896,[3] *'Mortalium Animos'* of Pius XI, 1928,[4] *'Mystici Corporis'* of Pius XII, 1943;[5] the *Monitum 'Cum Compertum'*, 1948,[6] and even the *Instructio 'Ecclesia Catholica'*, 1950,[7] all documents which take the line of a most uninviting 'integrism',[8] demanding

[1] In this book 'Catholicism' means the over-all ensemble of spirit, outlook, doctrine and attitude, which has shaped itself and expressed itself through the centuries in the Roman Catholic Church, and has come to be its distinguishing characteristic.

[2] G. Tyrrell, *Through Scylla and Charybdis*, 1907, cited by W. von Loewenich—*Der moderne Katholizismus—Erscheinung und Probleme*, Witten 1956², p. 408.

[3] *Acta S. Sedis* XXVIII, 1896, pp. 710f.

[4] *Acta Apostolicae Sedis* XX, 1928, pp. 5–16.

[5] *AAS* XXXV, 1943, pp. 217f.   [6] *AAS* XL, 1948, p. 257.

[7] *AAS* XLII, 1950, pp. 142–7. Cf. V. Subilia 'Una Istruzione della Suprema Sacra Congregazione del Sant'Offizio all'Episcopato di tutto il mondo sul "Movimento Ecumenico",' *Protestantesimo* V (1950), pp. 66ff.; G. Baum, *L'unité chrétienne d'après la doctrine des Papes de Leon XIII à Pie XII*, Paris 1961.

[8] We can trace two attitudes that are taken today in modern Catholicism on the question of Church Unity and relations with non-Catholic Christians. Both positions are essentially Catholic at bottom, but they differ in procedure. The first goes by the name of *Integrism*, the second is known as the process of *Integration*.

By *Integrism* is meant a pure and simple submission to the claims of Roman authority, the return of the prodigal sons to the father's house. This position regards the problems felt by Orthodox and Protestant as just a nostalgia for Rome, involving no need of any lessening on Rome's part of her traditional claims, to which sooner or later the non-Catholics are bound to pay attention. Such an attitude today is the form assumed by an almost chronic miscalculation of theology and psychology.

By *Integration* is meant a process of taking the gospel truths professed by non-Catholics and inserting them into the framework of Catholic doctrine and the Catholic hierarchical system and, so substituting for the formula of Return that of Encounter.

submission pure and simple as the condition of unity. If we set against these some—but not all!—of the utterances of John XXIII,[1] in which the integrist thesis *seems* replaced by an 'integrationist' one, in which the intention *seems* to be and to do precisely what the 1950 *Instructio* solemnly forbade (because of the perils of 'Indifferentism'), viz., to add the truths held by non-Catholics to those formulated in Catholic dogma, 'silently' to overlook controversial points of view, to concentrate on the things which unite, and to keep quiet on those which divide;[2] utterances, that is, in which the anti- or pre-ecumenical formula of 'Return' *seems* to be replaced by that of Encounter —one might then indeed have the impression of a radical change of attitude in Roman Catholicism. Such a view seems to be confirmed by a careful study of one specific point in the Pontiff's utterances. On several occasions, and in several ways, John XXIII has expressed the idea that the Council is first and foremost a domestic matter for the Catholic Church, in that its work 'is essentially all designed to bring again to the face of the Church of Jesus Christ, that splendour that was etched there at its birth in its simplest and purest lines, and to render it once more what its Divine Founder made it'. It should be a 'time to gather about the Church in a study of love, to rediscover the characteristics of her age of youth and vigour, and to set them together once more'.[3] This internal task has been set forth in language that seemed to premise the possibility of subsequent contacts with non-Catholics,[4] as if the common Father's house was being redecorated and remodelled, so as to be ready and fit to accommodate the new tenants who were to live there alongside the original ones. Even making all allowances for the fresh and homely savour of good fellowship that was characteristic of the temperament and language of John XXIII, we may go so far as to say that such a

---

[1] Cf. *Acta et documenta Concilio Oecumenico Vaticano II apparando*, Series I (Antepraeparatoria), vol. I—*Acta S. P. Joannis XXIII* (Vatican City, 1960).

[2] Beside the *Instructio*, cf. the Encyclical of Pius XII, '*Orientalis Ecclesia*' : 'The return of the erring children to a sincere and proper unity in Christ which we so long for, is not furthered by the point of view that a sufficient basis of faith is found just in those articles of doctrine in which all or the majority of the communities that glory in the name of Christian find themselves in agreement. Better that other theory, which without excepting any or lessening any accepts all revealed truths in their entirety' (*AAS* XXXVI 1944, (p. 134).

[3] Address 'In Petriana Basilica habita, post Sacram sollemnem Liturgiam, Byzantinoslavico ritu peractam', 13 Nov., 1960 (*AAS* LII, 1960, p. 960).

[4] Address 'Habita in Petriana Basilica ad consilia coetusque Concilio Vaticano II apparando', 14 Nov., 1960 (*AAS* LII, 1960, pp. 1004ff., esp. pp. 1009ff.). The context, and in particular, the phraseology of the Italian text published (*L'Osservatore Romano*, 14–5 Nov., 1960) are in favour of the interpretation put on it by various commentators, as given here.

pronouncement *seems* to mean that the supreme *magisterium* of the Catholic Church has accepted the Protestant thesis of Reform as a Precondition of Unity.

But we can detect divergences of attitudes, not just between the Catholicism of yesterday and that of today, but also inside the Catholicism of today. There is a manifest tension, which can only strike an outsider as irreconcilable. For example, the Dutch Archbishop Alfrink, subsequently made Cardinal, writes on the impossible absurdity of the formula of Return, and the need of a new style of interconfessional language;[1] and Hans Küng, a Swiss Theologian and Professor of the Catholic Theological Faculty of Tübingen, states in a book which carries forewords by two Cardinals, 'It is impossible to speak of a Return only for the others, as if *we* had no responsibility for separation, as if *we* had no resulting reparations to make, as if *we* had no duty to go and meet the others, as if the others had nothing to offer us, they who are our brothers, they who love Christ their Lord!... Such behaviour is too presumptuous and Pharisaical, even if we add prayer to it.'[2] On the other hand, Father Luigi Ciappi, Master of the Sacred Apostolic Palace, states that the Catholic Church 'has everything to give, and nothing to receive', 'the deposit of divine truth and the means of sanctification repose, in their entirety, alone in her'; he affirms that it is therefore impossible 'to pray and work effectively for Christian Unity, with any other goal except the reunion of the separated brethren with their old-time companions of faith, indeed, the return to Mother Church of her estranged sons'.[3] Similarly Father Marco Giraudo, O.P. has said: 'Put in crude terms, there will only be reunion if the Protestants give up their doctrines and accept those of the Catholic Church in their entirety.'[4] There is a tension, or even a direct contradiction, of belief between the attitude of the lofty prayer of the Abbé Couturier (so favoured in ecumenical circles) that return into unity

---

[1] Cf.: V. Subilia, 'Nomine cardinalizie', *Protestantesimo* 15 (1960), pp. 102ff.; *EPS*, 11 Dec., 1959; *Irénikon* 33 (1960), p. 201.

[2] H. Küng, *Konzil und Wiedervereinigung, Erneuerung als Ruf in die Einheit*, Freiburg 1960 [ET by Cecily Hastings, *The Council and Reunion*, London 1961, of 1961³, pp. 135, 141; American edition—*The Council, reform and reunion*, New York 1962].

[3] Fr L. Ciappi, O.P., 'La Chiesa Cattolica, perenne motivo di credibilità', *L'Osservatore Romano*, 29–30 May, 1961. *EPS*, 9 June, 1961 judges the article as giving a 'very different point of view', on the issues of Church Unity, from that of Catholic writers who favour ecumenical contact. On the other hand, *Unitas* XVI (1961), p. 269, calls the article 'an authentic description' of the attitude and doctrine of the Church in regard to the Separated Brethren.

[4] Fr M. Giraudo, O.P., 'Il Concilio e i Protestanti', in *Prospettive del Concilio Ecumenico—Quaderno 21—: Sacra Doctrina* VI (1961) N.S., p. 83.

be accomplished how and when God will wish, and the inflexible pronouncement of Father Charles Boyer, S.J., to the effect that such a formula is dangerous and unacceptable to the Catholic Church, in so far as the Catholic has precise knowledge of how unity will come about, namely, through the return of the separated churches to the Church of Rome, and their submission to its hierarchy.[1] Even in the matter of what the Pope himself has said, there are signs of the same dissidence. One might mention that famous sentence (of which the authenticity cannot be proved), said to have been pronounced by John XXIII on 29th Jan., 1959 to the parish priests of Rome, which seemed to echo a new attitude on the Catholic part to the Reformation: 'We are not going to put history on trial, and try to establish who is right and who wrong. Responsibility is divided. We are going to say: Let us reunite; let us end discussion.'[2] But alongside disputed statements of this sort, which, in the words of two Catholic bishops of the Greek rite, have not had the honour of commending themselves in certain bureaucratic circles in the Vatican, who have hastily whittled them down or explained them away,[3] John XXIII did one or two things which can only appear frankly disconcerting in an ecumenical context, and give rise to the reflection that any optimism used in interpreting his remarks about the Council must be kept within strict limits. For instance, having spoken of a *rapprochement* of doctrinal positions,[4] which a non-Catholic mind instinctively takes to mean a reciprocal process, he then put the labours of the Council under the protection of Mary the Immaculate, Queen of the Church and Mother of Unity,[5] and under the patronage of St

[1] C. Boyer, S. J., 'Le intenzioni della Settimana dell'unità', *Unitas* XV (1960), pp. 97f.; 'Tendenze attuali nell'ecumenismo cattolico', *Unitas* XVI (1961), pp. 202f., 255. Cf. (same author), 'Il prossimo Concilio Ecumenico', *Unitas* XV (1960), p. 8; *Unus Pastor—per la riunione alla Chiesa di Roma dei cristiani separati*, Rome 1951; *Unità cristiana e movimento ecumenico*, Rome 1955, etc. Mons. F. Charrier, bishop of Lausanne, Geneva, Fribourg, takes a similar line in a letter to parish priests, published in the Bulletin of the Diocese, July 1958.

[2] The statement reported in the Catholic newspaper *La Croix*, 31 Jan., 1959, has not been retained in the official text of *Acta et documenta*, Series I, vol. I, pp. 8f. Cf. P. Petit, 'Avant le deuxième Concile du Vatican', *Revue de Théologie et de Philosophie*, 1961, p. 174.

[3] S. B. Maximus IV, Patriarch of Antioch and of all the East, of Alexandria and Jerusalem, S. E. Zoghby, Greek Catholic Patriarchal Vicar General. Cf. P. Petit, *art. cit.*, p. 175 and *Irénikon* 33 (1960), p. 198f.

[4] Letter to the clergy of Venice: *AAS* LI, 1959, p. 380.

[5] Radio Announcement, 27 April, 1959: *AAS* LI, 1959, p. 314; Encyclical '*Ad Petri Cathedram*', 29 June, 1959, published *L'Osservatore Romano*, 3 July, 1959, cf. *AAS* LI (1959), pp. 497f.; Apostolic Letter *Motu proprio 'Maiora in dies'*, 8 Dec., 1959: *AAS* LII (1960), p. 26; speech delivered, 8 Dec., 1960, on the Feast of the Immaculate Conception at the Liberian Basilica of Sta Maria Maggiore: *L'Osservatore Romano*, 9–10 Dec., 1960. Fr S. Butler in an article in *L'Osservatore Romano*, 17 Jan., 1962 ('Il pensiero di P. Paolo

Joseph,[1] he gave his approval and authority for reciting the Rosary for the Council,[2] and proclaimed as Doctor of the Universal Church, Lorenzo of Brindisium (died 1619), one of the most biassed and bigotted anti-Lutheran polemicists of the seventeenth century.[3] Such facts should remind those Protestants who are more sentimental than analytical that the Pope always remained a Catholic. It can also be noticed that Papal utterances were progressively more explicit; they moved from the generalizations of the earliest announcements, which in the eyes of the uninitiated could, and did, lend themselves to arbitrary and groundlessly optimistic interpretations, to the very precise terms in which were couched the definite summons, first of the Preparatory Commissions, and finally of the Council itself.

One factor in the explanation of these contrasts turns on the place of origin of the speakers, depending on whether they came from Latin lands where Protestantism is simply the object of prejudice or misrepresentation (as regards its faith, theology, culture, churchmanship, ethics, politics or sociology), or from countries where Catholics are a small minority, and so always familiar with the Protestant point of view. Another factor may be the natural conflict between remnants of the Integrist Old Guard, and new tendencies in which profundity of scholarship is coupled with sensitive spirituality and ecumenical outlook. Protestants cannot but react with friendliness and sympathy, and with a constant interest, to those broadminded and understanding men who uphold such forthright views, and impress one with the respect they have for a man's own

Wattson sull'unità dei cristiani') used expressions which designate Mary as the 'Patroness of Unity': 'The union between God and his human creatures reaches its highest perfection and glory in the very person of Our Lady of Reconciliation, in that she thus has become the daughter of God the Father, the Mother of God the Son, and the Bride of God the Holy Spirit. Christ is the Good Shepherd and Mary's heart beats in unison with her son's heart, as it bleeds with compassion for our separated brethren, those lost sheep! . . . We may be sure that our Lady of Reconciliation sighs in her heart for their return. We call Mary the Shepherdess of the Straying Flock. We must then be constantly in prayer that this glad day come as soon as it may, that is, when not just the individual sheep shall return, but all sheep together into the one Fold.'

[1] Speech on 12 June, 1961 in the Hall of the Apostolic Palace at the first meeting of the Pontifical Central Committee for the preparation of the Second Vatican Council: *AAS* LIII, 1961, p. 498. Apostolic Letter, '*Le voci*': 19 March, 1961, in *AAS* LIII, 1961, p. 205f.

[2] Encyclical '*Grata recordatio*', 26 Sept., 1959: *Acta et documenta*, Series I, vol. I, p. 49.

[3] Apostolic Letter '*Celsitudo ex humilitate*' 19 March, 1959: *AAS* LI, 1959, p. 456. Cf. G. Maron, 'Laurentius von Brindisi, der neueste "Lehrer" der katholischen Kirche', *Materialdienst des Konfessionskundlichen Instituts* 10 (1959), pp. 41ff.; P. da Venezia, 'Il metodo polemico nei controversisti del sec. XVI e in S. Lorenzo da Brindisi', *La Scuola Cattolica* 88 (1960), pp. 202ff.

B

faith. Dialogue up to a certain point with them seems possible. But only up to a certain point. For suddenly and disconcertingly there is an impassible point, and we are forced to ask whether dialogue even with these Catholics who show an undoubted interest in the gospel, and can show themselves biblical scholars with Protestant biblicists, can be real, frank and unambiguous. One even wonders, paradoxically, whether it might not be better to have to deal with the brusque, rigid propositions of the Integrists, who do at least call things by their proper names.

The fact however remains, that while there is still question as to which of the opposing tendencies will prevail, we must resign ourselves to meeting the changing faces of Catholic ecumenism with a series of question marks, and to having to suffer some rude shocks in our continuous attempts to discover which wing is to be taken seriously, which is likely to win out in the end, which we should attempt to speak with, and whether either is truly representative or authoritative. One could note with some satisfaction, and seemingly with some grounds, that whereas formerly ecumenical gestures from the Catholic side were made by isolated and probably suspect innovators, they are now the prerogative of, and expressed in the most progressive form by, the Supreme Authority itself. Almost overnight, a subject hitherto whispered only among the most restricted and discrete circles, and always subjected to the scrutiny and approval of higher authority, has come to be broadcast with all the aids of dubious modern publicity.

We have then, on the one hand, the rigorous secrecy under the sacred bond of oath, for all that concerns the work of the commissions of the Council; which means that those 'who, while not sharing in the full profession of the Catholic faith, still have a sincere and bona fide desire for information' are invited to wait for the moment 'which shall be most opportune and proper for contacts on the highest level—mind, heart and vision of the supernatural—on which the Spirit of the Lord shall descend for the glory and love of Jesus Christ, Founder of his Church, holy and glorious'.[1] With this on the other hand, there has to be harmonized a subtle propaganda drive made by every possible means and on every possible occasion, which is obliged to collect its own information from sources not original and not official. This spectacular change of public image, which in

---

[1] Address already quoted of 14 Nov., 1960 to the members of the preparatory Committees: *AAS* LII, 1960, p. 1010; cf. P. Petit, *art. cit.*, p. 177.

some countries where Catholics are a majority has already resulted in juridical repercussions, is likely to prove an acute embarrassment for those who know that spiritual changes are never rapid. Ideas must be acquired slowly if they are to be accepted as true and sincerely held, as well as if they are to endure. In this present age of most rapid technical and social change this fact must never be forgotten.

On the other hand, it would ill become us not to suspend our prejudices and not give positive value to a change of attitude in interconfessional relations which have been poisoned for centuries by verbal, and at times more than verbal, polemics—we who know that, as the Apostle said, the truth of Christ is strong enough in its own persuasive power, not to need the might of anything that does not itself spring from the gospel and the gospel spirit of love.

What are the reasons for this change of course? Several have been and could be suggested.

2. *The Motivations of the Second Vatican Council*

The documents themselves reveal in essence two motives, one ecclesiastical, the other political. Both can be traced back to the original Encyclical of John XXIII, '*Ad Petri Cathedram*'.

Let us take a look at the ecclesiastical motive.

The prime aim of the Council itself will be to promote an increase of Catholic faith, a healthful renewal in the conduct of Christian peoples, as well as to revise church discipline in accordance with the needs of today. This will undoubtedly afford such a remarkable spectacle of truth, unity and charity as will present, even to the eyes of those who are separated from this Holy Apostolic See, a gentle invitation—so we hope—to seek and to find that unity for which Jesus Christ directed to the Heavenly Father so ardent a prayer.

We know well that recently, not a few Christian Communities separated from the Holy See have felt sympathetically drawn towards the faith and order of the Catholic Church, and have felt an increase of respect for this Holy See. The love of truth is finally dissolving certain prejudices and suspicions. We know too, that almost all who bear the name of Christians, though separated both from us and from one another, have several times held Congresses with a view to tightening the bonds between them, and have set up organizations for that very purpose. This indicates that they are moved by the desire to attain some form of unity.

But the unity of Christ's Church

must not be anything transitory, uncertain and passing,

left to the

caprice of men's varying opinions

that change with time.   It must be something

solid, stablished and sure; if other Christian communities lack this, certainly the Catholic Church does not, as anyone who will look closely at the matter can easily see.[1]

In order not to apply ecclesiastical terminology to non-Roman Christians, the Pope uses secular terms, calling their Churches communities, their Councils congresses, their World Council of Churches organizations, without naming or specifying any.[2] This procedure is in accordance with the dogma and practice of Catholic ecclesiology. Yet one fact we have here which is not to be overlooked —the recognition of the Ecumenical Movement. In this connection one can only make a comment in the light of historic fact on what has been the agelong policy of Rome. When faced with any new movement that touches the realm of religious or political sociology Rome, with her basically conservative outlook, usually takes an attitude of condemnation at first. However, should the movement succeed in gaining ground despite the initial anathema, Rome takes the forces that have given life to the movement inside the Catholic framework, pockets the movement, and goes so far as to claim its

---

[1] *AAS* LI, 1959, pp. 497ff.

[2] It is curious to note how the term Churches, to denominate non-Roman Confessions, appears in a document dated 11 Nov., 1961, but published in *L'Osservatore Romano*, 9–10 Dec., 1961, probably deliberately to time with the Ecumenical Conference at New Delhi (19 Nov.–5 Dec., 1961)—the Encyclical *'Aeterna Dei'*. The Italian text of the paragraph entitled 'Prayers for the Return of Separated Brethren', referring to Leo the Great, uses the phrase 'O that he might return to receive the plaudits of those who represent the ecclesiastical wisdom of Churches not in communion with Rome'. However in the Latin text—the only authoritative one—the word 'Churches' has been carefully avoided: 'O utinam ab iis, qui hodie vivunt, rerum ecclesiasticarum studiosis, a Romana Ecclesia dissidentibus, S. Leoni veteris communisque redintegrentur exsistimationis testimonia!'

The same phenomenon appears in the Apostolic Constitution *'Humanae Salutis'* dated 25 Dec., 1961, which announced and convened the Second Vatican Council for 1962. The Italian text published in *L'Osservatore Romano*, 26–7 Dec., 1961 uses the expression: 'We invite also all Christians of Churches separated from Rome, to join in this chorus of prayer, since the Council is meant to be for their benefit too.' However the Latin text runs: 'Extremum christianos omnes qui a catholica Ecclesia dissident enixe rogamus, ut Deo supplicent: nam ad eorum etiam fructum Concilium redundabit'.

Despite everything, it is a noteworthy phenomenon that in two important papal documents the word Churches is to be found in the Italian version published in the official newspaper of the Holy See. Pius XI in the Encyclical *'Mortalium Animos'* of 6 Jan., 1928, referring to the Churches taking part in the Ecumenical Movement, declared that these were: 'a false Christianity quite removed from the Church of Christ': *AAS* XX, 1928, p. 11. Cf. V. Subilia, *Il Movimento Ecumenico*, Rome 1948, p. 74.

paternity.[1] Now that the Ecumenical Movement is a historic fact and has gathered to itself all non-Roman Christendom, Protestant, Orthodox, Anglican, Old Catholic, i.e., practically two thirds of Christianity, Rome could not continue left in the minority, a passive spectator, running the risk of being by-passed by history. Hence she feels it necessary to initiate a grandiose process of bringing Catholicism up-to-date and improving its efficiency, with a spectacular playing up of the ecumenical theme. This reading of the situation is supported by the line adopted by the Central Committee of the World Council, and expressed at St Andrews in August 1960 in language sober and well-chosen. Alluding first to the Council, and noting the creation of the new Vatican Secretariat for promoting Christian Unity under the direction of Cardinal Bea, the Executive Committee underlines the contrast between this last action and the Encyclical 'Mortalium Animos' of 1928 with its 'flatly negative evaluation' of the Ecumenical Movement. 'Undoubtedly the Vatican has recognised that the Ecumenical Movement is not inspired simply by a vague humanitarianism, but springs from fundamental Christian convictions.' 'The Vatican has now decided to take an active part in the ecumenical conversation. It no longer wishes to leave to individual Roman Catholics all the initiative in this field; but it begins to speak and act directly in relation to other Churches and ecumenical organisations. In this way, to use a phrase of Father Congar, for the first time in history, the Roman Catholic Church, on the occasion of the Ecumenical Council, enters within the framework of dialogue.'[2]

After 'four hundred years of useless appeal to Protestants', after 'nine hundred years of useless appeal to the Orthodox',[3] after Protestant ecumenism had affirmed itself, and Eastern Orthodoxy been lost—a loss that must have been felt particularly badly[4]—Rome seems to have realized how necessary it is to try a new road.

[1] We find the same conception expressed in language very much akin to that used here in a work on the Council by a Catholic author, H. Küng, *The Council and Reunion*, p. 26. Küng says that often in the Church '. . . something will be condemned that is afterwards—all too late—permitted, and finally it will be blessed by and absorbed into the Church for the Church's advantage'.

[2] Report of the Executive Committee to the Meeting of the Central Committee of the World Council of Churches at St Andrews, Scotland 1960, in *The Ecumenical Review* 10 (1960), p. 46; *EPS* 27 (1960) 19 August.

[3] H. Küng, *op. cit.*, p. 135.

[4] Cf. V. Subilia, 'Da Utrecht a Venezia', *Protestantesimo* 14 (1959), p. 237. On several occasions John XXIII has made particular and explicit reference to the Churches of the East. We quote only a few phrases taken from his Address at Pentecost, 5 June, 1960, where the Pope speaks of Gregory Nazianzus and John Chrysostom as 'the two most

We have called the second motive political: the much-discussed necessity of a united front to defend Christian civilization against the subversive inroads of atheistic communism. Some assert it more or less openly, on the grounds that the danger justifies compromise. Others, both Catholic and Protestant,[1] in comment reject it as an unworthy motive, such as could only occur to the mind of a Philistine. Still one can trace in all the papal utterances the modern counterpart of that constant tradition in the Latin Church of a grand self-consciousness of a historic responsibility for society. We find in the Encyclical, '*Ad Petri Cathedram*', quoted above:

All have a duty to embrace the doctrine of the gospel. Reject it and the very foundations of truth, honesty and civilization are in jeopardy,

with the

disastrous inevitable consequence of there being no longer a place for religion, either in theory or in practice. From the pursuit of truth in its wholeness, fulness and purity, there must necessarily issue unity of mind, spirit and actions. . . . It is therefore necessary that all, both private citizens and those who direct the destinies of peoples, should love truth sincerely, if they wish to enjoy that peace and concord from which alone derives true prosperity in public and in private.[2]

Addressing on 14th November, 1960 the Preparatory Commissions of the Council, in contrast to the 'forgetfulness' and the 'laxity in caring for those principles of a spiritual and supernatural order, which had been the characteristics of the penetration and spread of Christian civilisation through the centuries', the Pope emphasized the 'necessity of restoring to its worth and splendour the substance of that human, Christian way of thought and life, of which the

---

authoritative voices to express the yearning for, the blessedness of, and the prayers for the return of the Eastern Churches into the bosom of the One Holy Catholic and Apostolic Church. O what an auspicious event would this be. What a flowering of human and divine love, to see the beginning of the gathering of the separated brethren of East and West in the one fold of Christ, the Eternal Shepherd. We should envisage such to be one of the most blessed fruits of the forthcoming Second Vatican Council, to the glory of the Lord on earth and in heaven, and with universal exultation the completion of the mystery of the Communion of Saints': *AAS* LII, 1960, p. 526. Just a year afterwards at New Dehli, the last great Orthodox Church that did not belong to it, the Russian Orthodox Church, was welcomed into the World Council of Churches. The member Churches of the World Council do not wish to be, and are not, one in any anti-Roman spirit, but they are certainly animated by a very different spirit from that of the Church of Rome.

[1] E.g. G. Tavard, A.A., *Petite histoire du Mouvement oecuménique*, Paris 1960, pp. 232f., quoted with consent by the Protestant P. Bourguet, 'Opinions sur le Concile', *La Revue Réformée* 12 (1961), pp. 65f.

[2] *Encycl. cit.*

Church through the ages has been guardian and instructor', because 'We know what we can expect at the hands of the foes of Christ and of Christian civilisation'.[1]

This second motive then is not just imaginary, but can be documented. In any case, both motives—the ecclesiastical and the political—are drawn together in the same Encyclical '*Ad Petri Cathedram*', in a revealing passage:

> Thus all the children are summoned into the one family home, built on the foundation stone of Peter, and therein must we seek to gather all peoples, as into the one kingdom of God.[2]

Can we then, or can we not, reconcile the old and the new styles of ecumenism in the Roman Church?—the contrasting tendencies that coexist in her today, the theory of integrism and that of integrationism, the ecclesiastical and the political motives? The answers we have so far given to the question of how to evaluate the different aspects of Catholic ecumenism have given us some idea of the climate of thought, but leave us still perplexed. What is behind the changing phenomena of varieties of form, procedure and ecclesiastical policy? What is the master principle which determines this complex of attitudes, so contradictory on the surface? The central Committee of the World Council of Churches at St Andrews gave its wise and considered verdict:

> We must remember that the creation of the Vatican Secretariat (for Christian Unity) in no way means that any of the fundamental differences that exist between the Roman Catholic Church and the Churches of the World Council have been abolished. The modification has been in procedure and climate. Opportunities for dialogue must be grasped, but this only means that the real problem remains to be faced just the same.[3]

What is the real problem?

3. *Foundation of Roman Catholic Ecumenism*

In 1943 in the Encyclical '*Mystici Corporis*', and again at the end of 1949, in view of the imminence of the Holy Year, Pius XII launched an appeal which he intended to be a moving one, for all prodigal sons, atheists, heathens, sinners, dissenters—a clear reference to the problem of unity—to return to the Father, whose mighty arms, open symbolically, awaited them in the same 'Father's house'.

[1] *AAS* LII, 1960.   [2] *Encycl. cit.*
[3] Report cited: *The Ecumenical Review* X (1960), p. 46.

1950, the year of Jubilee, was to be the year of the great return, and the great pardon for all men

our children,

even for those

who have abandoned us, offended us, brought us (and still bring) suffering. Distant children, erring ones, deluded and embittered ones, from this moment on, be sure that the paths that lead back to the Father's house are pleasant ones, and the embrace that awaits you is fully assured. We open the Holy Door, and with it paternal arms and paternal heart, in a fatherhood given us by Jesus the Redeemer, by inscrutable divine decree.[1]

If the expressions of John XXIII have been more guarded, more discrete, perhaps more diplomatic, they mean just the same:

Know that our affectionate invitation to Church Unity is not a call into a stranger's house, but into your own, and your Father's home.[2]

Here, in the way the parable is applied, is the essence of Catholicism. The line of distinction between father and prodigal sons is drawn on a very different axis from that of the Gospel version. But in this line of application, which sounds as edifying and Christian in Catholic ears, as it is distressing and anti-Christian in Protestant ones, is the nub of the issue. This is the point on which all the particular points of difference turn, and it must be said clearly, that modifications, reforms and any accord that might be reached over particular differences will mean nothing at all, and might indeed only create dangerous diversions, if one has not first gone down to the very root of the fundamental disagreement, which all today would agree lies precisely in the concept of the Church.

The Church has come to be conceived as the extension of the Incarnation, i.e., as the actual presence of Christ, as *totus Christus*. The phrase *Totus Christus, Caput et Corpus* (The Whole Christ, Head and Body), bears the hall-mark of the mature theology of the great Augustine, but derives originally from certain passages in Paul's Epistles, especially two parallel passages of the Epistles to the

---

[1] Pius XII, radio announcement, 23 Dec., 1949: *AAS* XLII, 1950, pp. 121f.

[2] Encyclical '*Ad Petri Cathedram*'. One of the Catholic theologians most forward in seeking to be comprehensive towards the 'positive principles' of the Reformation uses a metaphor from the Old rather than the New Testament to express the same thought. Speaking of the 'return' of the Protestants, he says that this means that 'like Abraham they are called to leave their country, their family, i.e., what they call "their Church"': L. Bouyer, *Du Protestantisme à l'Eglise*, Paris 1954, pp. 254f.

Ephesians and to the Colossians, whose origin, meaning and application have been debated in recent years with thoroughness and even passion. One interpretation, to whose distant and obscure origins we must return later, since it touches the very foundation of the Catholic-Protestant issue, turns on the analogy between the life of Christ and the life of the Church. According to this, the Church, as the Body of Christ and the contemporary manifestation in history of Christ, shares not only in the humanity, but at the same time in the divinity of Christ, as the Council of Chalcedon defined his Person. It is therefore a divine-human reality, living and developing in history, so that the Fact, the Event, of Christ (called by German theologians '*Christusgeschehen*') may be said to consist of the Incarnation plus the Church, the one conjoined with the other and inseparable from it.[1] The unique and unrepeatable nature of this event finds its expression as a universal concept in the Church, and its historical expression in the Church through the centuries. 'The unique individual fact of Christ, and his universal significance are at bottom only two different aspects of the same thing.'[2]

> So it happens, as one person comes from two, from head and body, from bridegroom and bride . . . Christ is called one, his head and his body . . .; because Christ is in Christ's members. . . . If two are in one flesh, why not two in one voice? Therefore Christ speaks, so far as the Church speaks in Christ, and Christ speaks in the Church, and the body in the head, and the head in the body.[3]

> You, the Apostle says, are the body of Christ and the members. Then, if he is the head and we are the body, one man speaks. Whether the head speaks, or the members, it is the one Christ who speaks. And it is properly the head that speaks, even in the person of the members.[4]

---

[1] E. Franz, *Totus Christus—Studien über Christus und die Kirche bei Augustin*, Bonn 1956, p. 22; E. Benz, 'Augustins Lehre von der Kirche', *Akademie der Wissenschaften und der Literatur—Abhandlungen der geistes- und sozialwissenschaftliche Klasse*, 1954, Nr. 2, Mainz and Wiesbaden 1954.

[2] E. Franz, *op. cit.*, p. 51.

[3] 'Fit ergo tamquam ex duobus una quaedam persona, ex capite et corpore, ex sponso et sponsa . . .; unus dicitur Christus caput et corpus suum . . .; quia in membris Christi Christus. . . . Si duo in carne una, cur non duo in uoce una? Loquatur ergo Christus, quia in Christo loquitur ecclesia, et in ecclesia loquitur Christus; et corpus in capite et caput in corpore': *Aurelii Augustini Opera* X, 1—*Enarrationes in Psalmos I-L, In Psalmum XXX, Enarratio II, Sermo 1, 4 (Corpus Christianorum*: Series Latina XXXVIII, p. 193—Turnholti 1956).

[4] '*Vos*, inquit apostolus, *estis corpus Christi et membra*. Si ergo ille caput, nos corpus, unus homo loquitur; siue caput loquatur, siue membra, unus Christus loquitur. Et capitis est proprium loqui etiam in persona membrorum': *op. cit.* X, 3—*Enarrationes in Psalmos CI-CL*, In Psalmum CXL, Enarratio Sermo ad populum 3 (*Corpus Christianorum*: Series latina XL, p. 2027—Turnholti 1956).

Our Lord Jesus Christ was man as perfect as entire, both head and body. The head we recognise in that man who was born of the Virgin Mary, suffered under Pontius Pilate, was buried, rose again and ascended into heaven; he sits on the right hand of the Father, whence we look for him to come and judge both the quick and the dead. This is the head of the Church. The body of this head is the Church, not the Church in this particular place, but the Church both in this place and throughout all the world. Not the Church of this moment, but from the time of Abel himself unto those who shall be born and shall believe in Christ unto the end of time, the whole people of the saints who belong to the one city. Which city is the body of Christ, whose head is Christ.[1]

. . . all of us in him are both of Christ and are Christ, in so much as the whole Church is head and body.[2]

What patterns of thought lie behind this language, and what do they mean? To offer any relevant critique would involve tracing their course from the New Testament message to the Augustinian system. And this is no place for tackling such research. Towards the end of our study we shall make allusion to the basic problems that result from, and the probable influences, immediate and remote that affected, the thought of the great Father of the Church of the West, and (more generally) to the forces that have shaped the evolution of ecclesiological thought in its trajectory from the second to the twentieth century.

At this preliminary point we merely indicate that the supreme *magisterium* today uses a classical Augustinian language, and with a somewhat alarming extension of its application, comes to speak of the Church as 'almost Christ's other self'.

It is in fact said in the Encyclical '*Mystici Corporis*':

To speak of the Body of Christ does not mean just that Christ is to be regarded as the Head of his Mystical Body, but also that he sustains

---

[1] 'Dominus noster Jesus Christus, tamquam totus perfectus uir, et caput, et corpus: caput in illo homine agnoscimus, qui natus est de Maria uirgine, passus sub Pontio Pilato, sepultus, resurrexit, adscendit in caelum, sedet ad dextram Patris, inde illum expectamus iudicem uiuorum atque mortuorum; hoc est caput ecclesiae. Corpus huius capitis ecclesia est non quae hoc loco est, sed et quae hoc loco et per totum orbem terrarum; nec illa quae hoc tempore, sed ab ipso Abel usque ad eos qui nascituri sunt usque in finem et credituri in Christum, totus populus sanctorum ad unam ciuitatem pertinentium; quae ciuitas corpus est Christi, cui caput est Christus': *op. cit.* X, 2— *Enarrationes in Psalmos LI–C, In Psalmum XC, Enarratio, Sermo* II, 1 (*Corpus Christianorum*: Series Latina XXXIX, p. 1266).

[2] '. . . omnes in illo et Christi et Christus sumus, quia quodammodo totus Christus caput et corpus est: *op cit* X, 1—*Enarrationes in Psalmos I–L, In Psalmum XXVI, Enarratio* II, *Sermo ad plebem* 2 (*Corpus Christianorum*: Series Latina XXXVIII, p. 155).

the Church in such a way, and lives in it in such a way, that it subsists as almost his second self.

Leo XIII's Encyclical '*Satis cognitum*' is quoted:

> Just as Christ, Head and Example of the Church, is not the Whole Christ if one reckons only his visible human nature, or his invisible divine nature . . . but is one with two natures and in two natures, so it is with his Mystical Body.

The result is a kind of application of the Christological doctrine of the *communicatio idiomatum* to ecclesiology:

> . . . our Saviour so shares with his Church his own properties, that the Church, in all its way of life, both visible and invisible, presents a perfect image of Christ.

With explicit reference to Augustine, it affirms:

> . . . the mystical head which is Christ, and the Church which represents on earth his person as a second Christ, constitute one unique new man, through whom heaven and earth are joined in perpetuating the salutary work of the cross. Hence we can express the synthesis: Christ, Head and Body, the Whole Christ.

Thus there follows naturally the admonition:

> '. . . to accustom oneself to recognize Christ himself in the Church. It is indeed Christ who lives in the Church, who by means of her teaches, governs, and distributes holiness. It is Christ who in a diversity of forms manifests himself in the various members of his society.[1]

Catholic theology is too circumspect to speak of the Church *secundum divinitatem* (under its divine aspect); that would be to fall really and truly into ecclesiological monophysitism. The accent is on *secundum humanitatem*, yet not in the opposite sense of an ecclesiological Nestorianism. In thinking of that most intimate, indissoluble tie that unites the divine with the human in the person of Christ and in the historical fact of the Church, it is quite possible, indeed obligatory, from the Catholic point of view, to use language that suggests a humanization of God in the Church, a homogenizing or assimilating, by which the Church has been assumed by the Word

---

[1] Pius XII, Encyclical '*Mystici Corporis*': *AAS* XXXV, 1943, pp. 217f. Cf. C. Journet, *L'Eglise du Verbe Incarné—Essai de théologie spéculative* II, *Sa structure interne et son unité catholique*, Paris 1951 pp. 126f.; E. Mersch, *Le corp mystique du Christ—Etudes de théologie historique*, Brussels-Paris 1951³, II, pp. 35f.; E. Mura, 'La dottrina del Corpo Mistico', in *Problemi e orientamenti di teologia dommatica*, Milan, 1957, II, pp. 373f.; G. Thils, *Orientations de la théologie*, Louvain 1958, p. 100.

of God, in the same way as the Word of God has assumed the man Jesus of Nazareth. Thus the whole institution of the Church becomes meaningful in relation to Incarnation; it is not just on the plane of spirit and faith, but 'bodily, and as by an extension of contact with his most holy body', that the Church manifests and actualizes in the process of history *the deeds, the sufferings, and the words of Christ in the flesh*.[1]

These premises make it possible for Catholic thinking to indulge in phrases that seem at the very least imprudent, and increase the likelihood of misunderstanding (e.g. the phrase 'the Whole Christ'), and to construct a divine-human ecclesiology, where veneration is widely recommended and cultivated, but no sort of criticism of the ecclesiastical institution is permitted or encouraged.[2]

Such premises enable the Church of Rome to point to itself as the expression of the living Christ, victorious in history, exempt for all time from the errors that cause individuals and peoples to lose the way, a refuge for the lost in their search for certainty and peace, the 'stone that has not been moved since the day the Lord laid it on solid ground, and declared it secure till the end of time'.[3]

Pope John XXIII has stated with typical insistence that the Council has the task of bringing things up-to-date, so that the Church shall be able to offer the 'separated brethren' the invitation to the great return:

[1] Y. M. J. Congar, O.P., *Christ, Our Lady and the Church* [ET], London 1957, pp. 13f, 54f.; *Esquisses du mystère de l'Eglise*, Paris 1953³, p. 139; 'Dogme christologique et ecclésiologie—Vérité et limites d'un parallèle', and 'Regards et réflections sur la christologie de Luther', in A. Grillmeier–H. Bacht, *Das Konzil von Chalkedon—Geschichte und Gegenwart*, Würzburg 1959,² III, pp. 239f., 475.

[2] Typical of this are the classic words of J. A. Möhler, *Symbolik oder Darstellung der dogmatischen Gegensätze der Katholiken und Protestanten nach ihrer offentlichen Bekenntnissschriften*, Mainz 1835⁴, pp. 335f.: '. . . here is his Church, his institution (*Anstalt*) in which he continues to live, in which the Word uttered by him continues to echo for ever. Thus the visible Church, seen from this point of view, is he who is continually seen among men in human form, who is ever renewing himself, the Son of God who is eternally being rejuvenated, his permanent Incarnation, the reason why believers are called in holy Scripture the Body of Christ. For this reason it can be seen that the Church, though composed of men, is still not just human. Rather, as in Christ the divine and the human though distinct, form one unity, so in the Church, Christ continues, entire and undivided. The Church, being the lasting manifestation of Christ, is at one and the same time human and divine, and is the unity of the human and the divine. It is Christ who acts in the Church, concealed under forms earthly and human: the Church has thus a divine and a human aspect. These two aspects exchange properties. The divine aspect, the living Christ and his Spirit, is the infallible element in the Church, the eternally sure: yet the human aspect is infallible and sure, because the divine is not present for us apart from the human.' These are 'the reasons for the Catholics' high veneration of the Church'.

[3] Address given 30 April, 1960, 'ad alumnos Pontificii Collegii Russici', *Acta et Documenta* Series I, vol. I, p. 83.

By the grace of God we shall then hold the Council, and we mean to prepare for it with an eye on those points where our Catholic family environment most needs reinforcement and reinvigoration, in the light of the pattern left by our Saviour. Then, when we have achieved that high endeavour, and when the road has been cleared, for our human part, of all that impedes its rapid passage, we shall hold up the Church in all her brightness, 'without spot or blemish', and say to all who are separated from us, 'orthodox', protestants, etc.: Behold, brethren, this is the Church of Christ. We have striven to be faithful to her, to ask from the Lord the grace that she might ever remain what He has wished her to be. Come! Come! This is the open road to encounter, to return. Come, take (or retake) your place, which for many of you is the place your fathers occupied years ago. And from such religious peace, from such a reunited Christian family, what joy, what prosperity—even of a political and social sort—may we not expect for all the world![1]

Other details may be found in documents of a later date in which the Pontiff has declared, without any possibility of misunderstanding:

The centre and fulness of all the visible unity of the Catholic Church is the Bishop of Rome in his office of successor to St Peter, and Vicar of Jesus Christ.

He had added:

We who, however unworthily, occupy the position on earth of the Divine Saviour, make his prayers our own

with respect to unity,

that he may grant to all Christians the grace to recognise the marks of his true Church, and become his devoted children.

Moreover the true Church

has ever been and remains one, holy, catholic and apostolic, as it was instituted,[2]

[1] Address 9 Aug., 1959 'Ad Moderatores diocesanis Actionis Catholicae Italiae', *op. cit.*, pp. 45f. The metaphor of the Church *without spot or blemish*, taken from Eph. 5.27, was used again in the Address already quoted, given at the conclusion of the celebration of the Byzantine-Slavonic rite, an occasion intended to demonstrate openness of spirit: *AAS* LII, 1960, p. 960. H. Küng refers to the papal expression [p. 6] and in a passage written in an almost Lutheran style, using modern exegesis as well as the Fathers of the ancient Church—especially a quotation from Augustine and one from Thomas Aquinas—seems to reject the idea of applying it to the visible and historic Church, and to suggest that it is a meaningful concept only *in statu patriae*, that is in a eschatological setting [p. 40]. In any event, this is to be sustained only with the use of partial texts . C. Journet *op cit.* II, pp. 115f., in a long *excursus*, has shown that Catholic tradition supports the historical application to the Church of today in its institutional aspect, if not in the person of its members.

[2] John XXIII, Encyclical *'Aeterna Dei'*, already quoted. Cf. *L'Osservatore Romano* 9–10 Dec., 1961. According to *EPS* 2 Feb., 1962, Dr W. A. Visser't Hooft, General Secretary of the World Council of Churches, has expressed the hope that the Vatican

that Church,

ever identical with itself

which can

contemplate itself in its stupendous oneness

and reveal itself

in all its splendour, as Mistress of truth, and Minister of salvation,[1]

in which it may be said,

> where Peter speaks, you know it is Christ who speaks, where the pastor who is Peter's successor, holds the place of him who is called *Bishop of our souls*.[2]

It is in the context of these fundamental ideas that we must examine and understand the attitudes, old and new, adopted by the Church of Rome vis-à-vis non-Roman Churches. The grand Pauline vision of 'summing up all things in Christ' (Eph. 1.10) has in this style of thought undergone a process of ecclesiasticization, in the sense that ecclesiology has to a certain extent taken on itself the prerogatives of Christology, or more precisely, those of one aspect of Christology—the glorious and the divine. Since the time of the Reformation, the Church of Rome has faced the crisis of seeing a non-Roman Christianity arise; since the Enlightenment, she has faced the advent of secular ideologies. Now, in the middle of the twentieth century, she is undertaking with the help of twentieth century methods, the task of thrusting upon a dechristianized world her great medieval tradition, and making a superhuman effort to draw everything under her aegis—heretics, unbelievers, separated Churches and godless peoples. She undertakes to be the Whole Christ, who can gather unto himself every element that entrusts itself to a fatherly guidance, like the Heavenly Jerusalem of the Apocalypse, to which 'they shall bring the glory and honour of the Gentiles' (Rev. 21.26).

Council will strike a different note from that of '*Aeterna Dei*', an Encyclical, 'which belongs definitely to the era of monologue rather than dialogue'. In the issue of 22 Dec., 1961, it had already been said that this Encyclical repeated 'the traditional Roman Catholic arguments'.

[1] John XXIII, Apostolic Constitution '*Humanae salutis*', quoted above. Cf. *L'Osservatore Romano* 26–7 Dec., 1961.

[2] John XXIII, Address, 25 Dec., 1961, published *L'Osservatore Romano*, 26–7 Dec., 1961. Pius XII in his '*Mystici Corporis*' had used similar language: 'We who, however unworthily, represent on earth the Person of Jesus Christ. . . . Christ and his Vicar form one single head. . . . They are thus in perilous error who think they can hold to Christ the Head of the Church, without at the same time holding faithfully to his Vicar on earth.'

We underline then this fact: the so-called new line in Catholic ecumenism differs from earlier lines in its dogmatic pre-suppositions only circumstantially and superficially, and not at all in depth; but it has this distinction—its outlook is much vaster, for those age-old ambitions of Catholicism now reassert themselves after being thwarted for four centuries by the social and religious reactions they had themselves aroused. '*Mortalium Animos*' and the pronouncements that followed it constitute the final utterances of that 'siege-mentality' theology which has prevailed in Catholic thinking and Catholic consciousness since the time of the Council of Trent, and especially of that historical complex of timidity or inferiority (it would be interesting to psychoanalyse the 1870 Dogma of Infallibility), which has lasted since the beginning of modern age, and now seems to be passing—though whether really so or not we do not pretend to judge. Let us only note that an undertaking to reconquer and to expand could be as much helped as it might be hindered at the outset, by that spiritual bankruptcy and apathy of which we see today, in unexpected quarters, such widespread and alarming symptoms. However, the fact is that Catholicism has been able to embark on this new course, because it is free of these complexes, and for that very reason there would be objective weight in the argument that this new line is more truly and more substantially catholic than the earlier ones.

We are now ready for the task of arguing and illustrating our thesis, by a consideration of that presupposition which seems most daringly pregnant with new possibilities: a presupposition that we will examine in those so-called *avant-garde* Catholic theologians who uphold that theory of integration that seems so radically different from that of integrism—the presupposition of Reform as the Precondition of Unity.

2

The Lines of Integration

1. *The evolution of Dogma*

THE Catholic position in the century that succeeded that of the
Reformation finds its classical expression in the words of Bossuet in
1688, in his famous *History of the varieties of Protestant Churches*, to
the effect that the essence of Catholic truth is its immutability, in
contrast with the essential mutability of heresy.

> . . . The Church, in professing only to speak and teach that which it
> has received, never varies at all. . . . On the contrary heresy, whose
> beginnings are in innovation, is always changing. . . . Catholic truth,
> deriving from God, has its perfection from the beginning. Heresy,
> feeble product of the human spirit, can never be anything but an ill-
> assortment of pieces. . . . These then are firm and unshakable principles
> on which I base my proposal to show the Protestants the falsity of their
> doctrines, their continual variations, and their inconstant ways of
> expounding their dogmas.

And the great Bishop of Meaux challenged the Protestants to
prove the contrary:

> If they can show the least inconsistency in us, or the least variation
> in the dogmas of the Catholic Church, from its origins to our time—
> that is from the founding of Christanity—I am quite ready to concede
> that they are right, and I shall myself erase all my history.[1] . .

This invariable-variable contrast has been repeated in a number
of pronouncements by the supreme *magisterium* up to recent times.
There is an echo of it even in the Apostolic Letter of 13th September,
1869, which Pope Pius IX addressed 'to all Protestants and non-
Catholics' on the occasion of the Vatican Council, to invite them,
'the erring children', to return to the Father's house. Contemplating

> the condition of mutual disagreement in which the religious societies
> separated from the Catholic Church find themselves,

[1] J. B. Bossuet, *Histoire des variations des Eglises Protestantes*, Lyon–Paris 1827, vol. I,
pp. 4, 5, 6, 25.

one realizes that

> the societies have continually differed in their doctrines, and such fluidity and instability never ceases in these societies. It takes little understanding to see clearly and obviously that this state of affairs is the exact opposite of the Church that the Lord Christ has instituted, in which truth remains ever constant, never liable to any sort of change, like a deposit entrusted to this Church to be kept in its perfect entirety.[1]

In the decree *'Lamentabili'* (3rd July, 1907), dogmas are described as 'truths fallen from heaven';[2] and in the Encyclical *'Pascendi Dominici Gregis'* (8th September, 1907), Pius X condemns the theory of the evolution of dogma explicitly, as a bundle of sophistries that wreck all religion:

> In this way, those formulae which we call dogma would have to suffer the same stresses and so be liable to change. That would indeed hasten the way to an internal *evolution* of dogma.[3]

Undoubtably this kind of outlook contains a nucleus of truth by way of faith in revelation; yet it tends to underestimate, if not to deny outright, the fact that dogmas do differ between one period and another in history, as well as to take no account of new ideas, nor offer any explanation of their dogmatic origin. It tends to regard every point of dogma as the expression of the same ancient, immutable, revealed truth. Faithfulness to dogma comes to be incompatible with a sense of historic criticism, and Catholic operations are reduced to mere apologetics. In the ecumenical field this means that the *massif* of Catholic doctrine is regarded as a fortress with raised drawbridge and no communications with the outside world.

However, the historical criticism of the eighteenth and nineteenth centuries had been able to penetrate far enough into the world of study to bring home the fact that this attitude of invariableness could not be further sustained. In its hour of need the Catholic position found timely help in Möhler,[4] and especially in the ex-

---

[1] Pius IX, Apostolic Letter *'Jam vos omnes'*, in J. D. Mansi, *Sacrorum Conciliorum nova et amplissima collectio*, Graz 1960, Tomo 50, col. 1259-60.
[2] H. Denzinger, *Enchiridion Symbolorum* Friburgi Brisg., Barcinone, 1952, 2022.
[3] *Ibid.*, 2079, cf. 2094-5.
[4] J. R. Geiselmann, *Johann Adam Möhler—Die Einheit der Kirche und die Wiedervereinigung der Konfessionen*, Vienna 1940; *Der Einfluss der Christologie des Konzil von Chalkedon auf die Theologie Joh. A. Möhlers*, in *Das Konzil von Chalkedon* III, pp. 341ff.; E. Hocedez, S. J. *Histoire de la Théologie au XIXe. siècle*, Paris 1949, I, pp. 231ff.; S. Jaki, O.S.B., *Les tendancies nouvelles de l'ecclésiologie*, Rome 1957, pp. 21ff.; E. Stirnimann, O.P., 'La Chiesa nella problematica presente,' in *Problemi e orientamenti di teologia dommatica*, Milan 1957, I, pp. 143ff.; J. R. Geiselmann, 'Les variations de la définition de l'Eglise chez Joh. Adam Möhler', in *L'écclésiologie au XIXe. siècle*, Paris 1960, pp. 141ff. It is interesting to note the definition of K. Barth—*Die kirchliche Dogmatik*,

Anglican Newman.[1] These introduced Catholic thought to the notion
of the seed-idea, gave credence to the concept of the evolution of
dogma[2] and gave rise to the remark that it was not Newman who
had been converted to Catholicism, but Catholicism that had been
converted to Newman.[3] It would certainly be an exaggeration to say
that such an idea was 'quite unknown to previous generations':
already 'St Vincent of Lerins, St Augustine, St Anselm and others
had already admitted a development of dogma'. But, 'having made
this reservation'—we use the phrase of a Catholic theologian—'it is
true to say that the work of applying the principles of evolutionary
theory to Catholic dogma, and to Christian events in general, is the
peculiarity of the nineteenth century'.[4] The idea had to overcome
not a little distrust and not a little opposition in so far as 'it seemed
difficult to reconcile the indubitable principle of doctrinal immutability with the evolutionary theory coined by Newman'.[5] But the
hour was bound to come when 'the conception of Catholic dogma as
a living organism, developing and growing without check through

---

I, *Die Lehre vom Wort Gottes* II, Zollikon-Zürich 1945[3], p. 624. on Möhler: 'The classic
figure of this theology that tries to carry the finest fruits of neo-Protestantism into
the Catholic granaries' [*Church Dogmatics*, 1956, p. 561].
  [1] Newman's theory can be traced back to 1845, i.e. the period of his conversion:
J. H. Newman, *An Essay on the Development of Christian Doctrine*, London 1845. Cf.
G. Tyrrell, *Christianity at the Crossroads*, London 1909 [1963, p. 41]; J. Guitton, *La philosophie de Newman—Essai sur l'idée de développement*, Paris 1933; M. Nedoncelle. *La philosophie religieuse de John Henry Newman*, Strasbourg 1946. L. Bouyer, *Newman*, Paris
1952; R. Schiffers, *Die Einheit der Kirche nach J. J. Newman*, Düsseldorf 1956; O. Chad-
wick, *From Bossuet to Newman— The idea of doctrinal Development*, London 1957; E.
Hirsch, *Geschichte der neuern evangelischen Theologie im Zusammenhang mit den allgemein-
Bewegungen des europäischen Denken*, Gütersloh 1951, III, pp. 291f.; S. Jaki, *op cit.*,
pp. 35ff.; R. Mehl, *Du catholicisme romain*, Neuchâtel 1957, p. 30; H. Fries, Die 'Dog-
mengeschichte des fünften Jahrhunderts im theologischen Werdegang von John
Henry Newman', in *Das Konzil von Chalkedon*, III, pp. 421ff.; 'John Henry Newman
—Ein Wegbereiter der christlichen Einheit', *Catholica* XV (1961), pp. 60ff.; J. H.
Walgrave, O.P., *Newman—Le dévelopement du Dogma*, Tournai-Paris 1957. For
Newman and modernism cf. also: G. Martini, *Cattolicesimo e storicismo*, Naples 1951,
pp. 141ff.
  [2] F. Marin-Sola, O.P., *L'évolution homogène du dogme catholique*, Fribourg 1924;
H. de Lubac, 'Le problème du développement du dogme', *Recherches de science religieusse*
35 (1948), pp. 130ff.; B. Bartmann, *Lehrbuch der Dogmatik*, Frieburg i. Br. 1932[8]
(Ital. trs. Alba 1950, I, p. 95), M. Flick, 'Il problema dello sviluppo del dogma nella
teologia contemporanea', *Gregorianum* XXXIII (1952), pp. 5ff.; R. Aubert, *La théologie
catholique au milieu du XXe. siècle*, Tournai-Paris 1954, p. 97; C. Journet, *op. cit.* [*The
Church of the Word Incarnate*], I, pp. 437ff. [vol. I, *The Apostolic Hierarchy*, London 1955,
pp. 339f.]; L. Ott, *Grundriss der Dogmatik*, Freiburg i. Br. (Ital. trs. Turin-Rome 1956,
pp. 16ff.); Ch. Boyer, S. J. 'Lo sviluppo del dogma,' in *Problemi e orientamenti di teologia dommatica*, I, p. 359; M. Schmaus, *Katholische Dogmatik*, Munich (Ital. trs. Turin
1959, I, p. 61).
  [3] O. Noordmans, *Das Evangelium des Geistes*, Zürich 1960, p. 180.
  [4] J. Bellamy, *La théologie catholique au XIXe. siècle*, Paris 1904[3], p. 122.
  [5] *Op. cit.*, p. 125.

the ages, would be hailed as one of the most important and most pregnant viewpoints of (Catholic) theological science'.[1]

It is a fact that immediately after the proclamation of Infallibility, in 1871, Newman, with remarkable insight, began to sustain one of the theses now passionately upheld by the modern Integrationists, by way of reconciling the prerogatives of the Papal primacy with the functions of the Episcopate:

> No truth stands by itself—each is kept in order and harmonized by other truths. Pius (IX) is not the last of the popes. The fourth Council modified the third, the fifth the fourth. ... The late definition (of Infallibility) does not so much need to be undone as to be completed. ... Let us be patient, let us have faith; and a new Pope, and a re-assembled Council may trim the boat.[2]

Here we have, thanks to Romanticism and the ideas of biology and nineteenth-century evolutionary science, a most interesting reversal of the classical Catholic thesis. Catholic theology slowly begins to assert that we must indeed consider that the revelation of truth was completed in the apostolic age,[3] but that truth has been revealed 'both explicitly and implicitly'.[4] This implies that 'all the dogmas that the Church has already defined, or will define in the future, are inevitably to be found in the thoughts of the Apostles' through divine illumination.[5] The Church of the centuries that follow has the task of rendering explicit the divine *depositum* it has received, whether in explicit or implicit form, and in any case, of defining it. This process of rendering explicit is the essential concomitant of preserving the content of divine revelation, conceived thus as a living thing. Its identity is maintained, not by leaving it inert like a mineral, but by letting it develop like a living organism.[6]

This biological principle is then used to explain the whole history of dogma, even to the extent of explaining the appearance of new doctrinal formulae. Even where, instead of a normal process of development, there is an abnormal transformation, even deformation; even where new and spurious elements are added to the original authentic ones—still, all is justified on the ground that no one can deny that in the beginning, it all existed in germinal form. We can see the dubious nature of this theory very strikingly in the Marian

[1] *Op. cit.*, p. 124.   [2] Quoted by H. Küng, p. 146 [pp. 235, 236].
[3] Denzinger, 2021.   [4] L. Ott, *op. cit.*, p. 13.   [5] F. Marin-Sola, O.P., *op. cit.*, I, p.57.
[6] C. Journet, *op. cit.*, I, p. 437 [I, p. 340]; L. Ciappi, O.P., 'Che cosa la teologia si attende dal Concilio?', *Sacra Doctrina* VI (1961) N.S. (*N.21, Prospettive del Concilio ecumenico*), pp. 89ff.

doctrine, which, even in its most improbable developments, can always refer back to its germ of origin, the fact that the mother of Jesus is certainly mentioned in the New Testament. In this way, any heresy whatsoever, granted that it has taken root slowly, almost imperceptibly, can be put forward as the recognition and the rendering explicit of some truth originally implicit, even if in its later stages of growth it has reached positions diametrically opposed to the original ones. As Brunner rightly observes, 'this kind of thinking involves nothing less than the abdication of the idea of truth itself before the movements of history'.[1]

And so we find ourselves at the opposite pole to Bossuet's thesis. Error, sign of death, lies in the Protestant fixity of faithfulness to the Word of God, and of harking back to apostolic origins; truth is in Catholic evolution, the sign of life.[2] The consequence of this attitude (which involves accepting, with proper reservations of course, the Modernist hypothesis) is that instead of affirming the irreformability of the Church of Rome because of what it uniquely is, and identifying it rigidly with the Church of Christ, there is now this new theory of making explicit the *depositum fidei*, which in practice amounts to a theory of relative reformability, or better, of the redimensioning of old truths through a complicated process of blending them with other truths as yet not rendered explicit, among which there might even be truths possessed by other Churches, in a broken and one-sided form of course, which are genuinely and essentially Catholic in value. This is the basis of the new Catholic ecumenism, which has for its goal a new Catholic fulness reached through a complex process of preserving, and at the same time rendering articulate, interpreting, and expressing in a new way, the *depositum fidei*, out of which it mines the most recondite and neglected implications. In this new fulness all the positive aspects of non-Catholicism, which past centuries of polemic and the interests of self-defence have perhaps suppressed or distorted in Catholic theological thought, will be put in their proper place and their proper dimensions.

Let us review some examples of this.

---

[1] E. Brunner, *The Misunderstanding of the Church*, London 1952, p. 41.

[2] Or rather a deeper knowledge of revelation and the work of the Holy Spirit acting in the Church, as it is called in: B. Poschmann, *Busse und Letzte Oelung*, Freiburg i. Br., 1951, p. ix, in *Handbuch der Dogmengeschichte*, ed. M. Schmaus, J. Geiselmann, H. Rahner, IV *Sakramente und Eschatologie*, fasc. 3. Cf. the remarks of W. Andersen, 'Desideria für eine evangelisch-kirchliche Dogmengeschichte', *Theologische Literaturzeitung* 84 (1959) col. 807ff.

2. Roman Catholic Biblicism

First there is the problem of the sources of the faith. The twin principles of the Council of Trent, Scripture and Tradition, have recently become the triad, Scripture, Tradition and the Teaching Authority of the Church, the first two being called the 'remote', the last the 'near' norms of faith. Now, it seems, one of these elements is to undergo a special reassessment rich with attendant possibilities. This is the element of Holy Scripture, which for four centuries fear of Protestantism had thrust into the background. Within certain limits, the contingency of self-defence is held responsible for the 'pari pietatis affectu ac reverentia suscipit et veneratur'[1] clause in which Trent joined Scripture and Tradition, and it is stated that 'only' Holy Scripture constitutes 'intrinsic and immediate evidence of God himself', and this gives it 'an irreversible precedence over tradition'.[2] Modern Catholic biblicism (and this is true both of academic study and devotional practice) now tends to follow this line, maintaining however the balance in favour of Catholicism, by producing a Catholic version of one of the points that had been the special object of Protestant attack, and thus eliminating one of the objectives of the polemic. Thus Protestant requirements would be met, without—as Father Boyer says so candidly—this introduction of the practice of using the Bible 'making any substantial difference'.[3] The Scripture is read in the Church, and understood in the sense that tradition has given it through history. It can be accepted as the '*normative norm*', and still require the light of another '*norm*' to explain and expound it. This is provided by Tradition and the Teaching Authority of the Church, i.e., by the testimony given by the Holy Spirit himself, not within the individual believer, but in the historic fact of the Church.[4] Pleasure is expressed at finding on the Protestant

[1] Denzinger, 783.
[2] H. Küng, *Rechtfertigung—Die Lehre Karl Barths und eine katholische Besinnung*, Einsiedeln 1957, pp. 116ff. Cf. J. R. Geiselmann, 'Das Missverständnis über das Verhältnis von Schrift und Tradition und seine Ueberwindung in der katholischen Theologie', *Una Sancta* XI (1956), pp. 131ff. (in French: *Istina* 1958, pp. 197ff.); P. de Vooght, 'Ecriture et Tradition d'après des études catholiques recentes'. *Istina* 1958, pp. 183ff., cf. pp. 191ff.; Y. M. J. Congar, 'Traditions apostoliques non écrites et suffisance de l'Ecriture', *Istina* 1959, pp. 279ff., cf. p. 296; *La tradition et les traditions*, Paris 1960; P. Lengsfeld, *Ueberlieferung, Tradition und Schrift in der evangelischen und katholischen Theologie der Gegenwart*, Paderborn 1961.
[3] C. Boyer, *art. cit.*: *Unitas* XVI (1961), p. 207.
[4] H. Küng, *op. cit.*, pp. 119–24; Y. M. J. Congar in *Le Concile et les Conciles. Contribution à l'histoire de la vie conciliaire de l'Eglise*, Paris 1960, pp. 293–323; J. R. Geiselmann, *Die lebendige Ueberlieferung als Norm des christlichen Glaubens. Die apostolische Tradition*

side an increased sense of the importance of tradition, and of the need to read the Bible in the light of the faith of the Church: this phenomenon is hailed as one more providential coincidence. Thus there is an increasing effort to exploit the use of biblical categories in speaking with Protestants, to promote useful dialogue, whilst all the time one knows that nothing essentially Catholic is being betrayed or compromised. Symptomatic is the way in which Küng frankly turns against the Protestants the charge of not being biblical, when he rebukes the Reformers for not being 'perfect hearers of the Word of God', in that basically they set their exegesis of the Scriptures 'above the Church and its Tradition', and thus rejected 'the teaching authority not only of the Popes, but even (after the Leipzig Disputations of 1519) of the Ecumenical Council'. Catholicism today wants, for its part, to be more biblical than the Reformers, showing its 'faithfulness to the gospel in its faithfulness to the Church that proclaims the gospel'. In fact, in the voice of the hierarchy one hears 'the very voice of the Lord', and 'obedience to him who alone we obey in our Christian liberty, is realised in obedience to the Church'. Today's emphasis on scriptural theology 'does not exclude, but implies' not mere alignment with, but a genuine and real subjection to, the authority of the Church's doctrine.[1] Every dogma that the Church has proclaimed, including the latest one of the Assumption of the Virgin Mary, has its basis in the Bible, and interprets the texts thereof without any addition to its contents, but merely by throwing a new light on them, and imparting to them certain impulses never realized before.[2] By way of demonstrating how faithful Catholicism is to the gospel, and in imitation of what the first Vatican Council did in enthroning the Holy Scriptures before the eyes of all the bishops, the second Vatican Council should formulate 'a solemn profession of faith' in 'the importance of the *word* of God for salvation'.[3]

We are thus faced with a paradoxical situation. While among Protestants (not, let it be said, on the academic level, where there is

in der Form der kirchlichen Verkündigung—das Formalprinzip des Katholizismus dargestellt im Geiste der Traditionslehre v. Joh. Ev. Kuhn, Freiburg 1959; 'Schrift—Tradition—Kirche—Ein oekumenisches Problem', in *Begegnung der Christen—Studien evangelischer und katholischer Theologen*, ed. R. Rösle and O. Cullmann, Stuttgart-Frankfurt am Main 1959, pp. 131ff.

[1] H. Küng, *op. cit.*, p. 123.
[2] M. Villain, *Introduction à l'Oecuménisme*, Tournai 1961, pp. 247–64.
[3] H. Küng, *The Council and Reunion*, pp. 152, 131, 268. Cf. the rapid but well informed and well presented survey of R. Martin-Achard, 'Le renouveau biblique dans le catholicisme romain,' *Revue de théologie et de philosophie* 1960, pp. 285ff.

again a constantly increasing awareness of the message of the apostles, such as must in due time bring forth its fruits, but on the level of church life), while among the very people of the Bible, there appears a lack of interest in the Bible, a fatal product of two centuries of reading it subjectively, or sentimentally, and not theologically, in Catholicism, on the other hand, one notes that the Bible is being used on a vast scale, and this, one day, may issue in undreamt-of developments, though this use is (and in Catholicism must ever be) bridled by the hierarchy. All which seems strangely to give the lie to that traditional Protestant conviction, that to bring Catholicism face to face with the Bible would mean the overthrow of Catholicism.

3. The doctrine of Justification

A second interesting example is afforded by the doctrine of Justification. Great stir has been caused by a book on this subject by Hans Küng, the Swiss Catholic Professor at Tübingen, another of whose works has already been mentioned.[1] Küng begins his study with an examination of the decrees of the Council of Trent from a historical, sociological and theological point of view. Called together in the age when Scholasticism was in decline, composed for the most part of Italians and Spaniards incapable of understanding the Lutheran mentality, scene of a conflict of theological tendencies, suffering from a *rabies theologorum* brought on by the attacks of the Reformers, Trent's formulae bear all the marks of a polemical spirit on the defensive, and their contents those of a degree of anthropo-centredness which is simply the reaction to the opposite exaggerations of the Reformers.[2] Yet Trent is only one moment in the evolution of dogma. It could not have, and never pretended to have, said all that there is to say on Justification. It saw one aspect of it, it denounced one peril of it. But Catholic doctrine is bigger than Trent, and more understanding of the fulness of truth. Today one must take up the task of making explicit the implicit, and putting all in a balanced perspective.[3] The doctrine of Justification has been saddled with misunderstanding from the beginning right up till today. The Reformers understood neither all its implications, nor the thought of Paul, nor Catholic dogma. This incomprehension persists still in

[1] H. Küng, *Rechtfertigung—Die Lehre Karl Barths und eine katholische Besinnung*, Einsiedeln 1957; 'Ist in der Rechtfertigungslehre eine Einigung möglich?', *Una Sancta* 1957, pp. 116ff.; 'Rechtfertigung und Heiligung nach dem Neuen Testament', *Begegnung der Christen*, pp. 249ff.
[2] *Op. cit.*, pp. 110ff. [3] *Op. cit.*, pp. 108, 112, 116, 123.

contemporary Protestant theology. Karl Barth, its greatest exponent, it even leads unjustly to call Catholic doctrine another gospel.[1] Any work of revision must begin with a definition of terms; by justification is meant on one side, the objective work of redemption done by God, and on the other, the appropriation of this, effected subjectively by man. The result is a dialogue of the deaf. The decrees of Trent must be understood to be complementary. Trent never intended to assert any objective co-operation on man's part in the (objective) work of redemption, but only a subjective co-operation to follow the objective work of redemption.[2] To realize this one only needs to look closely at the quotations in the decrees from Augustine on grace and on faith, the source of justification:

> We are said then to be justified freely, because none of the precursors of justification, either faith or works, merit justification. We are said to be justified through faith because 'faith is the beginning of human salvation', the ground and root of all justification, 'without which it is impossible to please God' and to enter the fellowship of his sons.[3]

Hence to protest at 'co-operation' is to bark up the wrong tree. 'How could Trent ever speak of co-operation in the objective fact of the cross?'[4] The notion 'at once just and a sinner' is also acceptable on the Catholic side. Indeed it is in an essentially Catholic statement, with a place even in the liturgy of the Roman Mass.[5] The same can be said of 'faith alone'. It is present in Catholic tradition both before and after the Reformation, as may be seen in the German Nuremberg Bible of 1483, and in three Italian versions, Genoa 1476, and Venice 1538 and 1546. 'Even the Council of Trent never meant to pronounce against the formula as such.'[6] In the same way 'To God alone be glory' is shown to be fully in accordance with synergism and the doctrine of merit. There is nothing pharisaic about it; its basis is grace, and it is implicit in the New Testament teaching of recompense.[7]

The conclusion is that there is thus no foundation for the Protestant, and especially the Barthian, attacks on the Council of Trent, and that it ought to be recognized today that there is no reason for

---

[1] *Op. cit.*, pp. 111–229. [2] *Op. cit.*, pp. 228–57f.

[3] 'Gratis autem iustificari ideo dicamur, quia nihil eorum, quae iustificationem praecedunt, sive fides, sive opera, ipsam iustificationis gratiam promeretur. . . . Per fidem ideo iustificari dicamur, quia "fides est humanae salutis initium", fundamentum et radix omnis iustificationis, "sine qua impossibile est placere Deo" et ad filiorum eius consortium pervenire' (Denzinger, 801).

[4] H. Küng, *op. cit.*, p. 229. [5] *Op. cit.*, pp. 231ff.

[6] *Op. cit.*, p. 243. [7] *Op. cit.*, pp. 257, 263.

any division between Catholic and Protestant over that doctrine which was the start of the Protest.[1] Hence to be really ecumenical, Protestantism should refrain from a negative anti-catholic attitude on this score.

Perhaps this survey has been too rapid, and one should have discovered more subtlety of meaning, yet alongside our intention to deal with the work elsewhere in greater detail, we cannot but remark that Küng's attempt is rather reminiscent of those spurious scholars who claim to have solved the question of Primitive Christianity, when they have discovered that this or that saying of Jesus or the Apostle Paul is to be found in the writings of late Judaism, or Qumram, or Stoic morality, or Hellenistic mysticism, yet who lack the power of synthesis and so miss the real nodus of the problem. Nor can we refrain from adding that no real ecumenical contribution is made by this sort of approach, in which Trent's semi-Pelagian phrases are subtly wrapped up in Augustinian ones, and by clever documentation Luther is made to look like a Catholic, and the Fathers of Trent like Lutherans, and the Catholic-Protestant antithesis is drained of its meaning, and reduced to an accidental if regrettable misunderstanding that no one in four centuries had ever noticed before Dr Küng. All this must be said notwithstanding a generous and courageous effort to point out overlooked evangelical principles, and to work again over the broken road that leads towards the Protestant position and up to a certain point repair it. One argument suffices. Were such a thesis valid and true, Catholicism would never have championed Mariology. It would on the contrary have rejected it, enshrining as it does the doctrine of creaturely co-operation in redemption. Illusory harmonies of this sort have their precedents in history (e.g., the Concord of Ratisbon on 2nd May, 1541, between Melanchthon and Contarini on Justification by faith), but they have no future. They recall the verdict passed by Fra Paolo Sarpi in his famous *History of the Council of Trent* on this same article of justification:

> He would probably be right, who said that in the debates between the opposing factions on the formulation of the article, each side rejected words that could bear a sense contrary to their ideas, and so all seized on words which each thought could mean what they wanted.[2]

---

[1] *Op. cit.*, pp. 256, 269, 271, 274, 276.
[2] Fra Paolo Sarpi, *Opere*, III, *Istoria del Concilio Tridentino*, ed. by Giovanni Gambarin, Bari 1935, vol. I, p. 368.

Küng's effort, however, is typical of a whole sector of Catholic thought that engages in the ecumenical dialogue.[1]

4. Mariology

Mention could also be made of Mariology, only by way of example. Here too there is an inclination, certainly not to reduce it to the proportions it bears in the N.T., but to redimension it by giving more space to Christology.[2] These efforts vary with the trends inside Catholicism that stress or minimize Marian doctrines.[3] It is suggested that the eccentricities of some Protestant sects, and the neo-paganism of some Protestant regions of the world should make Protestants cautious about throwing the first stone; it is pointed out too that in some Bible stories Jesus listens to appeals of a superstitious type (e.g., that of the woman who grasped the hem of his garment in order to be healed, Mark 5. 25–34), and, on that basis, it is asserted that 'superstition may still cover the hidden kernel of faith' which unbelief 'has utterly lost'; it is frankly admitted that there are excesses of Mariolatry, especially in Latin countries, but, it is at

---

[1] Nevertheless it is interesting to note the reaction of other writers on this theme, who cannot refrain—despite their proper esteem for their colleague—from expressing an 'uncomfortable feeling, after reading the book', and from saying that 'the author does not seem aware of the difficulties that lie unobserved behind expressions that look synonymous', which render the conclusion that 'the basis is the same on both sides, and the divergences arise only from differing emphases' hardly satisfactory: D. P. B., 'Karl Barth et les théologiens catholiques, *Irénikon* 30 (1957), pp. 337f. Thus D. T. Strotman, 'Justification et sanctification', *ibid.*, p. 408, expresses a courteous but definite reserve, saying that 'a book such as that of Küng, however enlightening and stimulating, ought not to leave us with illusions, but this on the whole is what this book does. The points of view of the two sides, or shall we say, their basic presuppositions, are still too far apart to be made to coincide with or complement each other.' Other Catholic writers are undoubtedly more exact and more far-sighted than Küng in assessing the Catholic-Protestant contrast over the doctrine of justification and in tracing its logical consequences for the conception of the Church, Grace and Sacraments. Cf. e.g., W. H. van de Pol, *Das reformatorische Christentum in phänomenologischer Betrachtung*, Einsiedeln–Zürich 1956, who states that Luther would never have arrived at his doctrine of Justification 'if he had not already lost his faith in the Church as a supernatural reality and in the mediation by sacrament of Christ's redemption in the Church and through the Church' (p. 391).

On the Protestant side, the fact that the letter that Karl Barth wrote to Küng has been printed as a kind of preface to the book, makes the author seem 'an Israelite in whom there is no guile', but one must ask with a polite smile 'if' the doctrine outlined by Küng is indeed official Catholic teaching. Cf. further the weighed and acute criticism of E. Schott, 'Annäherung an die evangelische Rechtfertigungslehre in der neuesten romisch-katholischen Theologie', *Materialdienst des konfessionskundlichen Instituts* 10 (1959), pp. 21f.; 'Trennt die Rechtfertigungslehre die Konfessionen noch heute?' in *Im Lichte der Reformation—Jahrbuch des Evangelischen Bundes* 1961, Göttingen 1961.

[2] For assessing the importance of Mariology in the Christology of Catholic dogmatics, cf. M. Schmaus, *Katholische Dogmatik*, V, *Mariologie*, Munich 1955.

[3] H. Asmussen, *Maria, die Mutter Gottes*, Stuttgart 1951[2]; H. Fries, *Antwort an Asmussen*, Stuttgart 1958, pp. 127ff.

once added, alongside a *sin of excess*, there may be also a *sin of defect*.[1] Here too, Protestantism is charged with not being sufficiently biblical, since the only use it makes of the passages in the Gospel that speak of Mary is that of an arsenal of polemics against Catholicism. It should rather have been able to deduce 'some positive creative factors for theology and devotion'.[2] It would be a grave psychological error, it is admitted, for Catholicism to raise new barriers against unity by putting out any new Marian formulae at the Council.[3] Yet the question is asked: 'Can we be Christian without being Marian? Can we make a Christian theology without making a Marian one? Could any return to unity in Christ be possible if one turns one's back on the mystery of Mary?'[4] One of the most able and cultured of Catholic theologians, Congar, has written with penetrating insight to show how essential for Catholicism is Mariology. It is impossible to think of the problem of Christ apart from that of the Church, and it is impossible to think of the problem of the Church apart from that of Mary.[5] Mariology and ecclesiology can and must be distinguished, yet 'only as two aspects of the same thing'.[6] In any case, Mariology cannot be considered as a mere excrescence on the total mass of Catholic doctrine and piety, to be tolerated today and dispensed with tomorrow. It has no marginal place in the system; it is not something pronounced in a popular accent; it belongs integrally, inasmuch as it represents the fundamental theological expression of the necessity of co-redemptive mediation on the part of the creature, as the essential concomitant of the mediation of redemption proclaimed in the gospel.[7] In Protestantism the Church has the function of proclaiming redemption in Christ: in Catholicism this becomes the function of transmitting redemption. While 'Protestants wish to see God only as Giver . . . and consider all interest shown in the gift itself as an act of disloyalty towards him who gives',[8] Catholics lay their stress on the reality of

[1] H. Küng, *The Council and Reunion*, pp. 182–6.   [2] *Op. cit.*, p. 187.
[3] H. Küng, *op. cit.*, p. 231.   [4] *Op. cit.*, p. 187.
[5] Y. M. J. Congar, *Christ, Our Lady and the Church*, London 1957. For the Catholic viewpoint in this regard, cf. (among much other literature): A. Mueller, *Ecclesia-Maria. Die Einheit Marias und der Kirche*, Freiburg 1951; *Maria et Ecclesia. Acta Congressus mariologici-mariani in civitate Lourdes anno 1958 celebrati*, Rome 1959.
[6] C. Journet, *op. cit.*, II, p. 393.
[7] *Op. cit.*, II, pp. 404f.; G. M. Roschini, 'La corredenzione oggettiva fondamento della corredenzione soggettiva', *Euntes docete* 1956, pp. 223ff. Cf. also the survey: 'Maria die Miterlöserin—ein neues Dogma?' *Materialdienst des Konfessionskundlichen Instituts* 12 (1961), pp. 6ff.
[8] Y. M. J. Congar, 'Marie et l'Eglise chez les Protestants', in *Bulletin de la Societé française d'études mariales*, Paris 1952, II, p. 99.

God's gifts in us, and this reality finds its symbol and centre in Mary, who expresses in the amplest and most absolute manner this co-operation on the part of humanity in the work of redemption. 'By her "be it done unto me", Mary enters co-operatively into the work of salvation in the name, and in the place, of all humanity.'[1] There is a profound, unseverable tie between Christ and her whom Bengel thought of as 'not the mother, but the daughter, of grace'. Against the Adam-Christ parallel, dogma needs to set the corresponding one between Eve and Mary. Eve co-operated in our fall, Mary in our redemption.[2] 'Perdition for all mankind had its origin in the disobedience of Eve that brought sin into the world. Salvation for all mankind had its origin in the obedience of Mary to God in bringing into the world the end of sin—the Redeemer.'[3] Now the new, the second, Eve, 'who generates the divine-human life of the faithful in her most spotless womb' who 'alone distributes the graces indispensable for salvation',[4] has her 'collective' realization in the Church, her 'personal' one in Mary.[5] In fact it is only in the Virgin that the Church can become a mediator (in the co-redemptive sense) of all the graces, *mediatrix omnium gratiarum*.[6] Not for nothing could Pope John XXIII say: 'He sets in jeopardy his salvation, who tossed in the storms of this world, refuses to clasp her helping hand',[7] since 'It is through Mary that we come to Jesus', and 'to love Christ means to love Mary his Mother and, in the light of redemption, our universal Mother'.[8]

If then the countersign for the recognition of the true Church of Christ is the veneration of Mary, because 'where Mary is not venerated, there is no Church of Christ';[9] if the condition of the restoration of the Church's unity is the rediscovery of the full gospel, i.e., the development and the unfolding of all its most recondite and unsuspected germs, then there must be 'bilateral

---

[1] R. Grosche, 'Fünf Thesen zur Mariologie', *Catholica* 1933, p. 38, quoted by Barth, *Die kirchliche Dogmatik*, I, *Die Lehre vom Wort Gottes* II, Zollikon–Zürich 1945[3], p. 158 [*CD*, 1956, p. 144].

[2] C. Journet, *op. cit.*, II, p. 412.

[3] A. Mueller, 'Maria als Bild der Gnade und Heiligkeit', *Begegnung der Christen*, p. 595.

[4] G. Miegge, *La Vergine Maria—Saggio di storia del dogma*, Torre Pellice 1959[2], p. 203.

[5] C. Journet, *op. cit.*, II, p. 397.   [6] *Op. cit.*, II, p. 409.

[7] John XXIII, radio sermon, 27 April, 1959: 'Quo locorum ordinarii et universi orbis christifideles adhortantur ad impensas supplicationes habendas, per maium mensem, ob oecumenicum cogendum concilium': *AAS* LI, 1959, p. 315.

[8] Address, 15 Feb., 1959: *AAS* LI, 1959, pp. 136–7.

[9] F. Diekamp, *Katholische Dogmatik*, 1930, II, p. 395, quoted by K. Barth, *op. cit.*, p. 156 [*CD*, p. 142].

reform'[1]—Catholicism must recognize the proper full stature of Christology,[2] but Protestantism, for its part, must treat Mariology with all the theological fulness necessary for a co-ordinated and complete understanding of gospel truth. On both sides

> we must acquire the sense of the balanced inter-relationships of the articles of faith that concern Christ, dead and resurrected, for this alone will save us both from undue exaggerations of and improper detractions from the implications of the Christian faith.[3]

5. The reassessment of Episcopacy

Let us take briefly a further example—the process of finding a counterweight for the papal primacy through a reappraisal of the episcopate. We have already alluded to the topic in speaking of Newman and the evolution of dogma. It is at bottom the question of the ministry and of authority in the Church. It is remarked that the first Vatican Council was forcibly cut short by events outside its control, and as a result could not deal with the episcopate's prerogatives and their systematic formulation. A good number of Catholic theologians of integrationist sympathies would say today that the dogma formulated in 1870 only partially represented the objective, in so far as only a part of the revealed doctrine was properly formulated, and that was the part that received 'thorough treatment' in the 'double definition of the primacy of jurisdiction and the personal infallibility of the Roman Pontiff'. There should also now be added to complete it, dogmatic formulation on 'the proper function of the Episcopate in the universal Church'.[4] There are some passages

---

[1] H. Küng, op. cit., p. 187; C. Journet, op. cit., II, p. 415.

[2] For Mariology seen as a consequence of the monophysite trends in Catholic Christology, cf. M. Thurian, 'Jésus-Christ vrai Dieu et vrai homme—Le concile de Chalcédoine et l'unité de l'Eglise', Verbum Caro VI (1952), p. 55; P. J. Emery, 'La Réforme du XVI siècle et les Conciles oecuméniques', in 1054-1954—L'Eglise et les Eglises, Chevetogne 1955, II, p. 276.

[3] M. J. Guillou, O.P., Mission et unité—Les exigences de la communion, Paris 1960, II, p. 90.

[4] C. Colombo, 'Il Papa e l'episcopato nel concilio ecumenico', in I concili nella vita della chiesa, Milan 1961, p. 69. This opinion is rejected by others (cf. e.g. Archbishop L. Jaeger, Das ökumenische Konzil, die Kirche und die Christenheit, Paderborn 1960, p. 68) who argue that the formulae of 1870 did not obscure, but rather throw light on the principle of unity that governs the Collegium apostolicum episcoporum. Cf. also the studies of Fr U. Betti, O.F.M., 'Natura e portata del primato del Romano Pontefice secondo il Concilio Vaticano', Antonianum XXXIV (1959), pp. 161ff.; 'La perpetuità del primato di Pietro nei Romani Pontefici secondo il Concilio Vaticano', Divinitas III (1959), pp. 95f.; La costituzione dommatica 'Pastor aeternus' del Concilio Vaticano I, Rome 1961; and G. Colombo, 'Il problema dell'episcopato nella Costituzione "De ecclesia catholica" del Concilio Vaticano I', La Scuola Cattolica 89 (1961), p. 344; G. Dejaifve, S. J., Pape et évêques au premier Concile du Vatican, Bruges, 1961.

to be met with in modern Catholic literature, which go so far as to say that only a relative value is to be set upon the dogma that was defined, and to give it a purely historical value which might be modified if new need arose. Thus a student of the authority of Geiselmann writes:

> This concentration round one single person is a historical necessity, but as such it admits of change. Were it to be a permanent phenomenon, it would disturb the whole balance of the Church, based as this is on the tension between primacy and episcopate. The primacy is the continuation of the fact that there was a Primus among the apostles. But the episcopate is no less a continuation of the apostolate, and, like the former, is by *divine right*.[1]

The objective foundation of such arguments is the recognition that conditions of history helped shape the thesis of primacy and infallibility. It was formulated under the external pressure of nineteenth-century liberalism with its 'disruptive tendencies',[2] and against 'the rights of the masses, *à la Rousseau*', in the interests of 'an *intrinsic* right' of divine authority.[3] It was formulated under the internal pressure of survivals of Conciliar and Gallican ideas which sought to limit the field of papal authority, and to make it harmonize with the voice of the whole Church expressed through Councils and the episcopate,[4] and being so formulated, the argument seems to run, it has a certain merely relative value in so far as these dangers have lost their substance today.

It is no isolated passage that criticizes the theological and ecclesiological unbalance, and the spiritual and ecumenical difficulties, that derive from the 1870 definition.[5] There is a constant note that this absence of dogma on the function of the episcopate and its bearing on the functions of the papacy, is providential. The memorandum of the preparatory commissions indicate that such a formulation

---

[1] J. R. Geiselmann, 'Les variations de la définition de l'Eglise chez Joh. Adam Möhler particulièrement en ce qui concerne les relations entre l'Épiscopat et le Primat', in *L'ecclésiologie au XIXe. siècle*, Paris 1960, pp. 141ff., cf. p. 194.

[2] J. R. Geiselmann, *art. cit.*, p. 194.

[3] Y. M. J. Congar, O.P., 'L'ecclésiologie de la révolution française au Concile du Vatican sous de le signe l'affirmation de l'autorité', in *L'ecclésiologie au XIXe. siècle*, pp. 77ff., cf. p. 110.

[4] Y. M. J. Congar, O.P., 'La Primauté des quatre premiers conciles oecuméniques—Origine, destin, sens et portée d'un theme traditionnel', in *Le Concile et les Conciles—Contribution à l'histoire de la vie conciliaire de l'Eglise*, Paris 1960, pp. 75f., cf. pp. 92ff. In the same volume, cf. also the articles: Fr de Vooght, O.S.B., 'Le Conciliarisme aux conciles de Constance et de Bâle', pp. 143ff.; R. Aubert, 'L'ecclésiologie au concile du Vatican', p. 245, cf. pp. 261, 265, 281.

[5] Cf. J. P. Torrell, O.P., *La théologie de l'épiscopat au premier concile du Vatican*, Paris 1961, p. 277; etc.

would have borne a 'stamp inadequately biblical, and much too sociological and juridical', with an almost total 'absence of interest in the communal aspect'. Today, on the other hand, Catholic ecclesiology has developed sufficiently to make possible a 'formula both precise and in harmony with Catholic teaching about the Church'.[1] This would mean a real possibility of resolving the problems of the ministry and of authority in such a way as eventually to modify the structure of the Catholic Church, and correspondingly to effect relations with separated brethren, who see in the papacy one of the greatest obstacles to reconciliation. It would answer, not merely the pressures of the moment, but to a large extent also, the objections of the Orthodox, the Anglicans and the Protestants in demanding some more federal, consultative and communal procedure, if some check were to be put on the centralization of powers in the Pope's hand, and if dogma legalized what has for quite a while been practice, the holding of prior consultations before making pronouncements of infallible content, if, that is, there really were a retraction—Catholic theologians would call it an 'explanation', or a 'making explicit'—of that famous phrase *ex sese, non autem ex consensu ecclesiae* (of his own self, and not with the consensus of the Church). Especially would this be so if one recalls how the germ of opposition to the Papacy derives from that moment of history when circumstances, some of them psychological, prevented the Papacy from showing itself in its purest light, whereas today its prestige stands so high that any feeling of reserve about it must ultimately pass and give way to its acceptance as a providential 'crucible of reunion'.[2] It is pointed out that the sense of the Church as a *collegium* is essential if it is ever to escape from the state where only monologue is possible, for the result of this is isolation both from other confessions and from paganism, hampering (both as regards the internal life of the Church and its mission to the world) any attempt to enter into either ecumenical or evangelistic dialogue;[3] in a word, essential if it is to be a Church really incarnate in men's lives.

[1] R. Aubert, *art. cit.*, p. 262.
[2] H. Küng, *op. cit.*, pp. 193f.; cf. G. Thils, *Primauté pontificale et prérogatives épiscopales*, Louvain 1961; G. Colombo, *art. cit.*, pp. 68ff.; 'Episcopato e primato pontificio nella vita della Chiesa', *La Scuola Cattolica* 88 (1960), p. 401.
[3] The expression of Y. M. J. Congar, O.P., 'La Chiesa e "gli altri"', in *Il Concilio Ecumenico*, Milan 1960, p. 123 (Italian translation of a special number of *Lumière et Vie* 8, 1959). 'It would be a truly great thing if, perhaps for the first time in history, the Catholic Church might, on the occasion of the Council, adopt the idea of dialogue and put it into practice.'

What are we to make of these theories? Can they really be regarded as 'a great step towards Christian unity'?[1] Could we really hope that the Catholic mind could set about a serious consideration of ideas of a *collegium* which if they were still to be found in 1870, have for 90 years been subjected to such exterminating processes as leave small hope of survival?[2]

First, we need to note certain historical facts. It would not be true to say that in 1870 a full discussion of the theory of 'ex consensu ecclesiae' was prevented by the pressure of political happenings outside the Council's power. The ideas embodied in the formula 'ex consensu ecclesiae' were quite explicitly discussed and after a lively debate were rejected in the Council thanks to the efforts of the prevailing party in the '*Constitutio dogmatica prima de Ecclesia Christi*',[3] a document polemic in tone just to counter the ferment in the other camp. It was not for nothing that the formula met with tough opposition, as is shown by the 88 votes of *non placet*, and by the 62 conditional votes of *placet iuxta modum* in the earlier stages of voting, as well as by the attitude of the 55 bishops who left the Council on the eve of the final vote, 'so as not to have to oppose it openly'.[4] That the opposition—apart from the element that formed the Old Catholic Church—did yield in the end to the opinion of the majority, is symptomatic. Here is no compliant conformism due to pressure such as an authoritarian regime might exert, as an unin-

---

[1] D. O. R., 'Dans l'attente du Concile,' *Irénikon* 33 (1960), p. 186.

[2] It is of interest to follow in the footsteps of Geiselmann and trace the mental processes of that great Catholic theologian who preceded the first Vatican Council, Möhler, the personality who dominated his age. At one time in the evolution of his thought, primarily because of his exegetical research, he felt he could not be sure of finding support in scripture for the primacy of the Pontiff, and his historical researches assured him that even before the breach with East, the bishop of Rome had never exercised rule over all the Church, and indeed never possessed legislative powers (*potestas constitutiva*) but simple executive powers (*potestas executiva*). Realising that originally the *presbyter* and the *episcopus* 'were one and the same thing', he believed that one must look for the cause both of the primacy of the Pontiff and the primacy of the episcopate in the sphere of historical, political and particularly spiritual reasons, in the sense that, in a slow and fateful process, authority was exalted to take the place originally held by love and the collective spirit of fellowship. Cf. J. R. Geiselmann, *art. cit.*, pp. 176, 177, 178, 182, 188, 190.

[3] The four successive texts of the *Constitutio*, known by their initial words '*Aeternus Pater*', are to be found in J. P. Torrell, O.P., *op. cit.*, pp. 287ff.

[4] P. Aubert, *art. cit.*, pp. 270f. After the proclamation of the dogma of 1870, Ignaz Döllinger, the church historian, wrote: 'All the Fathers of the Church without exception have expounded the passages in question (Matt. 16.18; John 21.17) in a sense totally different from the new decrees, and have never found in Luke 22.32 any vestige of the infallibility conferred on all the popes. Hence I should be guilty of perjury, were I compelled to accept with the decrees this exegesis, without which the decrees lack biblical justification.' Quoted F. Heiler, *Altkirchliche Autonomie und päpstlicher Zentralismus*, Munich 1941, p. 346.

formed observer might think. Here rather, is a matter of dogma which goes beyond all the conflicting opinions, and unites the opponents with their adversaries. For both, the voice of the Church is the voice of truth. In looking at this whole matter we must never be blind to this basic situation, which in the logic of Catholic dogma could never be otherwise.

Since 1870 no challenge has been offered to the principle of primacy. On the other hand it has been insisted on and given a supreme value as binding for salvation. The very formulae of the 'Constitutio' had already pronounced anathema all who dared deny that Peter was, in the persons of his successors,

> visible head of all the Church Militant (ch. I),
> column of the faith and foundation of the Catholic Church (ch. II),

so establishing of necessity that:

> the Church of Christ is one flock under one chief shepherd

and uttering the grave warning:

> This is the doctrine of Catholic truth, from which none may deviate without harm to his faith and his salvation (ch. III).[1]

Nor have successive Popes since 1870 failed to emphasize solemnly these basic points. Let us but cite two Popes of this century. Pius XI in his Encyclical '*Mortalium Animos*' said:

> True Christians afford exactly the same belief to the dogma of the Immaculate Conception as to that of the Holy Trinity, to that of the Infallibility of the Chief Pontiff as the Vatican Council defined it, as to the Incarnation of our Lord Jesus Christ.[2]

Pius XII in his Encyclical '*Mystici Corporis*' wrote:

> Christ and his Vicar constitute one single Head. . . . Thus they who think they can hold to Christ, Head of the Church, without holding faithfully to his Vicar on earth, are placed in dangerous error. If this visible head be taken away, and these visible bonds of unity be broken, the mystic body of the Redeemer is so obscured and marred that the haven of eternal salvation can no longer be either discerned or reached.[3]

Seemingly in contrast with some of his earlier acts which had been interpreted as a desire for the decentralization of power, John XXIII put out his Encyclical '*Aeterna Dei*'[4] on 11th November, 1961, and

---

[1] Cf. text reproduced in J. P. Torrell, O.P., *op. cit.*, p. 295, 297, 301.
[2] *AAS* XX, 1928, p. 13.
[3] *AAS* XXXV, 1943, pp. 218ff.
[4] Published by *L'Osservatore Romano*, 9–10 Dec., 1961.

D

in it (just at the time of the Assembly of the World Council of Churches at New Delhi) he proceeds to reaffirm in no uncertain way the Roman Pontiff's primacy in teaching and government. It so disappointed the Orthodox that they reacted by protesting in the name of history and ecumenicity against the position he assumed, and against his refusal 'to join in a dialogue of reconciliation, and recognise the synodal authority of the Ecumenical Councils, as was done by all parts of the undivided Church of the first centuries'.[1]

These official pronouncements, however discouraging, may be the effect of pressure on the part of the Curia. Tomorrow they may be whittled down, or, to be more exact, counterbalanced by noticeable correctives. In the process of systematization, it is always conceivable that the relationship between papacy and episcopacy may be codified. A doctrine already formulated can certainly be made to harmonize with another still to be formulated; in this particular case it is possible to reassemble and systematize today, in the total context of Catholic dogma, such elements of truth as were contained in a theory condemned yesterday. Paradoxical as the task may be, it is always possible to reconcile what Congar calls the poles of Pope and Church,[2] in as far as it does not modify the Catholic conception of the relation between Head and body.

As modern Catholic thought goes, the function of the Council and of collaborating bishops is to be viewed not so much dogmatically as practically, in the sense that the body of bishops in their entirety is potentially capable of teaching and governing to a degree not greater, but wider, than that of 'the Bishop of Rome alone considered by himself'.[3] It is in order that the latter may have all the information necessary for carrying out his duties fully, and in order that these duties may be effectively carried out in every sector of the Church in the manner appropriate for each, that the episcopacy must normally function in association with the papacy and vice versa. It is, then, extraordinary circumstances that make 'collaboration in an Ecumenical Council between bishops and pope necessary', when a solution must be found for critical and pastoral problems that press upon the Church, particularly at critical moments of history.[4] It is a necessity

[1] Statements by Bishop Emilianos, permanent representative of the Ecumenical Patriarchate at the World Council of Churches, appeared in a series of articles published at Istanbul, in the official organ of the Patriarchate, and printed in *EPS* 23 Feb., 1962, p. 3.

[2] Y. M. J. Congar, O.P., *Le Concile et les Conciles*, pp. 329ff. and *Il Concilio Ecumenico*, p. 111.

[3] C. Colombo, *art. cit.*, p. 79.   [4] *Art. cit.*, p. 80.

that belongs not to the *esse* but to the *bene esse* of the Church.[1] The
Council is an assembly of 'fellow-labourers and instruments of the
Holy Spirit' which has been communicated by Jesus to the apostles
and their successors by the imposition of hands 'in legitimate succession', and so it can be called 'a supernatural activity of the Church,
in which the *principal actor is the Holy Spirit*, sent by Jesus to the
hierarchy of the Church'. Its findings may, indeed *a priori* must, be
regarded necessarily and legally '*always as the work of the Holy
Spirit*', just because they result from the common efforts of 'all
within the Church who possess the Holy Spirit'.[2] But 'the Holy
Spirit cannot speak through the body of bishops apart from their
head'; the Bishop of Rome is the '*touchstone of apostolic tradition*',[3]
and bishops before the Pope are 'as pupils before their master'.[4] Even
more, the paragon can outrange these human limitations; episcopal
authority adds nothing to papal authority; 'it can only diffuse and
reflect its virtue', just as 'the creation of the universe adds nothing to
divine perfection, it is content to reflect it'.[5] Bishops in conjunction
with the Pope always indeed represent the 'supreme and infallible
authority of the Church',[6] multiplying to the degree of the sum total
of their different dioceses throughout the world, that other Christ on
earth which is the Pope.[7]
He is the

universal prince and pastor who guides the flock in Christ's own name.
It is into this process of government that Peter's successors will summon
and associate with themselves their brother bishops from all the world,
simply *in partem sollecitudinis* (by their own concern). At this chair shall
there ever be consecrated the episcopate of the Church, one, holy,
catholic, and apostolic. From Christ to Peter, from Peter to the individual pastors of the Christian flock, passes the power of the keys, sent
from heaven in the person of the Roman Pontiff, through the bishops,

---

[1] *Art. cit.*, p. 79.
[2] *Art. cit.*, p. 77, italics in the original. D.O.R. in the article quoted above from
Irénikon 33 (1960), p. 195, says that a Council sets 'before the eyes of all the faithful
the presence of the apostolic body in its entirety, the successor of the *collegium* of the
Twelve'.
[3] C. Colombo, *art. cit.*, p. 71, underlining as in text.
[4] J. P. Torrell, O.P., *op. cit.*, p. 190.
[5] C. Journet, *op cit.*, I, p. 530 [I, pp. 411–12].
[6] D.O.R., *art. cit.*, p. 186.
[7] C. Colombo, *art. cit.*, p. 81, says: 'What the bishops have by way of proper and
exclusive rights, is the gift of representing, and of personifying, each in his own diocese,
and all together in conjunction with the bishop of Rome and acting under his guidance,
in relation to the whole Church, the figure of Christ the Master and Christ the Shepherd.'

over the whole of Christian society, to guide and sanctify humanity redeemed by the blood of Christ.[1]

Enough seems to have been said to show clearly that any reappraisal of the relationship of papacy to episcopate is likely to produce only relative changes such as could not substantially alter the Catholic conception of the Church. The dogmatic principle of the Church as *Mother and Mistress* remains unchanged.

6. *The Discovery of the Laity*

At first glance we might really feel that at one point there is a substantial change in the Catholic conception of the Church, and that is the so-called 'theology of the laity'. Typical of this change of outlook is the title of a little book by the Archbishop of Chambery, L. M. de Bazelaire—*Laymen are also the Church*. The phrase goes back to Pius XII,[2] and is indicative of the existence inside that Church, despite its centuries-old reputation for clericalism, of a longstanding desire to correct a one-sided development in its ecclesiology.

Congar in his monumental study on the laity recognizes that in ancient Christian tradition, ecclesiology gave prominence to its corporate aspects. 'At least from the time of the Fathers', throughout the Scholastic age, up to the time of the Counter-Reformation, there is a constant emphasis 'especially on the idea that the Church consists of its members, and expresses their collective aspect'. Hence a prominent part is played constantly by the principle of the consensus of the whole body of believers, without however losing sight of the objective characteristics of what the Church essentially is.[3]

From the twelfth century onwards a hesitancy about the institutional nature of the Church had shown itself in currents, some

---

[1] John XXIII, Address given in the Vatican Basilica, 22 Feb., 1962 on the Feast of the St Peter's Chair: *L'Osservatore Romano*, 23 Feb., 1962.

[2] Pius XII, Address to the Sacred College, 20 Feb., 1946: *AAS* XXXVIII, 1946, p. 149. The Pontiff was maintaining that the laity 'should have an increasingly certain consciousness, not just of belonging to the Church, but of being the Church, i.e., the community of the faithful on earth under the guidance of the common head, the Pope, and the Bishops in communion with him'. The same Pope, however, in his Encyclical '*Mediator Dei*', 20 Nov. 1947, did not fail to point out that the priest 'represents the person of our Lord Jesus Christ', but 'the people for their part, since they neither represent in any sense the person of the Divine Redeemer, nor mediate in any way between themselves and God cannot in any way enjoy sacerdotal powers'. The thesis of the priesthood 'of all baptised' was put forward as a position very close to 'errors already condemned'; 'only the Supreme Pontiff. . . and with him the Bishops . . . have the right and the duty of governing the Christian people'.

[3] Y. M. J. Congar, O.P., *Lay People in the Church* [ET], London 1957, pp. 23, 27ff.

spiritual, some political, that tended to see the Church merely as an assembly of the faithful, to whose judgment both Pope and Council should have been subjected, and these currents issued in the one-sided ecclesiology of the Reformation. This ecclesiology is presented not as such, but as being at bottom the negation of all ecclesiology, because it lacks what is regarded in Catholic thought as the proper and essential function of the Church, i.e., the element of mediating between the Holy Spirit and the faithful. This being eliminated, there remain only the two extremes, the transcendental and the community, with the result that the laity are advanced to an immediacy of contact with the divine, such as was quite unknown in Christian tradition, and the priesthood of all believers comes in effect to mean the exclusion of any specific priesthood of the ministry, as can be seen particularly clearly in the Presbyterians, who entrusted all legislative functions to synods composed of pastors and laity.[1]

It was in reaction to this kind of ecclesiology that there arose another kind that has remained to this day, equally distorted in the opposite direction. The exaggeration of a Church composed chiefly of its members provokes the contrary exaggeration of a Church composed chiefly of its governmental, hierarchical, sacramental mechanism. This theory, reducing as it does the Church almost completely to terms of mediating through its hierarchy, practically eliminates from consideration 'the two poles it should mediate between, the Holy spirit on the one hand, and the faithful people (the religious object) on the other'.[2] The means by which the Church was to exist had come to assume such magnitude, that sight had been lost of the end to be attained, and consequently, the Christian laity were in danger of being considered 'a mere accident, an appendix to the Church, necessary only to its *bene esse*'.[3]

It is carefully pointed out that one-sidedness is erroneous and heretical only in one direction, i.e., on the Gallican and Protestant side. On the Catholic side, it amounts only to a matter of contingency, and does not involve the essence of the Church. The reasoning runs as follows:

Unilateralism in the Gallican and Protestant sense touches on the *structure* of the Church; here a misconception involves the Church's very *being*. Under such circumstances, faulty conceptions involve negation in the realm of essentials. Unilateralism in favour of the Church's institutional aspect, which we have seen never amounts to

[1] *Op. cit.*, pp. 23, 31, 36.   [2] *Op. cit.*, p. 39.   [3] *Op. cit.*, p. 45.

more than a question of emphasis, concerns the Church's *life*. If it affects anything, that thing is not the very essence of the Church, only its *completeness*. . . . Then supposing, in no way granting the possibility[1], that the two distortions were equal proportionately in onesidedness, they would certainly not be equal either in import, nor in importance.[2]

However, in face of additions and subtractions resulting from Confessional emphases, the call today is for a reassessment that will fill in the chronic lacunae in ecclesiology, since for the Catholic truth lies 'in the communion of all'.[3] 'Hierarchology' needs relating to 'Laicology' i.e., the institutional aspect, the pole of papal or episcopal hierarchy, needs integrating with the community, the laity, the believing people, so as to form one complete ecclesiology, satisfying every requirement. This will ensure that the Church will not be governed by *Diktat* from above, but with a due regard both for the proper ties between Head and body, and for all that the governed may contribute by way of reaction, interest, conscience, and perhaps even information and suggestion.[4] Such an operation could result in the blending of the typically clericalist ecclesiology of the Catholics with one of the chief elements of Protestant ecclesiology, the priesthood of all believers. One might find oneself face to face with something not just superficial and relative, but of incalculable importance for history and for dogma. Here might be a force capable of rejuvenating the old body of the Church of Rome: here something that might deprive, on the one hand, Protestants of some grounds of criticism that have divided the Church, and on the other, the laity of others that have produced a divorce between Church and world, with the resultant autonomy of thinking and secularization of society.

In proceeding to assess these ideas, we must first of all observe that this presentation of the so-called theology of the laity by modern Catholic thinkers[5] requires some correction from the historical and

---

[1] In Italian in the text: *dato non concesso*.   [2] *Op. cit.*, p. 44.
[3] Y. M. J. Congar, O.P., *Vraie et fausse Réforme dans l'Eglise*, Paris 1950, p. 264f.
[4] Y. M. J. Congar, *Lay People*, p. 252.
[5] Besides Y. M. J. Congar, cf. C. Journet, *op. cit.*, II, p. 1001f.; R. M. Spiazzi, O.P., *La missione dei laici*, Rome 1952; 'Il laicato nella Chiesa', in *Problemi e orientamenti di teologia dommatica*, Milan 1957, I, pp. 303f.; R. Aubert, *La théologie catholique au milieu du XXe. siècle*, Tournai–Paris 1954, pp. 52f.; G. Philips, *Le rôle du laïcat dans l'Eglise*, Tournai–Paris 1954; *Les laïcs dans l'Eglise—documents du XIIe. Congrés mondial pour l'apostolat des laïcs* (1957) Rome 1958; M. Schmaus, *Katholische Dogmatik*, III/I, *Die Lehre von der Kirche*, Munich 1958³⁻⁵, pp. 874f.; J. B. Bauer, 'Die Wortgeschichte von "laicus",' *Zeitschrift für katholische Theologie* 81 (1959), pp. 224f.; B. D'Arenzano, 'L'apostolato dei laici nelle prime comunità cristiane', *La Scuola cattolica* 89 (1961), pp. 101f.; G. Philips, 'L'état actuel de la pensée théologique au sujet de l'apostolat des

dogmatic points of view. It is not true to history to invert the relationships of the lay-community exaggeration on the one hand, and the sacerdotal-hierarchical one on the other, in saying that the first begat the second. The rise of the lay spirit, first in the religious and then in the political fields, was not due to spontaneous generation, but to a reaction to the clerical spirit long at work in the church. The New Testament and the primitive Church used the term 'klēros', to denote the 'heavenly gift assigned by God to every believer, an objectivization of his calling to have a part with all the sanctified'.[1] But in the Apostolic Fathers there have already appeared germs of change which could only lead to fatal consequences. In the Didache 13.3, the status of prophets (men vested with an itinerant, charismatic ministry) was considered equal to that of the priests of Israel, and they are granted the right of the first-fruits.[2] In his first epistle to the Corinthians (40.5), Clement of Rome lays down as a presupposition of the Christian ministry, the Old Testament right to legislate in matters of worship and priesthood.[3] The cause of this deviation is found in a failure to understand the theological implications of having passed from the dispensation of the Law to that of Christ. So we find that an ecclesiastical prerogative has been established, which derives neither directly nor exclusively from the Christian message, and threatens to impose on the Church an institutional structure whereby those who preside at worship are distinguished by divine right from the laity, and perform exclusively duties specified according to rank.[4] Consider that ominous expression ὁ λαικὸς ἄνθρωπος ('the lay man') to denote someone who must give heed to precepts for the laity (I Clem. 40.5) and be meek and submissive before his instructors (1.3; 2.1; 57.1-2), who symbolize

laïcs', *Ephemerides Theolog.–Lovanienses* XXXV (1959), pp. 877f.; K. Rudolf (ed.), *Der Laie—Rechte und Pflichten*, Vienna 1959; J. Hamer, O.P., 'L'apostolat des laïcs', *Foi et Vie* 59 (1960), pp. 415f.; L. C. Baas, 'Libres propos d'un laïc', in *Un concile pour notre temps*, Paris 1961, pp. 135f.; *Le sens du concile—Une réforme intérieure de la vie catholique—Lettre pastorale de l'épiscopat hollandais*, Bruges 1961, pp. 20f.; O. B. Roegele, *Was erwarten wir vom Konzil? Gedanken eines Laien*, Osnabrück 1961; E. J. de Smedt, *Le sacerdoce des fidéles*, Bruges 1961.

[1] W. Foerster, Art. κλῆρος, *Theologisches Wörterbuch zum Neuen Testament* (G. Kittel), Stuttgart 1933f., III, p. 763/15.

[2] *Corona Patrum Salesiana*: Series Graeca, vol. VII, *I Padri Apostolici*, ed. by G. Bosio, S.S., Turin 1940, I, p. 55.

[3] *Op. cit.*, I, p. 161.

[4] Cf. R. Bultmann, *Theology of the New Testament*, II, London 1955, p. 110; H. von Campenhausen, *Kirchliches Amt und geistliche Vollmacht in den ersten drei Jahrhunderten*, Tübingen 1953, p. 96; M. Goguel, *L'Eglise primitive*, Paris 1947, pp. 137f.; L. Goppelt, *Christentum und Judentum im ersten zweiten Jahrhundert*, Gütersloh 1954.

the Lord's authority with which they have been vested. So begins the slow fateful process which can only issue that great medieval distinction between clergy and laity.

There are two kinds of Christians. There is one kind set apart for divine service, and given to contemplation and prayer; it is fitting that these should cease from all the bustle of temporal things, since they are clerics, devoted (if you like, converted) to God. Κλῆρος is Greek for lot, in Latin *sors*. Hence men of this kind are called clerics, which means elected by lot. For God elected them to be his. For they are kings, i.e., they rule themselves and others in virtues, and thus possess the kingdom of God. And a crown on their heads implies this. . . .

Yet there is another class of Christian, the laymen. Λαός means people. These may possess temporal things, but only for use. For nothing is more wretched than to despise God for the sake of money. These are allowed to marry, cultivate land, judge between man and man, go to law, lay oblations on altars, give tithes, and they may be saved, if only they avoid vice by doing good.[1]

Congar rightly comments that in this description 'the state of the laity is depicted as a concession to human weakness', and further, 'that its spirit points towards the idea that the laity, being given to temporal affairs, have no active part in things of the sacred order'.[2]

The distinction between clerical and lay is complicated by the division of the clergy into secular and regular. Basil the Great had already used the same phrase as the Epistle to the Philippians 3.20, 'our citizenship is in heaven', not however, as the apostle did, to indicate the state of all believers in Christ, but the monastic life; 'the spirituals' are no longer the believers in so far as they have received the Spirit and are called not to conform to this world but to make their lives a service (Rom. 12.1–2), but instead, the monks who separate themselves from the world and live an 'angel's life',

---

[1] 'Duo sunt genera christianorum. Est autem genus unum, quod mancipatum divino officio et deditum contemplationi et orationi, ab omni strepitu temporalium cessare convenit, ut sunt clerici, et Deo devoti, videlicet conversi. Κλῆρος enim graece, latine sors. Inde hujusmodi homines vocantur clerici, id est sorte electi. Omnes enim Deus in suos elegit. Illi namque sunt reges, id est se et alios regentes virtutibus, et ita in Deo regnum habent. Et hoc designat corona in capite. . . .
Aliud vero et genus christianorum ut sunt laici. Λαός enim est populus. His licet temporalia possidere, sed non nisi ad usum. Nihil enim miserius est quam propter nummum Deum contemnere. His concessum est uxorem ducere, terram colere, inter virum et virum judicare, causas agere, oblationes super altaria ponere, decimas reddere, et ita salvari poterunt, si vitia tamen benefaciendo evitaverint': Gratian, *Decreta sive Concordia discordantium canonum, c.* 7, *c.* XII, *q.* 1 (*c.* 1140); cf. H. E. Feine, *Kirchliche Rechtsgeschichte*, I, *Die katholische Rechtsgeschichte*, Graz 1955³.
[2] Y. M. J. Congar, O.P., *op. cit.*, p. 9.

a life which, like that of the angels, is one unbroken service.[1] There is a further classical description of the monastic state in the Thomist definition of the 'States of Religion':

> Religion is the way by which we render duty to God.[2]

> Those called 'religious' are those who dedicate the whole of their lives to God, keeping themselves from any worldly business. Those who live in religion are they who yield themselves and theirs to God.[3]

All this in time will be codified in the *Codex Juris Canonici*, and this will lay down that this distinction is by divine right:

> It is by divine institution that in the Church clerics are distinguished from laymen.[4]

The basis of this is ordination conferred on the one, and from which the other is excluded:

> By Christ's institution ordination distinguishes cleric from layman in the Church, for ruling the faithful, and for ministry in divine service.[5]

It follows that the laity owe the clergy a reverence based on sacred order. It is sacrilege to violate this untouchable and infallible dignity with which they are vested:

> All the faithful owe the clergy reverence, by reason of their rank and prerogative, and they defile themselves with sacrilege should they inflict personal injury on them.[6]

The function of the laity in the Church is simply to be, not persons responsible for their faith and Christian duty, but passive objects administered and governed by the clergy. Such very passivity is described as a right, a privilege granted by the clergy:

> Laity have the right to receive from the clergy, according to the norms

---

[1] Basil the Great, *Serm. asc.* 1.2, cited from F. Heiler, *Der Katholizismus—Seine Idee und seine Erscheinung*, München 1923, p. 437. Cf. L. Vischer, *Basilius der Grosse— Untersuchungen zu einem Kirchenvater des vierten Jahrhunderts*, Basel 1953, who sets out clearly the positive and responsible part of Basil in the Constantinian Church.

[2] 'Religio est per quam redditur debitum Dei'—Thomas Aquinas, *Summa Theologica* I/II, q. 60, a. 3.

[3] '. . . religiosi dicuntur, qui totam vitam suam divino cultui dedicant, a mundanis negotiis se abtrahentes. . . . Illi vero qui vivunt in religione, se et sua tribuunt Deo', *op. cit.*, II/II, q. 186, a. 5 *ad* 1.

[4] 'Ex divina institutione sunt in Ecclesia *clerici* a *laicis* distincti'—*Codex Iuris Canonici* (Rome 1934), can. 107.

[5] 'Ordo ex Christi institutione clericos a laicis in Ecclesia distinguit ad fidelium regimen et cultus divini ministerium'—*op. cit.*, can. 948.

[6] 'Omnes fideles debent clericis, pro diversis eorum gradibus et muneribus, reverentiam, seque sacrilegii delicto commaculant, si quando clericis realem iniuriam intulerint' —*op. cit.*, can. 119.

of Church Discipline, spiritual goods, and especially the necessary aids to salvation.[1]

It was precisely this domination of the Church by the clergy, and their monopoly of spiritual responsibility, with the resultant limitation of the laity to 'secularia negotia' ('the business of the world'), and their exclusion from 'ecclesiastica negotia'[2] ('the business of the Church') which gave rise 'by way of opposition' to those medieval movements of protest, which began a history whose last word has not yet been written even in our times. It has been noted that the characteristic of medieval heresies is their lay inspiration: 'The thirteenth century saw the rise of a multitude of tiny sects, more or less heretical, more or less radical, nearly all of them characterized by evidences of lay-inspired action and policy. . . . They were trying to give the layman a sense of his value and his dignity, his ability to direct, by himself, his own religious life.'[3] In the political field also, there were similar tendencies, though different in inspiration and ends, aimed no less at freeing the laity from the dominance of the clergy. The remark of Philip the Fair, the opponent of Boniface VIII, is interesting. Taken out of its context, it could be used as a slogan for this completeness of real Catholicism that is sought today:

The Church is made up, not only of clergy, but of laity too.[4]

[1] 'Laici ius habent recipiendi a clero, ad normam ecclesiasticae disciplinae, spiritualia bona et potissimum adiumenta ad salutem necessaria'—*op. cit.*, can. 682.

[2] The formula is of the Cardinal Umberto de Selvacandida, *Adversus Simoniacos* III, 9, in: *Monumenta Germaniae Historica—Libelli de Lite*, I, p. 208: 'Laici sua tantum, id est saecularia, clerici autem sua tantum, id est ecclesiastica negotia, disponant et provideant. . . . Sicut clerici saecularia negotia, sic et laici ecclesiastica praesumere prohibeantur.'

[3] G. de Lagarde, *La naissance de l'esprit laïque au déclin du Moyen Age*, Saint-Paul-Trois-Châteaux et Paris 1934–46, 6 vols., (Italian translation of 4th French edition: *Alle origini dello spirito laico*, Brescia 1961, vol. I, *Bilancio del XIII secole*, pp. 121–7).

[4] 'Ecclesia non solum est ex clericis sed etiam ex laicis': manifesto '*Antequam essent clerici*', quoted by W. Ullmann, *Medieval Papalism*, London 1949, p. 214. The most contemporary and original expression of political laicism is that of Marsilius of Padua, in his *Defensor Pacis*, where he also treats other aspects, asserting the principle that the faithful are not to be considered the subjects of the priests (II. 3–4), and that it is in the competence of all Christians to make church law and interpret revelation (II. 20–1). A Dutch theologian, Albert Pighius, raised the question of these ideas in 1538, by asking whether Luther had gone to school with Marsilius of Padua, or vice versa. Cf. E. Staehelin, 'L'edition de 1522 du "Defensor Pacis" de Marsile de Padoue', *Revue d'histoire et de philosophie religieuse* 34 (1954), p. 220. On these influences, cf. an article which we have not been able to see: J. Heckel, 'Marsilius von Padua und Luther', *Zeitschrift der Savigny-Stiftung für Rechtsgeschichte*, Kan. Abt. 44, 1958, 268–336, cited by H. Grundmann in the bibliography to the article: 'Marsilius von Padua', *Die Religion in Geschichte und Gegenwart* (*RGG³*), Tübingen 1960, III, cols. 776f. On the position of Marsilius, see F. Battaglia, *Marsilio da Padova e la filosofia politica del Medio Evo*, Florence 1928; A. Passerin d'Entrèves, 'Rileggendo il "*Defensor Pacis*"', *Rivista storica italiana* 4 (1934), pp. 1f.; *La filosofia politica medioevale*, Turin 1934 (cf. also by the same,

It would be even more interesting to compare modern Catholic ideas with some of the things said on the subject of the lay conscience and lay responsibility in early Lutheranism. Of the 95 theses he fastened to the door of the Schlosskirche at Wittenberg on 31st October, 1517, Luther made the 81st and the 90th echo the reaction of the laity to the preaching of Indulgences:

> This scandalous preaching of Indulgences makes it difficult for even the learned to defend the reverence due to the Pope from the slanders or, if you prefer, the subtle resistence of the laity.

> To resolve by force alone without reasoning the very dangerous issues raised by the laity, is the very thing which exposes the Church and the Pope to the jibes of his enemies, and makes Christians so unhappy.[1]

In the famous Appeal to the Christian Nobility of the German Nation of 1520, this lay revolution (with Christian, not secular, ends) is referred to in terms more fully positive:

> All Christians have status in the Church, with no distinction between them, save in the office that each performs.[2]

Catholic thought is guilty of a grave error of judgment over the ecclesiology of the Reformation in regarding it as self-contradictory and as retaining only the elements of divine immediacy and community. Divine Immediacy is an idea that belongs to those mystical, rationalizing and spiritualistic schools which the sixteenth-century Reformers attacked with the same vigour they used against the Roman position. Let this not be overlooked, even if from the eighteenth century to the time of Barth, these notions made large inroads into evangelical Churches, and even came to be regarded as

the article; 'Senso e limiti del laicismo', *Protestantesimo* 14 (1959). p. 197; Marsilius of Padua, *Studi raceolti nel VI centenario della morte*, ed. by A. Checchini and N. Bobbio, Padua 1942; C. de Lagarde. *op. cit.*, vol. III, *Marsile de Padoue ou le premier théoricien de l'état laique*, 1948². On other interesting influences, cf., E. S. Molnar, 'Marsilius of Padua, Wyclif and the Hus', *Anglican Theological Review*, 1962, pp. 3f. However, we think that the verdict on Marsilius passed by A. Passerin d'Entrèves, remains valid—*art. cit.*, p. 35: 'His is a vision certainly at the opposite pole to that intimately and profoundly religious one held not only by the great medieval thinkers, such as St Thomas or Dante, but also by a Luther or a Calvin, to whose doctrine attempts have been made to relate his teaching.'

[1] D. Martin Luther's *Werke—Kritische Gesammtaussgabe*, Weimar 1883f., I, p. 229, *Disputatio pro declaratione virtutis indulgentiarum*, 1517, cf. pp. 237 and 238: 'Facit hec licentiosa veniarum predicatio, ut nec reverentiam Pape facile sit etiam doctis viris redimere a calumniis aut certe argutis questionibus laicorum.' 'Hec scrupolosissima laicorum argumenta sola potestate compescere nec reddita ratione diluere, est ecclesiam et Papam hostibus ridendos exponere et infelices christianos facere.' Cf. E. Muelhaupt, 'Luther und der Klerikalismus', *Luther* 30 (1959), pp. 32f.

[2] M. Luther, *op. cit.*, VI, pp. 381f. *An den christlichen Adel deutscher Nation von des christlichen Standes Besserung*, 1520, cf. pp. 407/18f.: 'Dan alle Christen sein warhafftig geystlichs stands, unnd ist unter yhn kein unterscheyd, denn des ampts halben allein.' Cf. H. Storck, *Das allgemeine Priestertum bei Luther*, Munich 1953.

authentic Protestantism, both inside and outside Protestantism.[1] The confusion made possible the production of several Protestant books in the nineteenth century in which the social element in the Church survives (so it seems) only because of a pragmatic need to have some sort of constitutional organizational structure. It is perhaps these Liberalistic writings that have inspired Catholic thinkers to find in confessions of Faith of the sixteenth century only the element of 'congregatio sanctorum', and not to take account of the other elements that made up the idea of 'congregatio' itself.

In the seventh article of the Augsburg Confession:

> They teach that the one holy Church shall abide for ever. The Church is the congregation of the saints wherein the gospel is purely preached and the sacraments rightly administered,

the element of association is not to be separated from the objective element that determines it, viz., the gospel preached and signed in sacraments. Not only this, but Article VII, 'De Ecclesia' cannot stand without Article V, 'De Ministerio Ecclesiastico', which precedes and explains it:

> That we may attain this faith, the Ministry hath been instituted for teaching the Gospel and offering the Sacraments. For it is through the instrumentality of the Word and the Sacrament that the Holy Spirit is given, which makes our faith effective in those that hear the Gospel, where and when it pleases God. . . . They condemn the Anabaptists and others who feel that the Holy Spirit makes contact with man without the external word.[2]

---

[1] Cf. G. Miegge, *Protestantesimo e spiritualismo*, Torre Pellice 1941; R. Prenter, *Der Protestantismus in unserer Zeit*, Stuttgart 1959; V. Subilia, 'Libertà e dogma secondo Calvino e secondo i riformati italiani', in: *Ginevra e l'Italia*, All'Universita di Ginevra nel IV centenario della sua fondazione. Raccolta di studi promossa dalla Facoltà Valdese di Teologia di Roma, ed. by D. Cantimori, L. Firpo, G. Spini, F. Venturi. V. Vinay, Florence 1959, pp. 191f.

[2] 'Est autem ecclesia congregatio sanctorum, in qua evangelium pure docetur et recte administrantur sacramenta.'

'Ut hanc fidem consequamur, institutum est ministerium docendi evangelii et porrigendi sacramenta. Nam per verbum et sacramenta tamquam per instrumenta donatur spiritus sanctus, qui fidem efficit, ubi et quando visum est Deo, in his, qui audiunt evangelium. . . .

'Damnant Anabaptistas et alios, qui sentiunt spiritum sanctum contingere hominibus sine verbo externo. . . .'—*Die Bekenntnisschriften der evangelisch-lutherischen Kirche*, Göttingen 1956[3], pp. 58–61. Cf. E. Schlink, *Theologie der lutherischen Bekenntnisschriften*, Munich 1946[2]; R. Prenter, 'L'Eglise, d'après le témoignage de la Confession d'Augsbourg,' in *La Sainte Eglise Universelle—Confrontation oecuménique*, Neuchâtel–Paris 1948, pp. 93f.; F. Brunstaed, *Theologie der lutherischen Bekenntnisschriften*, Gütersloh 1951; R. Josefson, 'Das Amt der Kirche', in *Ein Buch von der Kirche —Unter Mitarbeit schwedischer Theologen*, ed. by G. Aulén, A. Fridrichsen, A. Nygren, H. Linderoth, R. Bring, Göttingen 1951, pp. 386ff.; E. Kinder, *Der evangelische Glaube und die Kirche—Grundzüge des evangelisch-lutherischen Kirchenverständnisses*, Berlin 1958, pp. 81ff., 85ff.

Statements as clear and theologically well-balanced as these, which stress with equal emphasis the double aspect of the Church, are reinforced and enlarged upon in Calvinistic writings. In the fourth book of his *Christian Institutes*, Calvin uses an ancient Christian expression and calls the Church the Mother of all who have God for Father,[1] and makes it clear that since God is not present among men '*par présence visible*', he uses the mediation of his ministers—

> not to endow them with the honour and superiority that is his, but only to work through them, just as a workman uses the aid of a tool.[2]

The Reformed Confessions of Faith maintain the same line, and keep a healthy balance between God's action and that of his ministers.[3]

Having said this much to put in proper perspective the specific functions of the ministry and the priesthood of all believers, it is clear that in the thought of the Reformers these last were all by equal right members of the people of God, and all endued with the

[1] J. Calvin, *Institution de la religion chrestienne* IV/1/1, Edition critique publiée par J. D. Benoit, Paris 1961.

[2] '. . . non point pour leur résigner son honneur et superiorité, mais seulement pour faire son oeuvre par eux, tout ainsi qu'un ouvrier s'aide d'un instrument': *op. cit.*, IV/3/1. For Ecclesiology of the Reformed Churches, cf. amongst others: H. Clavier, *Etudes sur le Calvinisme*, Paris 1936; *Die Kirche Jesu Christi und das Wort Gottes, Ein Studienbuch über das Wort Gottes als Lebensgrund und Lebensform der Kirche*, ed. by W. Zöllner und W. Stählin, Berlin 1937; A. Lecerf, *Etudes calvinistes*, Neuchâtel–Paris 1949; R. Newton Flew (ed.), *The Nature of the Church*, London 1952; H. Berger, *Calvins Geschichtsauffassung*, Zürich 1955; W. Niesel, *Die Theologie Calvins*, Munich 1957²; P. Jacobs, *Theologie reformierter Bekenntnisschriften*, Neukirchen Kreis Moers 1959; G. MacGregor, *Corpus Christi—The Nature of the Church according to the Reformed Tradition*, London 1959.

[3] Enough to quote the clear language of Chapter XVIII of the *Confessio helvetica posterior*: 'Dieu a tousjours usé de Ministres et en use encore aujourd'hui, et usera tant qu'il y aura Eglise en terre, pour se recueillir et establir une Eglise et la gouverner et conserver. Et pourtant l'origine des Ministres et leur institution est très ancienne, establie de Dieu mesme, et non point par quelque nouvelle ordonnance inventée des homme. Vray est que Dieu usant de sa puissance pourroit, sans aucun moyen, se choisir une Eglise entre les hommes: mais il a mieux aimé traitter avec les hommes en se servant des hommes. Pourtant faut-il avoir esgard aux Ministres, non pas simplement comme estans Ministres: mais comme estans Ministres de Dieu, par lesquels il ameine les hommes à salut. Et pourtant nous admonestons un chacun de se garder d'attribuer tellement à la vertu secrete du S. Esprit ce qui est requis pour nous convertir et bien dresser, que nous aneantissions le ministere Ecclesiastique. . . . Au demeurant, il nous faut bien donner garde d'attribuer trop aux Ministres ni au ministere. . . . Croyons donc que Dieu nous instruit par ses Ministres au dehors par sa parole: mais qu'il esmeut interieurement par le sainct Esprit les coeurs de ses eleus afin qu'ils croyent: qui est la cause pour laquelle nous devons rapporter à Dieu l'honneur d'un tel bien fait': *La confession helvétique postérieure*, Traduction française de 1566—Introduction et notes par J. Courvoisier, Neuchâtel–Paris 1944, pp. 101f. For the latin text, cf.: *Bekenntnisschriften und Kirchenordnungen der nach Gottes Wort reformierten Kirche*, ed. by W. Niesel, Zollikon–Zürich n.d. (2nd ed.), p. 253 (under title: 'Confessio et expositio simplex orthodoxae fidei 1566').

Spirit who alone originates our calling, faith and service. And these functions were not to be used as distinctions in dignity and authority —for these belong to God alone—but with the proper division of particular responsibilities, as among colleagues, with an eye to the purity of faith and the government of the Church.[1] The words of Jesus are not to be twisted into their contrary meaning:

> You know that in the world the recognised rulers lord it over their subjects, and their great men make them feel the weight of their authority. That is not the way with you; among you, whoever wants to be great must be your servant, and whoever wants to be first must be willing to be slave of all. For even the Son of Man did not come to be served, but to serve (Mark 10. 42–5).

The Church is the community of those who are in the service of one sole Lord. It has no superiorities of hierarchy, but there is one and the same spirit of communion and brotherhood, of mutual help in proper duties for the common good. Even appointments to government are appointments of an executive nature, intended to ensure that only One has government in the Church. The prerogatives of the Head remains his, the functions of the Body are performed by the members who recognize their organic colleagueship.

What has been happening in the Catholic world, so that in this present century, words such as these can still be heard from the lips of its supreme religious authority:

> In the pastoral body alone resides the right and authority necessary to move and direct all the members towards the goal set for society. As for the masses, they have no right other than that of letting themselves be led, and of following their pastors as a docile flock?[2]

Are we then to assume that all at once, something unthinkable even yesterday has happened, and that under the pressures of this century of political revolution and social change, there has blossomed within the Church of Rome a sudden capacity to listen to secular criticism of the clericalization of the Church? Has the secularization

---

[1] Cf. the study of T. F. Torrance, *Royal Priesthood*, Edinburgh 1955, on which however we should have to express some reserve over the author's concept of episcopacy. And especially the very full presentation to the ecumenical discussions of today by C. Eastwood, *The Priesthood of all Believers*, London 1960. For a more general survey, cf. J. R. Nelson, *The Realm of Redemption—Studies in the Doctrine of the Nature of the Church in Contemporary Protestant Theology*, London 1956³, p. 144. For the New Testament basis, cf. E. Schweizer, *Das Leben des Herrn in der Gemeinde und Ihren Diensten. Eine Untersuchung der neutestamentlichen Gemeindeordnung*, Zürich 1946; cf. *Church Order in the New Testament*, London 1961.

[2] Pius X, Encyclical *'Vehementer nos'*, 11 Feb., 1906: *ASS* XXXIX, 1906–7, p. 12.

of life become a phenomenon imposing enough to evoke, even four centuries too late, corrective action that will give the laity some real Christian responsibility, such as yesterday was reserved for religious specialists only? Interest depends on receiving understanding, responsibility and a proper sphere of action. Protestantism too is at grips on a world scale with the expanding secularization on life. But if this is happening inside Protestantism, it is to be charged against two centuries of defective theological understanding of the gospel. In other words, it is something that has happened in a highly complicated nexus of events, *despite* its own principles. In Catholicism on the other hand, the principles involved work just the other way. If the laity are to have a proper effective function, Catholicism would have to reverse all of 'its history and its system',[1] since the very conception of the Church and the whole of Christianity are involved. Is this an attempt to give the great masses of Catholic laymen the responsibility of thinking out the implications of their own faith, before the traditional machinery of the Church falls beneath the blows of a modern Nebuchadnezzar? Is it inspired by the sight, as old as it is new, of Christianity spreading and surviving without priests in the People's China of the twentieth century as in the Rome of the first?[2] Or is it just a device to promote the ascendancy of the hierarchy, by giving the laity the task of making the hierarchy's voice heard in the various sectors where they work in the world,

echoing image-like the voices of their masters.[3]

If the operation amounts to this, it would in effect make Catholicism more Catholic than ever, but would this internal reinvigoration really answer the fundamental problem raised by the transformation of the baby, which till now has slept in the safety of the cot under the watchful eye of Mother Church,[4] into a restless adolescent full of questions, and (all too soon) into a mature responsible adult, capable of making his own judgments in matters of faith, and of giving an account of the faith that is in him? When grave problems

---

[1] H. Barion-G. Wendt, Art. 'Klerus und Laien', *RGG*[3], III, col. 1663.

[2] Y. M. J. Congar, O.P., *Lay People*, pp. 173f.

[3] The expression is used of the Apostolate of the Laity by Leo XIII in the Encyclical 'Sapientiae Christianae', 10 Jan., 1890: Denzinger, 1936c. John XXIII in the address to the leaders of Italian Catholic Action, 10 Dec., 1961 (reproduced in *L'Osservatore Romano*, 11–12 Dec., 1961) finished his passage on the Apostolate of the Laity with the words: 'To the good apostolate that derives from the column and fount of unity that is the Church of Rome, victory is assured.'

[4] The image is Congar's, *op. cit.*, pp. xxxi, 252.

are at issue, is a serious, adequate renewal possible without a complete rethinking of that ecclesiology which makes the Church, in the persons of the hierarchy and the priesthood, the immediate norm of faith and mediator of salvation? Has the light of her experiences in the thirteenth and sixteenth centuries made Catholicism alive, in this new crisis of history, to the dangers of suppressing the germs of gospel truth that are making a ferment within it?[1] 'The insertion of the Church into the world depends largely on having a theology of the laity'[2] soundly put together. If present Catholic declarations about the laity are going to be made only in conjunction with others, contradictory and stultifying, about the divinely authorized distinction between clergy and laity, they will lose all their power to reinvigorate.

7. Ecclesia Reformanda

We reach the end of our list of examples. The line of procedure seems already obvious. Both implicitly and explicitly in the language of Catholic ecumenists, the principle that Catholicism is never to be touched, never to be reformed, is shown to be so much undermined, that some theologians are driven to the seeming paradox of claiming the traditionally Calvinist principle of *Ecclesia semper reformanda* to be really a Catholic one.[3] We find concepts quite surprising:

> The papal intention is that the Ecumenical Council should have as its task the renewal of the Church, as the preliminary condition for its return to Unity.[4]

One hears it said that it is not in accordance with the best Catholic tradition to assume attitudes that exclude Reform of the Church; on the contrary the best Catholic tradition demands an attitude in favour of it.[5] Hence the slogan new to Protestant ears, 'The Catholic

---

[1] There are still some laymen in Catholicism today whose supreme aspiration is 'obedience' and 'submission to the ecclesiastical authority': cf. J. L. L. Aranguren, *Cattolicesimo e Protestantesimo come forme di vita*, Brescia 1961, p. 280. But there are also laymen of spirit who raise their voices to demand more effective responsibility in the Church even in view of the Council, and indeed because of it: cf. articles in *Témoignage Chrétien* 17 June, 1960 and 17 Feb., 1961, cited by P. Petit, *Revue de théologie et de philosophie*, 1961, p. 185; the studies cited of L. C. Baas and O. B. Roegele; a group of Catholic laity in Italy in anticipation of the Council, in *La Missione* 1960, p. 161; G. Mollard, in *Esprit*, 1961, p. 719, special number on 'Voeux pour le Concile—Enquête parmi les chrétiens'; the review on 'I laici e il Concilio', in *La Civiltà Cattolica* 113 (1962), p. 495, etc. In the preparatory Commission for the Council, that on the Apostolate of the Laity does not contain a single layman, 'not even as a consultant': cf. the study cited of P. Bourguet, p. 54.

[2] C. Crespy, in *Esprit* 1961, p. 858.   [3] H. Küng, *op. cit.*, pp. 11, 51.
[4] *Op. cit.*, pp. 5, 133.   [5] *Op. cit.*, p. 12.

Church ever in Reform'[1]—a slogan that becomes 'The Catholic Church "of our time" (be it noted that these words are used even before the Council has begun its undertaking to renew) deserves "on all sides" to be known as the "Reformed Church", so as to lead to a providential *rapprochment* with the other "reformed" community.'[2]

Such expressions give the *prima facie* impression of novelty and improbability and remind one of the bland way in which contemporary Italian Catholicism claims responsibility for the Risorgimento, anti-Catholic as it was. Nor is it a matter of isolated statements; they are much more widespread than one might think,[3] and a closer analysis shows a remarkable corroboration from history, in so far as one's *prima facie* impression is produced by a limited historical outlook. But if one uses a viewpoint that reveals more than just the last four centuries of Catholic history, one discovers in the centuries immediately prior to the Lutheran reformation how effective and frequent was the motif of *Church Reform in Head and Members*, and one understands Erasmus' complaint in 1526 that Luther's proclamation of Christian liberty had had the counter-effect of a massive recrudescence of authority in the Church.[4] Congar has stressed how the Church of Rome suppressed its sense of self-criticism, and adopted instead an attitude of suspicion towards any sort of discussion, first because of the biblical objections raised by the Reformers, and then because of the rationalistic sarcasm of the Age of Enlightenment.[5] That the Church of Rome, after centuries of disdain of any kind of criticism or change, should feel again something stirring, and should be listening to the sound of such words as reform and renewal, is one of the most typical symptoms of that Catholic reawakening to which we have referred already. It is an indication of liberation from a psychosis that has paralysed it for four centuries, and bears the possibility that it may rediscover itself in its most essentially Catholic meaning. As happens when we discover all the wealth of cordial humanity that has been shut up inside a shy man, in those rare moments when he succeeds in breaking out of his inferiority complexes and being his real self.

---

[1] *Op. cit.*, p. 86. [2] *Op. cit.*, pp. 133, 146.
[3] Cf., *inter alia*, Y. M. J. Congar, O.P., *Chrétiens désunis—Principes d'un oecuménisme catholique*, Paris 1937, p. 339 [Engl. trs., *Divided Christendom*, 1939]; J. Lortz, *Die Reformation als religiöses Anliegen heute*, Trier 1948, p. 212; Y. M. J. Congar, *Vraie et fausse réforme dans l'Eglise*, Paris 1950; S. Tromp, S.J., 'De futuro Concilio Vaticano II', *Gregorianum* XLIII (1962), pp. 10f. (Tromp is Secretary of the theological Commission of the Council).   [4] A. Renaudet, *Etudes érasmiennes*, Paris 1939, pp. 261–84.
[5] Y. M. J. Congar, O.P., *Réforme*, pp. 30f.

E

3

Reforming Tendencies in Roman Catholicism

WHAT are the range and the theological boundaries of this contemporary urge to reform in Catholicism? Once more we must resort to the analogy between Christ and the Church that always underlies Catholic thought. Applying the categories of the Chalcedonian dogma to ecclesiology, there is a human side to the Church, and this it is that is to be reformed. It is opportune here to recall again the typical phrases of the Encyclical '*Ad Petri cathedram*', where the aims of the Council are defined in terms of a domestic event inside the Catholic Church, which takes place however with an eye to the 'sweet hope' of the 'return':

> The prime aim of the Council itself will be to stimulate a growth of the Catholic Faith, a healthful reshaping of the practices of Christian people, and a revision of ecclesiastical discipline in the light of modern needs.[1]

Spiritual and ethical failings on the part of the Christian people and the anacronism of some ecclesiastical practices, are to be no more obstacles or stumbling stones on the road of 'return'. Just as in the sixteenth century the Council of Trent brought new health to

[1] Translation used in *L'Osservatore Romano*, 3 July, 1959. In addressing the last session of the first phase of the works of the central Pontifical Preparatory Commission for the Council, the Pope said: 'We shall go forward with the help of the Lord, still in the sense we have understood from the first announcement, i.e., a general stirring up of Catholic energies, and setting them to serve Christian people and their needs. To say it briefly and to say it all, the Council aims at making the clergy put on a new splendour and holiness; that the people be effectively instructed in the truths of Christian faith and morality; that the new generation that grows up in the hope of better times be properly educated; that our social mission be cared for; that Christians may be missionaries from the heart, which is to say, fraternal and loving to all and with all. . . . What should we do for our separated brethren? What for the ever so many who do not bear the mark of Christ on their foreheads, and yet are children of God? . . . The house that we decorate again for the festa, that is renovated in the springtime brightness of her precious ornaments, is the Church which invites all men to itself.' The Latin text with an Italian translation was published in *L'Osservatore Romano* of 21 June, 1961. For the official text, cf. *AAS* LIII, 1961, p. 499.

the ailing body of the Church of Rome, in the matter of religion, ethics and church discipline, so the Second Vatican Council is given the duty of reawakening and bringing up to date the Church that is so far behind the times in structure and in methods, in the face of the religious apathy and the ethical laxity of the dechristianized masses of the twentieth century.

1. *Subjective faults*

Many Protestants do not always understand how Catholic theology, with its concepts of infallibility, can, and indeed is theologically obliged to, speak of a church of sinners.[1] Yet these sentences of Father Beaupère may serve to illustrate it:

> It may well be that a Protestant, let us say a Lutheran, in his Lutheran Church, sharing to the utmost possible extent at the very depth of his heart in what is transmitted of the truth and life of Christ through that Lutheran Church—it may well be that this Lutheran brother is in the last analysis nearer to Christ than I am, or any Catholic at all. Do not confuse the plan of personal sanctity with the objective plan of the relative positions of the different Christian communities. On the personal level, it may well be that a Reformed or Anglican brother is more intensely nearer Christ than I. Because one is a Catholic, one is not automatically more deeply sanctified. I believe that I have in my Catholic Church a fulness of the life of Christ which my Lutheran brother does not objectively have in the Lutheran Church, but it may well be that within the Catholic Church, I am totally unfaithful, totally sinful, totally a bad Christian. That is another question.[2]

Statements of this sort must be carefully weighed and given their proper theological bearings, for they are capable of being interpreted with misleading optimism by a certain Protestant mentality which emphasizes ethics and sentiment, and in turn arouses the attention of

---

[1] Of interest is the work of K. Rahner, S.J., *Kirche der Sünder*, Freiburg i. Br. 1948. Fr S. Tromp, S.J., *art. cit.*, p. 10, speaks of 'humana fragilitas, etiam possibilis in nobilioribus Ecclesiae membris.' 'Aliud autem sunt individui, aliud munus divinum ad quod sunt electi; aliud singula Corporis Christi membra, aliud organismus ipse socialis, a Christo ipso conditus et in Cruce sanguine eius consecratus et aeternaliter stabilitus: organismus, in quem Salvator iugiter gratias ac dona spiritualia influit; organismus quem per Vicarium suum visibiliter regit ac dirigit; organismus Spiritu Sancto unificatus, vivificatus, vegetatus indesinenter.'

[2] Paper given by R. P. Beaupère, O.P., Director of the Centre St Irénée (Lyons) at Agape on the occasion of the Ecumenical Camp, 30 August to 1 September, 1961, at which there were also present Dr W. A. Visser 't Hooft, General Secretary of the World Council of Churches, and Bishop (Orthodox) E. Timiadis, representative of the Patriarchate of Constantinople at the World Council of Churches. The subject of discussion was: Unity and Disunity in the Church from the Roman Catholic point of view. The quotation is taken from a recording, and is published with the kind approval of the speaker.

certain Catholic commentators, who wrongly interpret the phenomenon as meaning that once the Catholics reform their behaviour,
Protestants will no longer protest. This however is very far from the
outlook of a Protestant who knows his fundamentals, and certainly
far from the mind of the Reformers. Serious Catholic students, such
as Lortz or Adam, know this well, and remember a typical remark
of Luther's on the matter:

> I would not trouble myself with the Papists, if only they taught rightly.

The Holy Spirit

> condemns false doctrine, and bears with those who are weak in faith
> and in living.[1]

2. Institutional faults

To indicate the institutional defects, one might cite the distortions
imposed by bureacracy, legalism and formalism on that Christian
spirit which alone gives form to and sustains 'the life of the Body of
Christ'.[2] It is superfluous to give examples, for such distortions
threaten every Church, as every servant, of Christ. If the proof of
a man's worth is his ability to withstand the distorting pressures his
profession may cause, the same sort of thing can be said of Churches,
without however in any way affecting the question of the truth or
otherwise of their messages. The mistake of rigorist movements of the
sectarian and anti-totalitarian type is that they do not realize this.[3]

It is however one matter for the process of ecclesiastical bureaucracy to make merely marginal inroads, over which the Christian

---

[1] J. Lortz, *Die Reformation in Deutschland*, Freiburg i. Br. 1941², I, p. 390; K. Adam,
Vers l'unité chrétienne—Le point de vue catholique, Paris 1949, p. 52.

[2] H. Küng, *op. cit.*, p. 18.

[3] It is however disturbing to note the reception afforded a book which contained quite
innocuous suggestions, and which merited a warm approval, that of Fr L. Lombardi, S.J.,
Concilio—Per una riforma nella carità, Rome 1961, which phrased most respectfully ('on
the knees before the assembled teaching Church . . . as if I beheld Jesus himself, her
who is his mystic body through the ages', p. 6) some modest requests for vigilance to
eliminate the risk of careerism in the Curia, and to place the right persons in posts of
responsibility, without being influenced by the fear of replacement or demotion to
positions of less importance if age or the interests of the public good demanded it (with
the exception of the Pope, 'Head for life, beyond control and indeposable', to whom
'God himself' has assured 'the efficiency he needs until his death', p. 212). In a considered
but harsh article 'Verso il Concilio in unione col Romano Pontefice', on the front page
of *L'Osservatore Romano* of 11 Jan., 1962, the book was passed off as merely 'private,
personal'. At the same time was reiterated the necessity of 'a perfect submission to the
judgment of the legitimate authority' and 'those who by divine right are Masters in
matters of faith, custom and sacred discipline'. Pope John XXIII himself intervened to
emphasize the condemnation in the concluding address of the third session of the Central
Preparatory Commission, published in *L'Osservatore Romano*, 24 Jan., 1962. The book
was not named, but the references are clear. The consequence of all this was that the
book itself after a few days disappeared from circulation.

spirit of the love of the Lord watches unceasingly and has the victory, and quite another for it to be exalted as a matter of principle, and come near to transforming the spirit of service into that of domination, with all the apparatus of worldliness that naturally goes with it. Denunciations of the pomp of Papal courts are of ancient date, and originated in Catholic quarters, but have gone unheeded for centuries. Symptomatic is the fact, we may recall, that Luther in his *Appeal to the Christian Nobility of the German Nation*, in 1520, puts among the points that 'the Council' should deal with—even then they spoke of this as the means of renewal for the Church—this very issue, which even if it seems a superficial one, is nevertheless, because of its very superficiality, the apparent sign that the authentic spirit of Christianity is in danger of being turned into its precise opposite.[1] And today it is Catholic voices, conscious of the urgency, in our dechristianized world, of restoring to the insipid salt its lost savour, that seem to re-echo those ancient protests.[2] But have such

[1] M. Luther, *op. cit.*: *WA* VI, p. 415: 'It is a terrible and fearful thing to realise that the head of Christendom, who calls himself vicar of Christ and successor of St Peter, lives in such pomp and worldly magnificence that a king or an emperor cannot pretend to nor attain the equal; and while he has himself called "holiest" and "spiritual", he is a being more earthly than the very earth itself. He wears a triple crown, while the greatest kings wear only a simple one; he compares himself to the poverty of Christ and St Peter, and this is a truly novel and strange comparison. They shout heresy if any speak against him, but they won't understand that such a custom is anti-christian and anti-divine . . . such pomp is cause of scandal, and for the sake of the blessedness of his soul the Pope is bound to lay it off.'

[2] Father Lombardi, *op. cit.*, p. 227, writes, e.g., 'In all earthly hierarchies it is by now accepted that there are hardly any outward signs of different rank, such differences being reduced to slight symbolic indications: the general dresses much as the private soldier, the minister as the humblest clerk. But amongst us in the other hand—in the very society where the first should be "as he who serves", and especially among the ecclesiastics—there are still varieties of dress and several pomposities to indicate the different positions. . . . It would be edifying for the people to see all ecclesiastics dressed simply. . . . . If a man does not laugh at seeing it otherwise, it is perhaps because he is by now so bemused that he hardly understands any more what we mean by it.'

A French parish priest, G. Mollard, in *Esprit*, 1961, p. 723, after speaking of all the ecclesiastical trappings, vestments and titles of Eminence and Excellence, and asking 'Where is the gospel in all this?', writes: 'Ecclesiastical trappings do much harm, and, with money, are one of the obstacles to faith, for many say: I believe in Jesus Christ, but I do not believe in the Church. . . . If the Pope took note of the harm done by his Court, which is borne by the most loyal and loving of his children as a family shame, he would not hesitate to dismiss the noble guard, the Swiss guard, the bearers of his chair; he would rid himself of the intolerable weight of his museum, and give his treasures to some international institution. If the Council takes this road, which after all does not require great courage, it will be upheld by the wide approbation of Christian people, an approbation of a different sort from that represented by kisses for episcopal rings, and cheers in Piazza San Pietro. A Christian friend said to me one day: "When the medicine becomes serious, it means the doctors no longer deceive themselves: the Church one day will refuse to accept anything that is not serious." '

Father S. Pelaya, *I preti sono uomini*, Rome 1962, p. 43, writes: 'Soon faith in Christ will be eliminated from the mind and thought of men, while in the Vatican they will

protests, ancient and modern, any real hope of being effective, unless they go to the very root of the system? We are sure that not even under the pressure of a political revolution, would the cleansing of the Temple effectively take place, unless it were the outcome of a reform inspired by the gospel itself. Political revolution might sweep clean obvious anachronisms, just as the unification of Italy abolished the Papal States, and the Lateran Pacts of 1929 resolved the last shreds of the Roman problem by drawing the boundaries of the Vatican City. However, in the Catholic mind, as Pius XI observed in the year of the Reconciliation, such a geographical limitation is regarded as an assurance against every embarrassment,[1] in so far as the little Vatican City remains 'exalted above the temporal plane', to incarnate and symbolize 'the apostolic authority of Christ's Vicar over all governments and his inalienable right to independence in matters of international politics—in a word, the absolute liberty of the spiritual over every political power'.[2] The germ of the idea remains insulated, as far as history is concerned, from anything that ever has or ever will happen. And so, for any Catholic who possesses the *sensus Ecclesiae*, that word of Bernard of Clairvaux[3] to the effect that the Pope in his temporal power is successor not to Peter but to Constantine, still remains valid. What remains of this Constantinian power in the shape of present-day formalities, is interpreted as a transfiguration. The Catholic mind finds no absurdity, but rather harmony and appropriateness, in the

continue to amuse themselves and deceive themselves amid the flourish of silver trumpets and the sparkle of palace uniforms, amid the discussion of the tiny reforms of liturgy and bureaucracy and the gold of heavy archaic vestments, amid the applause and admiration of exotic pilgrims and the fatuity of Roman nobility, amid the servility and the sullen rebellion of the bussolanti, the chairbearers, the knights of cloak and sword, and a world of hypocrisy and mustiness, of obsolete titles and customs.'

According to news published in *La Stampa*, 23 March, 1962, Pelaya was Provincial Father of the Friars Minor of Catanzaro and has been expelled from the Order. The writer of the article, N. Adelfi, commented: 'Though it may have been impetuously and brusquely, the monk of Calabria has nevertheless had the courage to speak out on certain issues which today are felt most vividly on the consciences of believers, even though they speak little of them and that in whispers.'

The passages quoted in this note are not taken from text books, but they represent careful thought, because they, with many others, are symptomatic of an unrest and a ferment which are not anticlerical, they profess full submission to the Teaching Authority of the Church, they do not put forward criticism in matters of dogma; yet they are moved—especially the last two—by a Christian passion that commands respect and accord.

[1] Pius XI, Address to the Lent-preachers of Rome: *AAS* XXI, 1929, p. 109.

[2] C. Journet, *op. cit.*, I, pp. 605, 609 [I, pp. 466, 469].

[3] Bernard of Clairvaux, *De consideratione* II VI, 10 and 11: Migne—*PL* 182, col. 748, quoted by C. Journet, *op. cit.*, I, pp. 600-8 [462-8]. Cf. E. Staehelin, *Die Verkündigung des Reiches Gottes in der Kirche Jesu Christi*, Basel 1955, p. iii.

contrast between the temporal expression of the Lord's sovereignty in the glory of his Vicar, and the qualities more directly evocative of the Gospel seen today in the ascetic rigours of the poverty and the obedience of the monastic orders, and tomorrow, who knows, perhaps also in the simplicity of the evangelical Churches.

3. *Historical faults*

Defects in the understanding of history in this age of social change, can be illustrated by the phenomenon known to Catholic and Protestant Churches alike, of the westernization of Christianity, and the difficulties felt in the mission field consequent upon the frequent confusion of the content of the gospel with the Americo-european forms of expression in which its message and the faith are couched, and upon the failure to realize that this Gospel can find credence and expression in forms alien to our cultural tradition. Proof of Catholic sensitivity to the problem, and of their search for a fuller Catholicity can be found in the appointment of coloured Cardinals as members of the Supreme College, and the use of non-latin rites of consecration by the Pope himself. The method which Cardinal Paolo Marella has called that of the *tabula rasa*, is to be replaced by the 'adaptation method'. The first

> consists in making little or nothing of a people's heritage prior to their conversion; rather, in erasing it and making the neophytes forget it, and substituting en bloc alongside the Christian religion, the culture, usages, and even in certain cases, the language of the nation to which the missionaries belong. In short, to make the convert a fellow-citizen of the missionary.[1]

In face of the impressive phenomenon of a new ethnic consciousness among people of colour, the second method consists in the attempt to assimilate

> everything not contradictory to faith and morals.[2]

The theological principle behind these two successive methods, and the preference for the second over the first, is fully in keeping with the Integrationist line, but in this case, it does not mean syncretizing the Christian heritage with that of non-Christian peoples, i.e., it is a question not of adapting dogma, but of adapting methods of missionary presentation under new pressures. There is a higher

[1] Card. P. Marella, 'Il Concilio sulla via dei popoli non Cristiani', in *Concilio Ecumenico Vaticano II*, Genoa n.d. (1962), p. 72.
[2] *Op. cit.*, p. 75.

synthesis of the natural with the supernatural, and the reaffirmation of the Catholic, i.e., the supernatural and universal, character of the Church finds a wider and more coherent expression than in the past. In other words, here one finds a modern manifestation of that traditionally Catholic principle that grace does not destroy but perfects nature, so that reason and natural religion represent the point of entry for faith in the Gospel.[1]

4. *Inter-confessional relations*

In the field of inter-confessional relations there are more direct references, and we find new attitudes that seem to modify noticeably age-long practices. One could hope that these might issue in real and proper inter-confessional understanding even in countries with a Catholic majority, and so gradually lead to habits of mutual politeness and respect, evidenced both in law and in custom, so ending the chronic state of incivility among Christians. Foremost among these new attitudes, one finds a recognition of the free, never to be coerced, nature of faith of any sort, such as should have been obvious for the last twenty centuries, wherever messengers of a Lord not self-evident were at work. One finds also an acceptance of the fact that there is a plurality of denominations in the modern world, and that this has come to be a feature of the modern State since the end of the Wars of Religion. Now that the Constantinian pretence is over, this shows itself as the right to choose one's belief and equally one's disbelief. But it is best here not to go to any depth into this new outlook, nor express any critique of it, since it does not arise naturally from Catholic dogma, and is certainly motivated by the over-riding hope that sooner or later this plurality will be a thing of the past.[2]

[1] For the new Catholic Missionology, cf. Encyclicals of Pius XII, '*Evangelii praecones*', 2 Jan., 1951, '*Fidei donum*', 21 April, 1957, John XXIII, '*Princeps Pastorum*', 28 Nov., 1959, and with regard to this last: 'In Litteras Encyclicas "Princeps Pastorum" Ioannis P.P. XXIII Commentari', *Euntes Docete* 1960, nos. 2–3. Also two volumes already quoted, of M. J. Le Guillou, O.P., *Mission et unité*; Card. C. Costantini, *Réforme des Missions au XX siècle*, Tournai 1961.

[2] Cadier-Couturier-Pribilla-Thurian, *Unité chrétienne et tolérance religieuse*, Paris 1950; R. Aubert, L. Bouyer, L. Cerfaux, Y. M. J. Congar, A. Dondeyne, A. Leonard, J. Masson, A. Moliter, B. Olivier, H. D. Robert, *Tolérance et communauté civile— Chrétiens dans un monde divisé*, Paris-Tournai 1952; Pius XII, Talk to the Union of Italian Catholic Jurists, 6 Dec., 1953, in *L'Osservatore Romano*, 7–8 Dec., 1953 (cf. comment of L. Salvatorelli, 'Ipotesi o tesi?', *Il Mondo*, 29 Dec., 1953); J. Lecler S.J., 'A propos de la distinction de la "thèse" et de l' "hypothèse",' *Recherches de Science Religieuse*, 1953, pp. 530f.; A. F. Carrillo de Albornoz, *Roman Catholicism and Religious Liberty*, Geneva 1959; C. Boyer, in: *Verità e Libertà—Relazioni introduttive al XVIII*

However where these changed relationships towards other Confessions have legal implications, they deserve close study. He would show that his knowledge of Catholicism is ingenuous and superficial, who would attribute this new course to some irresistible impulse of cordiality that might be in the air, touched off by the goodness and joviality of John XXIII, that wipes out all the censoriousness and abuse of the past, and engenders a radically changed mental outlook towards non-Catholics. Catholicism is not to be turned out of its age-long course by any matter of temperament. The new climate of our times in inter-confessional and international relationships has had undoubted weight in a Church as endowed with historical understanding as is that of Rome, but there are some motives for these new attitudes that can be accurately charted in the fields of theology and canon law.

Protestants have been for centuries, in Catholic eyes, the epitomy of heresy. Today the word is used no longer; it has been changed to 'separated brethren'. However, the insistence that truth is on their side alone proves that the concept itself remains. Nor is this all. The juridical and the moral viewpoints intertwine in a complicated casuistry that makes precise definition difficult. In Catholic thought, heresy is error in the matter of faith, and schism dissent. Yet both error and dissent may or may not be tainted with an element of guilt, which may or may not be laid at the door of the erring or dissenting person.[1] Indeed the Code of Canon Law lays it down that heresy is sinful when a doctrine erroneous in itself is upheld with 'pertinacity'.[2] Is the category of guilt applicable to the present inter-confessional situation, or does it apply only to the initial stages of rupture in the Church? Cardinal Bea, President of the Secretariat for Union, has made himself the mouthpiece of the present attitude, in saying that 'schism and heresy, as such, separate from the mystical body of Christ which is the Church, that is, from a full participation in the life which Christ communicates to the Church. But this applies to

Congresso nazionale della Società filosofica italiana, Palermo 1960; V. Subilia, 'Verità e libertà', *Protestantesimo* 15 (1960), pp. 161f.; G. Peyrot, 'Cattolicesimo romano e libertà religiosa,' *Protestantesimo* 16 (1961), pp. 44ff.; A. Hartmann, S. J., 'The Principles on which *Religionsfreiheit* is based in Catholic Theology', *The Ecumenical Review* 13 (1961), pp. 427f.
[1] Cf. the Scholastic documentation in C. Journet, *op. cit.*, II, pp. 708f.
[2] *Codex Iuris Canonici* (Rome 1934), can. 1325 §2: 'Post receptum baptismum si quis, nomen retinens christianum, pertinaciter aliquam ex veritatibus fide divina et catholica credendis denegat aut de ea dubitat, haereticus; si a fide christiana totaliter recedit, apostata; si denique subesse renuit Summo Pontifici aut cum membri Ecclesiae ei subiectis communicare recusat, schismaticus est.'

those who personally and knowingly separate themselves from the Church, and certainly not to those who in good faith find themselves separate as a result of the legacy they receive from their fathers.'[1] Thus there come into play the concepts of 'good faith' and 'invincible ignorance'.[2]

Bellini writes

> Protestants of today are not those who began the Reformation, and the Orthodox of today not those who made the schism; they were born, grew up, and were shaped in this situation. One must realise that their minds were not only instructed in a certain doctrine, but were born in it, and also brought up in it, so that there has been created in them a mentality which binds them to their belief, and renders them practically incapable of understanding the true demonstrable force of contrary statements and their arguments. . . . The recognition of such good faith has important bearing upon the possibility of the salvation of the separated brethren, and upon their sharing in the mediating reality of the Church. Dissenters in this position cannot be held guilty of personal sin in heresy when it separates them from the Church. Though they are in a state of incompleteness and of doctrinal error, they are not personally in a state of sin for heresy, for which always personal guilt is involved.[3]

Hence Protestant Churches would always be Churches composed of believers of the same faith and the same doctrines, some of whom however would be innocent of the sin of heresy, since their heresy is one of birth, whilst others are guilty, because their heresy has been acquired. The first have not been able to know, and therefore have not yet been able to embrace, Catholic truth, the others have known it, and have rejected it. This would create inside the Protestant Churches a very serious line of demarcation among people who have equal rights to share in the Communion of Christ. A Catholic theologian has even proposed as an ecumenical expedient that Canon 2314 of the Code of Canon Law be emended, so that excommunication for heretics should be limited to Catholics who have abandoned

---

[1] Card. A. Bea, 'La grande chiamata all'ovile di Cristo'—Conference held 22 Jan., 1961 in Rome at the Pontificio Ateneo Angelicum. Our quotation is taken from a summary published in *L'Osservatore Romano*, 27 Jan., 1961. Cf. *La Civiltà Cattolica*, 21 Jan., 1961, p. 113. Pius XII had already said in his Message to German Catholics, with reference to the 'separated', 'Only God knows how many are they who stand afar through no fault of their own': *AAS* XL, 1948, p. 418.

[2] Cf. copious documentation gathered by F. J. Leenhardt, *Le Protestantisme tel que Rome le voit*, Geneva n.d., and: *Eglise et Royaume de Dieu—Réflexions sur l'unité de l'Eglise et sur le salut des non-catholiques*, Geneva n.d.

[3] A. Bellini, *Il movimento ecumenico*, Padua–Rome–Naples n.d., pp. 139–141. Cf. E. Chavaz, *Cattolicesimo ed ecumenismo*, Milan 1957, and A. Bea, conference referred to above.

the Church, while those who are Protestant by tradition might be considered as partially belonging to the Church, i.e., as subjects whose relationship to its authority is not either fully comprehended or complete, and so they are 'brethren' waiting to be possessed of their full rights.[1] It may be that this proposed amendment will be considered in the envisaged revision of the Canon Law in connection with the Council. Clearly present trends are in that direction. For that reason, Protestants have a corresponding duty to form clear concepts of the principles behind these trends, however far from simple may be their logic. Perhaps the matter might be reduced to the formula: Non-catholics *are to be taken seriously not in respect of what they believe, but only for the good faith with which they believe it.* That means, their sincere ignorance of Catholic truth would be more valuable than their knowledge of Gospel truth; indeed, more valuable than the intrinsic worth of this truth, independent of their knowledge of it, or their sincerity. What they believe—i.e., their very motive principles which count with them much more than their personal fate and their personal feelings—*the dogmatic content of their faith, is discounted no less today than it was yesterday.* There can be no doubt in the matter. One accepts the persons, even the collective groups of Protestants; one shows them kindness, understanding, brotherliness; one recognises that there is a genuinely religious and Christian content in their convictions. But one rejects the substance of their faith. The old adage—Augustinian, if we mistake not—of hating the error and loving the erring one, is here applied with appalling thoroughness; the question of the person and the question of the dogma are at one and the same time superimposed and kept apart. Certainly, when one asks the why and the wherefore one certainly does not know if one should feel repelled or rejoiced at the sight of this new 'brotherliness'. One hardly knows any longer whether to believe and take seriously all these fine statements on 'what unites us'. And a sense of perplexity and disquietude prompts

---

[1] G. Colombo in *La Scuola Cattolica*, 1949, p. 297, cited by A. Bellini, *op. cit.*, p. 141. Cf. G. Vodopivec, 'Membri *in re* ed appartenenza *in voto* alla Chiesa di Cristo', *Euntes Docete* X (1957), pp. 65f. Vodopivec adds: 'Not all those subject to the power of the Church are *eo ipso* also true members of the Church. The Church herself considers the separated as subject to her power, but refuses to consider them as real members in the true sense of the word. This means that the concept of member implies a concept of a fulness and of a reality higher than that of merely being subject, and that of the juridical personality of the Church' (p. 89). Canon 2314 of the *Codex Iuris Canonici* reads (§1): 'Omnes a christiana fide apostatae et omnes et singuli haeretici aut schismatici: 1° Incurrunt ipso facto excommunicationem. . .' and §3: 'Si sectae acatholicae nomen dederint vel publice adheaserint, ipso facto infames sunt. . . .'

the query whether one ought not to reject with revulsion such dubious courtesy, for it recalls certain phrases of a letter of Luther written to Spalatino, 9th September, 1521, which have the roughness, but also the solidity, of granite:

> Erasmus is very far from knowing what grace is, for in everything he writes, he has his eye not on the cross but on peace. On that basis, he thinks that everything can be solved by courtesy and good will.... With that method no one ever changes heart.[1]

It would not be wise to dismiss the dangers of courtesy with the naïve remark that Luther's phrase only indicates an obsolete state of mind, or that the polemics of the recent past have proved an indifferent strategy. Jesus, Paul, even the Apostle John, according to the New Testament were not courteous when the truth of the Gospel was at stake, either in dealing with doctrine or with persons. From remotest Christian antiquity, it has been impossible to dissociate 'We believe' from 'We condemn'. Papal documents of the phase before the present justly contained warnings against the perils of Peace for Peace's sake. To this theme we must return later, since it is basic to our disagreement, and is of a piece with that discerning of the spirits, to which the Gospel calls believers, in order to distinguish between the spirit of truth and that of error (I John 4.6). For the moment we may be content with observing how in every Church, Christian charity at times takes on some dubious and disconcerting shapes, and with the best intentions in the world assumes attitudes that are out of place, not to say offensive. The Catholic mind is inspired by a quite positive and—we frankly admit—loving (in the Catholic sense of the word) desire to come out and meet us and remove obstacles, but it does not realize that reasonings and gestures of this kind, however magnanimous in intent, produce only pain and disappointment to the Protestant spirit.[2] Naturally and inevitably we find ourselves once more up against the fact of Catholicism, i.e., up against a fundamental issue of dogma which determines a psychological attitude. Sentimentalists in ecumenism are in for a rude awakening when brotherhood is regimented and subordinated to a legal casuistry that makes the question of truth or falsehood depend on the entire and exclusive interests of Catholicism.

[1] M. Luther, *WA* II, p. 387.
[2] We have found a happy exception in an important article by A. Prandi: 'Il Movimento ecumenico delle Chiese non cattoliche', *Il Mulino* 9 (1962), pp. 384f. Speaking of the Catholics, Prandi remarks: 'The theme of "return under one Shepherd" cannot be eradicated from the Catholic point of view, but it is also true that today they realise how repugnant it is for the separated brethren' (pp. 385f.).

And yet for all that, such reactions must not blind us to the existence of a new factor. There is a modification, there is—to use the biggest word—an unmistakable reformation of the old attitude of inquisition and condemnation. Not that the fundamental dogmatic bases in themselves have been discarded, but there is a change at the point of impact in human and inter-confessional relationships. The debates of the sixteenth century gave way unhappily to a confessional rigidity on both sides, which made its lasting mark on history, and left each side strangers and unknown to each other. Even the very memory of a time of contact was lost. It is a matter of tremendous importance if it is again possible to talk together in an atmosphere immeasurably less contaminated by non-theological considerations, and more fit for the dignity of the faith. Even if that 'psychological recovery' which the Abbé Couturier spoke of,[1] 'by means of prayer, goodness, the mutual esteem of individuals and all their human and Christian values', is conditioned by all the disturbing presuppositions we have alluded to above, and is motivated by a frankly declared missionary interest,[2] it still is pregnant with a promise whose limits are not to be measured. This change of confessional outlook is charged with new possibilities for Christendom, which may carry far beyond their calculated range, and indeed backfire on their very promoters, sending sky-high the dykes which they now think can contain the force. By a slow and seemingly imperceptible change of levels on both sides, there could creep in a spirit of humble quest in place of prejudice—in the theological sphere it is largely already there; in place of scorn, the desire for colloquy; in place of patterns already fixed, an interest in something that suddenly is realized to be an unknown quantity. Walls, behind which wasteful wars, offensive and defensive, have been waged for centuries, are thrown down, to permit a pacific circulation of ideas, values, interpretations and viewpoints quite different from one's own. This opens up the possibility of realizations and reactions which in the long run will work against the operation of any restrictive principle which claims the *a priori* right to trace out their course or fix their limits. One comes to discover the Christianity of the other and the reasonableness of his faith, as well as to assess his faith

---

[1] M. Villain, *L'Abbé Paul Couturier, apôtre de l'Unité Chrétienne—Souvenirs et documents*, Tournai, 1957[3], p. 57.

[2] 'Animi missionale studium alant: illud inquimus studium, quo fratres et amicos omnibus et cum omnibus se demonstrent': talk already quoted of John XXIII: *AAS* LIII, 1961, p. 499.

no more by external judgments, no more by prejudice and dogma, but as far as is humanly possible, one assesses it from within, by forcing oneself to think in concepts proper to the other's faith, and to express it objectively in such a way that he can recognize it. Here there is the recognition that there exists a Christianity that is not Catholic, even if the recognition is accompanied with every safeguard and reservation, and even if it is insisted on over and over again that this Christianity is not intrinsic, but is Christian only in that it contains some Catholic truths, only in that 'there are present and at work within it, elements of the true and only Church'.[1] However inconsistent it may seem with what we have remarked before, it is now admitted that there may be, imperfectly and incompletely, Christians outside Catholicism, not 'despite' their own Confession, but 'precisely by means and virtue of' their own Confession.

'The dissenting Churches are not imperfect Churches alongside the perfect Church; they are not even part of the Church; they are an incomplete participation in that complete Church whose historic manifestation has ever coincided, and shall ever coincide, with the Catholic Church.'[2]

Even if this statement may seem to contradict what we have ourselves just said, it must be affirmed that these changes of climate are historically so significant, and so pregnant of possibilities, that they cannot be properly evaluated. Both sides must be careful to avoid slighting them and to acquire the art of not hurting or offending the other's confessional feelings, unless the most pressing reason demands it—a difficult art, and the foregoing is evidence that we ourselves practise it but indifferently.

---

[1] A. Bellini, *op. cit.*, p. 142. This would be the place to consider (would the treatment not take us too far from our theme) the problem of 'vestigia ecclesiae'. Cf. T. Sartory, O.S.B. *Die oekumenischen Bewegung und die Einheit der Kirche—Ein Beitrag im Dienste einer oekumenische Ekklesiologie*, Meitingen bei Augsburg 1955, pp. 147f.; G. Thils, *Histoire doctrinale du Mouvement Oecuménique*, Louvain 1955, pp. 142f.; R. Mehl, 'Ecclesia quoad substantiam', *Revue d'histoire et de philosophie religieuses* 36 (1956), p. 326; G. Miegge, 'Vestigia Ecclesiae—Storia di un concetto ecumenico', *Protestantesimo* 12 (1957), pp. 117f.; G. Vodopivec, 'La Chiesa e le Chiese', in *Problemi e orientamenti di teologia dommatica*, Milan 1957, I, pp. 537f.; G. Thils, 'Tendenze ecumeniche nel Protestantesimo attuale', in *Il Protestantesimo ieri e oggi*, ed. by Mons. A. Piolanti, Rome 1958, p. 572.

[2] A. Bellini, *op. cit.*, pp. 142–4.

5. The Reforms of Forms

We have examined some aspects of this reform movement in catholicism, yet before we reach our main thesis, we must prolong a little the lines of our study by considering indications of changes of a formal type.

One immediately thinks of the concession, already hinted in the pre-Conciliar documents, of some limited autonomy in the field of liturgy. The question of the language used in worship seems at first sight a mere matter of form, hardly worthy of special treatment. However, a closer look reveals that this is an ecumenical problem, with a bearing indeed on interconfessional relationships,[1] but also involving the way in which Christianity itself is to be interpreted.

When Luther in 1520 urged that the words of the Mass, i.e., of the Testament of Christ, should be pronounced 'in a loud and distinct voice' in the language of each people, so as better to rouse their faith,[2] he certainly based his request on theological premises that he understood well. Today a like request is made in many parts of the Catholic world, yet one may question whether those who make it realize fully what long-term consequences (such as might change the very shape of their faith) are inherent in what seems, innocently enough, a matter of form. Today's agitation is inspired by a missionary concern. Faced by a world drifting away from Christ, a pastoral mind does not wish to leave it any longer famished for the word of God. It is considered absurd that the man of today, free from prejudice, with a mind capable of a critical research into the fundamentals of things, should be presented with still one more obstacle to faith in an archaic language that makes gospel truths seem foreign. These demands are supported by the observation that the use of Latin is not a dogma of the Church, and that the matter is 'still open to a free discussion':[3] against the objections of those who 'desire to retain Latin as an element of unity', the retort is that 'the unity of the Church is in its faith and not in its language'.[4] In the face of the grave difficulties arising from the use of a language unknown to the people to whom it is addressed,[5] there is expressed the hope of a definite de-archaizing

---

[1] H. Clavier, 'L'action du langage sur la diversité et sur l'unité de l'Eglise', in Die Kirche Jesu Christi und das Wort Gottes—Ein Studienbuch über das Wort Gottes als Lebensgrund und Lebensform der Kirche, ed. by W. Zöllner and W. Stählin, Berlin 1937, pp. 222f.
[2] M. Luther, De captivitate Babylonica ecclesiae praeludium, 1520: WA VI, p. 524.
[3] Cf. Etudes 1961, p. 225.   [4] G. Mollard, art. cit., Esprit, 1961, p. 726.
[5] P. Winninger, Langues vivantes et liturgie, Paris 1961.

which will permit the gospel to be made really contemporary for the man of our age:

> Shall we too soon have the joy, especially on the Feast days, of being able to read to our members the word of God in their own idiom, and so to nourish them so much more effectively on the bread of the revealed truth? That is our vivid hope, and we also look to the day when such a reading may be not merely permissive, but mandatory, as the normal and proper way of preaching the gospel and the doctrine of the apostles, prophets and Moses. Then we shall have laid a better and surer foundation for a more vital pastorate.[1]

The campaign must have been an extensive and obstinate one to have aroused such vigorous opposition,[2] as culminated in the Apostolic Constitution, '*Veterum Sapientia*'.[3] This papal document, referring explicitly to representations made to the Holy See, voices solemnly the decision:

> to deal at once with the matter in principle, and so ensure the maintenance of the ancient and unbroken use of the Latin tongue, and where it has lapsed into almost total disuse, its absolute restoration.

Pronouncements of Pius XI[4] are the basis for declaring that since

> *every Church must originate* in the Church of Rome, and the Supreme Pontiffs have *true episcopal authority, ordinary and immediate, not only over all and every church, but also over all and every pastor and member*

---

[1] C. Oggioni, 'L'uso della lingua volgare nella liturgia', *La Scuola Cattolica* 88 (1960), pp. 56f. Cf.: V. Subilia, 'La lingua parlata nel culto cattolico', *Protestantesimo* 16 (1961), pp. 171f.

[2] The prospect of a gradual substitution for Latin, or at least a reduction of it, was glimpsed in a discourse of the Pope given 13 March, 1960, in the Church of Sta Maria del Soccorso, according to the news published in certain papers. *L'Osservatore Romano*, 14–15 March, 1960, contained only an indistinct reference, and official sources give nothing. Indeed they only document the opposition. The signal of the counterattack was given in an anonymous but undoubtedly authoritative article in *L'Osservatore Romano*, 25 March, 1961: 'Il Latino lingua della Chiesa.' The article denounced 'the campaign at present conducted against the Latin liturgy, a campaign that is very often cloaked under false pretences, and which is conducted most disloyally with an audacity which has been adjudged as iconoclastic fanaticism'. The attitude of the article was described in the Review of the Benedictines of the Monastery of Chevetogne, *Irénikon* 34 (1961), p. 182 as 'une dureté pénible', that ran the risk of 'd'indisposer plutôt que de convaincre'.

[3] John XXIII, Apostolic Constitution '*Veterum Sapientia*', 22 Feb., 1962, published *L'Osservatore Romano*, 24 Feb., 1962.

[4] Pius XI, Motu Proprio '*Litterarum Latinarum*', 20 Oct., 1924: *AAS* XVI, 1924, p. 417, in which Latin is described as 'splendid vesture for heavenly doctrine and most holy laws'; Apostolic Letter '*Officiorum omnium*' of 1 Aug., 1922: *AAS* XIV, 1922, p. 452. The Encyclical '*Mediator Dei*' of Pius XII is not cited, wherein Latin is described as 'a clear and noble sign of unity, and an effective antidote against all corruption of pure doctrine'. For the contribution of this Encyclical on the subject, cf.: H. Hermelink, *Die katholische Kirche unter den Pius—Päpsten des 20. Jahrhunderts*, Zollikon-Zürich, 1949, p. 105.

of every rite, people and tongue, it follows that the means of communication between them must be *universal* and uniform.

Not only universal, but also *immutable*, must be the language used by
the Church.

The reasons alleged are that 'the truths of the Catholic Church'
cannot be entrusted to the 'constantly varying languages of today,
none of which can claim any superiority over the others' because
their meanings cannot ever be expressed 'with sufficient exactness
and clarity'.

There must therefore be one language that can serve as 'a common,
unvarying norm, whereby to regulate the exact meaning of the other
languages', and as a 'door which opens directly onto Christian truths'.

Since the Catholic Church, inasmuch as it is founded by Christ the
Lord, far surpasses in dignity all human societies, it is proper that it
should not use a *popular* tongue, but rather one noble and august.

Such strange arguments are not easily understood, unless they
are seen in their setting of Catholic thought. Then they are seen as a
protraction as far as the realm of language of that hierarchical pattern
and that dogmatic codification of truth (all with the object of guaran-
teeing it against risk of error, and of keeping it out of the way of
discussion) which is the distinguishing pecularity of Catholicism.
Hence gospel truths come to be given a fixity even of form, in a way
never to be reconciled with the tension of dialectic, nor with the
problematic nature of the whole Christian message, which is a
message of a piece of history. The Latin language, in short,
defined as it is in this document as the 'living language of the Church',
seems as it were to assume that prerogative of being the norm, and
that function of interpretation, that Christian tradition attributes to
Holy Scripture and the Holy Spirit.

The Constitution '*Veterum Sapientia*' has caused disappointment
in some Catholic quarters, which seems to persist despite some
isolated denials.[1] According to its provisions, any 'integration' could

---

[1] According to *EPS*, 16 March, 1962, a group of 30 prominent Catholics of the Low
Countries, among them M. L. Baas, national president of Catholic Action, sent a letter
to the Dutch bishops expressing their own feelings of unrest at the fact that the Pope's
publication, anticipating decision by the Council, seems to block all discussion and all
hope in the matter. The same source (6 and 13 April, 1962) states that Bishop W. Kampe
and Cardinal F. König have tried to quieten these apprehensions. But the language of
'*Veterum Sapientia*' is so strong as not to seem to admit of any doubt: according to its
verdict 'both bishops and Superiors General of Orders' must be on guard lest 'any of
their subjects, in a foolish desire for innovation, write against the use of Latin either for
teaching the sacred discipline, or for the sacred rites of the liturgy, or moved by prejudice

F

only take place, one assumes, through 'indulging' Protestant practice, as is done at the moment in certain limited sections of Catholicism.[1]

A facile explanation of the Papal intervention would see it as a piece of conservative anachronism, resulting from pressure from reactionaries in the Curia. However, behind these words can be detected a motivation consistently Catholic, lying deeper than any merely contingent, and hence negligible, consideration. Behind the question whether to use or not to use the common tongue, lies the question whether Christianity is to be interpreted as a living message addressed to the consciences of men involved in the problems of their age, or as a sacred mystery whose sphere is a rite celebrated by initiates who stand in a special relation to the divinity. Hence it is of a piece with the impossibility, for dogmatic reasons, of doing away with the distinction (established by divine institution) between cleric and layman. The clergy share in some sense in this inaccessible otherness of the divinity, and embody it. The incomprehensible language, as also the solemn uniform different from that of other men, as also too the life of celibacy indicative of the abolition of sex, all set up a frontier designed to separate sacred from profane, divine from human. It is by means of the use of these unfamiliar forms that the sacred and the divine manage to maintain their supernatural and ineffable character.

In worship man reaches out beyond his normal existence. When he speaks of God, or to God, he automatically uses sublime words, such as do not normally rise to his lips. Now it is precisely the ancient languages that possess in their own selves, even today, a strength and a dignity that derives from their objective and solemn changelessness, and achieve what cannot be achieved by any living language, all of which

minimise at all the force of the will of the Holy See's directive in the matter, or change its sense'.

If in any country the authority of Latin 'has been at all lessened' everything is to be made to conform once more to the traditional pattern, on which is based instruction in theology. 'However, those who teach these subjects in Universities and Seminaries are required to speak in Latin, and to use texts written in Latin. Where ignorance of the Latin language makes it impossible to conform with these requirements of the Holy See, these teachers must be gradually replaced by others more apt in the matter.'

Thus one might comment, theological competence and the scientific worth of a teacher must ultimately take second place to the superior capacity of a less capable scholar to speak Latin. The document has all the air of the anti-modernist condemnation of the early part of the century. It concludes thus: 'What we have in our Constitution established, decreed, ordained and enjoined, we will and command by our authority to stand definitely fixed and sanctioned, and that no other directive, concession or custom, even though worthy of special mention, shall have precedence over this order.'

[1] Cf. the review already cited, *Protestantesimo* 16 (1961), pp. 171f.

is particularly appropriate for a sacred language. By them there is spread over the act of worship the splendour of eternity free from the tie of time.[1]

Here one is not thinking, much as one might like to, of the use of one language for all the Church, as if it were the language of the Spirit, whose objective was the spread of the knowledge of the gospel, and as if it were to be known by all men of the Spirit as 'the tongue in which they were born' (Acts 2.8)—a kind of Pentecost eternally renewing itself, and overcoming the confusion and dispersion worked by Babel. On the contrary the age-old Protestant contention that the language used in the Church must always be understood, smacks of the rationalism of the Enlightenment in Catholic ears.

> Silence full of mystery, which ultimately is what the use of an unknown tongue involves, expresses the holiness of God more purely than the most effective instruction.[2]

Connected in the Catholic mind with this line of thought, is the insistence that in the Liturgy the soul should learn to free itself from any utilitarian outlook, which makes it always act with some end in view, and ultimately with the idea of learning some religious truth. It must not look any more at itself but contemplate the glory of God. The Liturgy

> is not a means to be used to arrive at a determined end; rather it is— at least to a certain extent—an end in itself. It is not, in the eyes of the Church, a stage on the road that leads to a goal outside itself; rather it is a world of living realities that abides in itself. . . . The liturgy cannot have any 'aim' . . . since it has its raison d'être properly considered not in man but in God. . . . The meaning of the liturgy then is this, that the soul stands before God, unfolds itself before him, inserts itself into his life, into that holy world of reality and truth, of divine mysteries and divine signs.[3]

Protestantism's constant concern with man and its insistent desire to give him an understanding of his faith, and so lift that faith out of its infantile state and make it mature and theologically competent, is perhaps due to the anthropological interests of the Humanism of the Renaissance in the context of which it had its origin. It may be that in remembering the admonition of the apostle to know him in whom we have believed (II Tim. 1.12), and the things which we have been given by God (I Cor. 2.12) such as render the spiritual man able to judge all things (I Cor. 2.15), Protestantism

---

[1] O. Casel, *Die Liturgie als Mysterienfeier*, Freiburg 1922, p. 147.
[2] *Op. cit.*, p. 147.
[3] R. Guardini, *The Spirit of the Liturgy*, London 1930, p. 96.

has forgotten, or given only marginal attention to that sense of adoration possessed so richly by the New Testament with its recurrent doxologies. This could be true, even if the Reformation was precisely a protest against the way in which Christianity was being made anthropocentric in not dissimilar if in different ways by both Catholicism and sixteenth-century Spiritualism, and even if it represented an effort aimed precisely in the opposite direction, to set God at the centre, and displace man with his reason, his works, his piety. At any rate Calvinism, reckoned as it is the most pedagogic of all the Reformation Confessions, has as its key-note, alongside *sola scriptura, soli Deo gloria*.[1]

However, on the other hand, it might be that Catholicism has imbibed from the historical and cultural environment in which it arose, conceptions of divinity that belong to the ancient world, and has undergone processes of assimilation on a vast scale to the worship patterns of the Jewish-Christian world and those of its own historical environment, with the result that Catholic worship (in terms of Heiler's classification) has taken on the notes of the esoteric, the archaic, the ritualistic, aesthetic, symbolic and dramatic.[2] Why have all attempts, past and present, to adopt the vernacular in the Roman Church failed? Should we not seek the answer in this contamination by elements that do not belong to the gospel, but have been so naturalized and incorporated into Catholicism that it no longer knows how to rid itself of them? These accretions have come to affect not only forms, but the very conception of God himself. Thus, once again, a question seemingly a matter of form like the others has led us back to the basic question. The use of a dead, uncomprehending tongue is no *adiaphoron*: it impinges on one of the fundamental Christian conceptions, for the God of the Gospel is a God of Revelation and Word, and not of Mystery and Silence.[3]

[1] Cf. the fine presentation made by J. Cadier of the marks of reformed piety, in: *Foi et Constitution—Actes officiels de la deuxième Conférence universelle*, Edinburgh 3–18 Aug., 1937, Paris 1939, pp. 95ff. It is also noteworthy that M. Mezger, art. 'Anbetung', in *RGG*[3] I, col. 358, puts the praise of God as the central note of Protestant worship.

[2] Cf. F. Heiler, *Der Katholizismus*, chapter: 'Die Mysterienliturgie', pp. 373ff.

[3] The function of silence is known in the world of the history of religion: cf. F. Heiler, *Prayer* [ET], New York 1932, pp. 336, 354, 358f.; G. Mensching, *Das heilige Schweigen*, Berlin 1926; art. 'Schweigen', in *RGG*[3] V, cols. 1605f. The first appearance of the idea in a Christian setting is in Ignatius of Antioch—*Magn.* 8.2, in *Corona Patrum Salesiana: Series Graeca*, vol. XIV, *I Padri Apostolici*—Turin 1942, II, p. 75. All students of the thought of Ignatius note, even if with different reactions, the resemblance of his formula of the Logos proceeding out of silence, to later ones of the Gnostic Valentinus.

6. *The intellectual framework*

Still a matter of form, but one of immeasurably greater import, is the question of the language, the conceptual formulae and the philosophic ideas in which the theological content is clothed.

Contemporary Catholicism, especially in France, has sent out innumerable pressing demands for 'de-archaising'. In the decade that preceded the middle of this century, there appeared from the pens of some of the most learned and acute theologians, especially Jesuits, volumes and articles that were symptomatic of a widespread spiritual unrest. These writings protested against the way in which Christian theology was subordinated to a philosophic system which in origins and inspiration was not Christian, i.e., the Aristotelian philosophy which had figured the concepts of God, of grace, and of sacrament basically in terms of cause and substance. Thomism, the central theology of Catholicism, has all the defects of this mode of thought, and possesses only the value of an outworn medieval doctrine, no longer capable of properly expressing gospel truth in language which answers to the needs of modern problems.[1] Hence the attempt, on one hand to go back to the period before Scholasticism had hardened ideas, to the sources of the Bible or to the Fathers; and on the other, to seek points of contact with the ways of thought of modern man, shaped as they have been by modern culture, and its scientific and sociological interest. Not indeed with the idea of substituting a new philosophy for an old one, and so presenting one more case of making Christian thought captive in a prison of non-Christian thought-forms, but with the aim of injecting the leaven of the gospel into the spiritual categories which man in his present social conditions uses in thinking about his real problems.[2]

In these writings the criticism was not pushed home to its full consequences for Protestantism, although the influence of Kierkegaard, Barth and Cullmann could be detected. It followed the undoubted Catholic party line, and never deviated from the wholly Catholic tradition of the great consonance of reason and faith,

[1] Cf. the final chapter of the work of H. Bouillard, *Conversion et grâce chez St. Thomas d'Aquin*, Paris 1944. The same author was to publish several years later a three-volume work on *Karl Barth*, Paris 1957. Besides this criticism of Thomism, cf. also: H. de Lubac, *Corpus Mysticum—L'eucharistie et l'Eglise au moyen âge*, Paris 1944 (a criticism of the juridical conception of the Church, and the substantialist conception of the Eucharist); same author, *Surnaturel—Etudes historiques*, Paris 1946 (a criticism of anti-Jansenist theology).

[2] Cf. article of J. Daniélou, 'Les orientations présentes de la pensée religieuse', *Etudes*, April, 1946.

systematized by Thomism, and canonized in the declarations of the First Vatican Council. The authors intended merely to initiate discussions over the immutability of one fixed way of formulation which had been considered valid in its time of origin, but which no longer responded to modern thinking. As against their colleagues who gave Thomism a constant valuation, and saw in it 'the truly scientific expression of Christian thought',[1] these theologians revealed a more tractable and more dynamic mind when they asserted that Christian thought had not stopped short in the thirteenth century, and when they refused to accept the contention that the thought of the Church could be enclosed in a system, on the grounds that, according to the gospel, Truth is a Person.[2] In other words, as Mons. Bruno de Solages has put it, they want to do just what Thomas himself did in his time: in the face of the discovery, 'sensational for that epoch', of the works of Aristotle himself, Thomas broke with the Neoplatonic tradition of Augustine which had for centuries dominated theology, but instead of letting himself become, as many contemporary theologians did, completely absorbed with the new problems posed by that discovery, and so passing 'more or less into complete Aristotelianism, which is, when all is said and done, paganism . . ., he had the courage to look the issue full in the face, and to resolve it', by using the categories of Aristotelian thought in the interests of the Church. As then, so today, in the face of the world with its changes, there are three camps: 'that of the theologians who refuse to take any notice of evolution, that of those who end up in Relativism, with loss of faith, and finally the camp of those who in face of the modern world, adopt an attitude analogous to that of St Thomas to Aristotle.'[3]

Yet should anyone, in faithfulness to the Catholic principle of adapting the different cultures of successive ages, project a new and more up-to-date synthesis between Christianity and the thought-forms of the man who lives through this present cycle of civilization, he would come up against a specific regulation in the Canon Law which seems to endow Scholastic concepts with a permanent validity:

[1] M. M. Labourdette, O.P., 'La théologie et ses sources—Etude critique', *Revue thomiste*, 1946, pp. 353-371.
[2] The collective reply of the Jesuit theologians to the Dominican Labourdette: 'La théologie et ses sources—Réponse', *Recherches de science religieuse*, 1946, pp. 385-401.
[3] B. de Solages, 'Pour l'honneur de la théologie', *Bulletin de littérature ecclésiastique*, 1947, pp. 65-84, cf. pp. 82f.

Let teachers ever be guided in the study of Rational Philosophy and Theology, and in the instruction of pupils in these disciplines, by the reason, doctrine and principles of the Angelic Doctor, and hold soundly to them.[1]

In fact charges of Modernism were speedily made, and seemed to presage a massive reaction.[2] They were serious charges in view of the condemnation of Modernism without appeal in the early years of the century,[3] and the continuance of the oath against it.[4] But such charges merely meant that the issue had not been solved, but only shelved. Yet they succeeded in being upheld by the supreme *magisterium*. On 17th September, 1946, Pius XII in receiving the twenty-ninth General Congregation of the Company of Jesus, had alluded to the 'new theology', and its tendency to be 'ever on the go, never getting anywhere', and he had warned them not to disturb and overturn what must never be altered.[5] A few days later, on September 22nd, he received the General of the Dominicans, and said that Thomas' system remained the permanently settled foundation of theology and philosophy, and the guarantor of its progress.[6] Such words were but the prophetic forerunners of the alarmed official pronouncement of 1950. In the Encyclical 'Humani Generis', the Pope condemned as Relativism the attempt to reformulate doctrine and affirmed on the contrary that the doctrine of Aquinas 'is consonant with Divine Revelation' and so no one might look slightingly or disrespectfully on the eternal validity of that philosophy 'confirmed and accepted by the Church'. Thus one would avoid the danger of substituting for it

certain hypothetical notions, and unstable and vague expressions of the new philosophy, which, like the grass of the field, today is and tomorrow withers away. This is the way to make dogma itself like a reed shaken by the wind.

There was no mistaking the allusions to the old Modernist position and the new tendency to modernize thought-forms, and the

---

[1] *Codex Iuris Canonici*, can. 1366 §2.
[2] R. Garrigou-Lagrange, O.P., 'La nouvelle théologie, ou va-t-elle?', *Angelicum*, 1946, pp. 126f.; 'Necessité de revenir à la notion traditionelle de vérité', *ibid.*, 1948, pp. 185f.; 'L'immutabilité des vérités définies et le surnaturel', *ibid.*, 1948, pp. 285f.
[3] Decree of the Holy Office '*Lamentabili*', 3 July, 1907: *ASS* XL (1907), pp. 470f.; Pius X, Encyclical '*Pascendi dominici gregis*', 8 Sept., 1907: *ASS* XL (1907, pp. 593ff.
[4] Pius X, Motu proprio '*Sacrorum antistitum*', 1 Sept., 1910: *AAS* II (1910), pp. 660f.
[5] *L'Osservatore Romano*, 18 Sept., 1946.
[6] *Ibid.*, 23-4 Sept., 1946.

parallel was made in a way that seemed to ignore, or at least under-estimate, the complete difference of theological climate between the two movements:

> Just as once there were those who questioned whether the traditional apologetic of the Church did not prove a hindrance rather than a help in drawing souls to Christ, so today there is no lack of men who go so far as to ask seriously whether theology and its methods, as used in the Schools and approved by the ecclesiastical authorities, stands in need of being, I do not say perfected, but completely reformed, if Christ's Kingdom is to be propagated more effectively in all the world, amongst men of every culture and every religious opinion.

The conscious need to measure 'the doctrine of the Holy Fathers and the supreme *magisterium* against that of Holy Scripture' must be turned in the opposite direction, in the sense that Holy Scripture 'is expounded in accordance with the mind of the Church, which has been appointed by Christ the Lord as the guardian and inter-preter of all the deposit of revealed truth'.

This deposit has not been entrusted by the Divine Redeemer

> by way of authenticity of interpretation, either to individual believers, nor to the very theologians, but only to the *magisterium* of the Church.

Theologians may certainly discuss among themselves questions not yet decided, but their real task is not one of interpretation, nor of dogma, but rather apologetic; that is in

> indicating how the teachings of the living *magisterium* 'are to be found either explicitly or implicitly' in Holy Scripture and Divine Tradition.

In performing this task they must invariably keep to the 'imme-diate and universal norm of truth' which is indeed the *magisterium*.

Now the wish to modify the way in which truth is to be presented, by replacing ancient patterns approved by this sacred *magisterium* with new schemes, may mean removing oneself, either obviously or not, away from its guidance. This was a danger whose reality had been so disquietingly demonstrated, and the Pope was fortifying himself against any attempt to use Relativism against the authority of his Encyclicals. The teaching of these 'is of the ordinary *magis-terium*, of which the words apply: "He who hears you, hears Me".'

So were the roads blocked against the generous hopes that

> Dogma, trimmed of those elements which are (in their phrase) foreign to divine relation, may issue in fruits that may be set alongside the dogmatic opinions of those who are separated from the Church, and so

there may gradually come about an assimilation between dogma and the opinions of the dissenters.[1]

One need only think of the consequences of some attempts made in the Protestant camp during this century and the last to establish contact between the theology of the Church and the culture of the world, to recognize that the caution of the Encyclical about new experiments in transmitting the Christian message was understandably justified. There can indeed be a spirit that seeks to evangelize by following, more or less unknowingly, the path of adaptation to the spirit of the age and its ways of thought, sidestepping the necessity inherent in the gospel to break off at the point where there appears a risk of negating the very content and the very meaning of the gospel it seeks to impart. Yet on the other hand, when the free play of contrasting ideas is blocked from above, and precaution against human error takes the form of an *a priori* veto by decree, then there enters the risk that in sheltering the gospel from secular winds, one may make it a gospel no longer vigorous and healthy, but torpid, mummified and incapable of travelling the roads of this life. Neither one solution nor the other is to be recommended by its results, however much each may have been inspired by the intention to be faithful in evangelism. At any rate, faced with this reactionary Encyclical, which looks as if it must paralyse any move to renovate the thought-forms of Catholic theology, the question to be asked is: Can so uncompromising a statement ever be modified? Must we completely exclude any hope of a future opening? In

[1] Pius XII, Encyclical 'Humani Generis', 12 Aug., 1950: AAS XLII, 1950, pp. 561–578. Italian translation that of L'Osservatore Romano, published in extract by Gregoriana Editrice, Padua 1950. For the 'new theology', cf. K. Guggisberg, 'Moderne Strömungen in der katholischen Theologie', in Die Strömungen im moderne Katholizismus und die evangelische Stellungnahme, Zollikon–Zürich 1953, pp. 36f.; R. Aubert, La théologie catholique au milieu du XXe. siècle, Tournai–Paris 1954, pp. 47f., 71f.; W. von Loewenich, op. cit., pp. 281f.; H. H. Schrey, art. 'Frankreich', in RGG[3] II, col. 1045; G. Thils, Orientations de la théologie, Louvain 1958, pp. 57f. On the Encyclical, cf. P. Parente, art. 'Humani Generis', in Enciclopedia Cattolica VI, cols. 1502f.; K. G. Steck, art. 'Humani Generis', in RGG[3] III, col. 477; C. Boyer, 'Les leçons de l'Encyclique "Humani Generis"', Gregorianum XXI (1950), pp. 526f.; C. Colombo, 'Il significato teologico dell'Enciclica "Humani Generis"', La Scuola Cattolica 78 (1950); M. Flick, S.J., 'L'Enciclica "Humani Generis". Vero e falso progresso del pensiero cattolico', La Civiltà Cattolica 101 (1950), pp. 577f. (in the same year appeared articles by Father Bea on biblical problems, and by Father Selvaggi on the relation of science and faith); A. Perego, S.J., 'La nuova Teologia. Sguardo d'insieme alla luce dell'Enciclica "Humani Generis"', Divus Thomas 53 (1950), pp. 436f.; A. Dondeyne, Foi chrétienne et pensée contemporaine, Louvain 1951; 'In Litteras Encyclicas "Humani Generis" Pii PP. XII Commentarium', Euntes Docete, 1951, pp. 1–254; C. Muller, L'Encyclique 'Humani Generis' et les problèmes scientifiques, Louvain 1951; G. K. Steck, 'Die Bedeutung der Enzyklika "Humani Generis" für das Problem von Kirche und Lehre', Evangelische Theologie 11 (1951–2), pp. 549f.

support of the contention that pressure still persists, because the problem has not been, and is not to be, resolved by a stroke on the part of authority, one may quote this significant passage from Father Villain:

> When the Church through the voice of the *magisterium* defines a dogma, its intention is by its definition to lay down authentically a *datum* of faith. Yet that does not mean that the Church's expression of it does not bear the impress of a particular system of thought, which as such has no absolute value, and is never to be regarded as irreplaceable. Let us be quite clear what is meant. We do not claim that a definition might one day be suppressed or passed over in silence. It possesses naturally an eternal character. But it could be that a definition might have need of reinterpretation, should the context of the problem and the language used have come to be modified.[1]

Villain draws a parallel between missionary necessities and ecumenical necessities. If whole continents, utter strangers to the area of Christian civilization were to gravitate tomorrow towards Christianity, then one would have to 'furnish these new Christians with a complete system of equivalents' in order to put across the Christian message in the categories of their thought. In the same way, in dealing with Protestants accustomed to thinking in biblical categories, it is useless to go on with Scholastic categories. This is not a matter of compromise by accepting the principle of *sola Scriptura*, but of sacrificing language and method in the interests of ecumenical charity, as a provisional step to making oneself intelligible to Protestants, and so setting them on the road of Catholic truth. It involves 'a constant progress through comprehension to revelation —which God will complete in his own time'.[2]

The author accordingly arms himself against '*Humani generis*':

> What I set out here, and I need not stress it, makes no common cause at all with the relativism of dogma. In the situation I speak of, dogma itself remains unchanged; all that is in question is its formulation, and its exposition in categories of new and varying thought. The Ecumenists fervently hope that a day will come, and come soon, in which the mystery of Christian unity which is both a 'revealed *datum*', and a 'becoming' will pose to the Church problems on which it has never pronounced

---

[1] M. Villain, *Introduction à l'Oecuménisme*, p. 249. The passage is taken from the 1961 edition of the work, and is thus eleven years after '*Humani Generis*'.

[2] *Op. cit.*, p. 257. The text of the French does not translate well: 'un progrés constant vers une saisie semblable de la Révélation, qui aboutira quand Dieu voudra'. The parallel between mission and unity has been developed in the two volumes already cited of M. J. le Guillou, O.P., *Mission et unité*.

in the sense I have suggested, and that the principle of equivalents will be generously allowed by the Church itself.[1]

There is no doubt that the language problem transcends the difference between Catholic and Protestant, and colours the difficulty of presenting the gospel to the men of our time, and both Confessions give attention to it.[2] To see how important this is, one need only take an example that concerns both Catholic and non-Catholic theologians—a concept central to Christianity, and present in Holy Scripture itself—that of Redemption. A close look reveals that here we have an image capable of evoking response in 'an age in which there were slaves to be redeemed'.[3] Today, however, it awakes practically no echo, and we must ask whether its content must not be radically rethought, and fresher expressions found, more fitted for the outlook of modern man and nearer to his feelings.

It is not just a question of adequacy. In confessions of faith of the traditional type, couched in language which no longer corresponds to their content and so compromises the testimony they must give before the world, it is truth itself that is at stake. A classic example, a problem for Catholicism and Protestantism alike, can be seen in the doctrine of the Trinity. Doubtless in the fourth century to speak of three 'persons' of the Trinity, meant using a language certainly inperfect and contested; yet all said and done, it did express the truth of revelation. But to speak of three divine 'persons' now that we have modern anthropological sciences, is nothing less than to speak of three Gods, unless we use the phrase as a conventional cypher in a sense different from its universal meaning. The use of the ancient term has already become impracticable. Instead of explaining the revealed truth, and imparting a theological understanding of it, it makes it incomprehensible, and turns it into a non-Christian doctrine, teaching polytheism. We are faced with the necessity of changing the language, not in order to whittle away or to modify orthodox doctrine, but just to explain it as it is. Yet up

[1] M. Villain, *op. cit.*, p. 250.

[2] In the Protestant field cf. K. von Bismarck, 'The Christian Vocabulary: an Obstacle to Communication?', *The Ecumenical Review* 9 (1957), pp. 1f.; H. Kraemer, *The Communication of the Christian Faith*, London 1957; I. T. Ramsey, *Religious Language*, London 1957; A. Malet, 'Le problème des concepts et du language dans la théologie et dans la prédication', *Foi et Vie* 58 (1959), pp. 25f.; *Das Problem der Sprache in Theologie und Kirche—Referate vom deutschen evangelischen Theologentag 1958*, ed. by W. Schnee-melcher, Berlin 1959; P. Tillich, *Theology of Culture*, New York 1959; H. Noack, *Sprache und Offenbarung—Zur Grenzbestimmung von Sprachphilosophie und Sprachtheologie*, Gütersloh 1960.

[3] R. Aubert, *op. cit.*, p. 47.

to now, no theological genius has discovered a language more satisfying, or has shown himself capable of a process of theological rethinking equal to the dogmatic effort made by the Church of the
fourth century. This is but one of the many points where a theological undertaking with vast ramifications is required, if the common
deposit of faith is to be transmitted to future generations.[1]

But just as many are the points of misunderstanding that create
barriers between the Churches. It would be well not to underestimate
their reality, and to realize that their removal will involve on each
side a revision of traditional habits of thought established for centuries. On the Protestant side, the very spirit of Protestantism bears
within it the possibility of such revision, and this century has seen
tremendous movements in theology of this pattern, and once the
dangerous trends towards excess have subsided, we may see tomorrow some fascinating, not to say daring, possibilities for communicating the gospel carefully without disturbing the balance between
content and form. On the non-Protestant side, if the Catholic Church
could tomorrow admit the possibility of rethinking its dogma, and
frankly allow alongside that relative pluralism of liturgies, a plurality
of theologies, or at least, of theological expression (all on the basis
of a principle already admitted, that of the reinterpretation and the
elaboration of dogmas), then we should certainly be faced with a
situation so new that no one could predict in advance the lines of
its development, and it might bring about an incarnation completely
new to history of unity in diversity and not in uniformity. This
would be one of the most desirable forms of that 'bringing up to
date' that John XXIII spoke of, and such as would liberate Catholicism from some of the heaviest ecclesiastical drags inherited from
the Middle Ages, that thwart the possibility of communicating her
message to the men of our time, who are contemporaries with
nuclear physicists, Marxist sociologists, with Jaspers and Sartre and
with linguistic analysts. There is no sense any longer in speaking
to them of natural and supernatural, of substance and accidents, in
categories which may have been valid in the eleventh or the thirteenth centuries, in the days of Anselm of Aosta or Thomas Aquinas.
Even more; it would mean an end to that Latin provincialism of
theology, which in a world remarkably extended as ours is, merely

[1] At the third Assembly of the World Council of Churches at New Delhi, December
1961, the desire was expressed for the formation of a Commission for theological
language, to study in this light the division between Confessions, and the possibility of
offering the gospel to the world in an up-to-date form. Cf. *EPS*, 6 Dec., 1961, p. 5.

limits, and in a sense renders illusory, the idea of the catholicity of Catholicism. The most aware of Catholic theologians have for a time now been alive to this need, and in the realm of high Catholic theology, there is such a zeal for inquiry and such a determined effort at rethinking, that the prospect of new and vaster horizons depends only on the lack of further hindrances and vetoes from above.[1]

As regards Catholic-Protestant relations in particular, the theological hub of the disagreement might in many cases be isolated as a mass of fused philosophical ideas, which in the last analysis turns out to be an element not at all essential to division and which has been the cause of quite unnecessary disagreement. Well known are the studies that have been made on the Greek mode of thinking of the Divine presence as used by the Catholic Church, which uses chiefly visual means; and on the Hebrew method, favoured by the Protestants, which chiefly stresses hearing. The bearing of these divergent points of view on the apprehension of the faith, on the presentation of the message, and so on the inter-Church discussion, affect theological ways of thinking far more than one might suppose.[2]

Equally known are some of the attempts at re-expression of dogma on particular subjects, as for example that of the Lord's Presence in the Holy Communion. Father de Baciocchi has proposed that, because of its doubtful meaning in the realm of modern culture, the term *transubstantiation* should be dropped, whilst of course maintaining the dogma it is meant to express.[3] The present writer has tried to show that it is possible to think of arriving at an ecumenical agreement upon the Real Presence, by liberating theological statements from their state of captivity to language that lies too much

---

[1] H. Fries, 'Die theologischen Studien—Stand und Hoffnungen', in *Begegnung der Christen*, pp. 527f.

[2] Cf. e.g., the article of F. J. Leenhardt, 'Des raisons et de la façon d'être Protestants', *Verbum Caro* VII (1953), pp. 24f., and the book of T. Boman, *Hebrew Thought compared with Greek* (Engl. trs. of 2nd ed.), London 1960. On the Catholic side, cf. (among others) the essay of C. Tresmontant, *Essai sur la pensée hebraique*, Paris 1953, with its thesis of the necessity of assimilating the contribution of the various cultures, pp. 167f.

[3] J. de Baciocchi, S.M., 'Le Mystère eucharistique dans les perspectives de la Bible', *Nouvelle Revue Théologique*, 1955, pp. 551f. Cf. same author, 'Présence eucharistique et transsubstantiation', *Irénikon* 32 (1959), pp. 139f.; *La vie sacramentaire de l'Eglise*, Paris 1959; G. Colombo, 'Bilancio provvisorio di una discussione eucarisrica,' *La Scuola Cattolica* 88 (1960), pp. 23f. The attempt of Fr de Baciocchi was answered from the Protestant side by the not-too-happy book of F. J. Leenhardt, *Ceci est mon corps— Explication de ces paroles de Jésus-Christ*, Neuchâtel–Paris 1955 [ET in *Essays on the Lord's Supper*, 1958] and the article 'La présence eucharistique', *Irénikon* 33 (1960), pp. 146f.

under the power of philosophic premises.[1] The great problem lies
in seeing if the new formulae proposed, or others like them, preserve
in the concepts of the presence of God the eschatological tension
between the various times of God's work that the New Testament
establishes, or if on the other hand, they amount only to a more
polished and up-to-date method of affirming sacramentally what is
one of the constants of Catholicism. The presence of the Lord then
becomes once more just an *object* to be manipulated ecclesiastically,
theologically, liturgically. Even if the ponderous language of substance were abandoned, and replaced with something more modern,
the basic issue would still remain in all its seriousness.

In general, it is quite foreseeable that certain doctrines which
Protestants are accustomed to reject as non-biblical will tomorrow
appear decked out in a biblicity that makes them at first sight
unrecognizable. But the change would in reality be only 'the affirmation of an abiding identity'.[2] Thus the one and the same phenomenon of language-transformation and a plurality of theologies
could prove to be basically only another aspect of the process of
making Catholicism more catholic, freeing it from too many
particularities, with an eye to a greater fulness in its catholicity,
such as is the prayer of those Catholic theologians of today who are
most acutely conscious of their task.

The Dominican Le Guillou writes:

> The encounter with separated communions constitutes for the Catholic
> Church an appeal to display her Catholicity in its dynamic nature,
> taut and alive to carry her specific and proper principles to a wider
> range of expansion; a challenge to be true to her missionary situation,
> to affirm in the world the Kingship of Christ, in faithfulness to tradition
> lived out in a vision of Catholic fulness.[3]

Then we can understand, and recognize the high significance of
these words of this same Dominican, a Roman Observer at the
Ecumenical Assembly at New Delhi:

> We believe that the present Catholic effort can have no better guide
> than St Thomas in working out its passion for catholicity.[4]

Synthesis in the Thomist style is the pole-star that sets the course

---

[1] V. Subilia, *Gesù nella più antica tradizione cristiana*, Rome-Torre Pellice 1954, pp.
182f.
[2] M. J. le Guillou, O.P., 'Plénitude de catholicité et oecuménisme', *Istina*, 1959,
p. 272.
[3] *Art. cit.*, p. 278.   [4] *Art. cit.*, p. 272.

of Catholic ecumenism towards its dream-goal of gathering up all of worth in every outlook, every culture, every civilization, every confession. 'The Church lays hold on the world to consecrate it and offer it to God', says Father Daniélou.[1]

Formal questions have led to theological questions; to be more exact, to the great fundamental theological question.

7. The Dogmatic reformation

We now come to the key point of our excursus, where a greater effort of sustained criticism is required. Every aspect of Catholic reformism so far passed under our review could be classified as concerning merely human, contingent aspects of the Church of Rome. Is it possible to think of any reforms in dogma itself?

Without entering the realm that Congar calls that of 'theology-fiction',[2] is it not possible to imagine that the vast efforts to produce a new pattern of theology made by the most penetrating and progressive Catholic minds may result in a sudden transformation of the theological landscape of Catholicism, in the same way that a landslide, by shifting vast masses of earth, changes the whole appearance of an area? If its dogmatic structure were to be totally recast, would there not result a movement in Catholic theology (incalculable in its historic effect) that would correct the chronic tendency to displace central matters to the periphery—a new theologically centripetal process, such as would entail giving new proportion to all the parts? This sort of thing has already happened in Protestant theology, and could develop there on a vaster scale, conditioned as it was in its origins—this is especially true of its Lutheran branch—by a prevailing interest in sixteenth-century piety, theology and culture, and sometimes distorted in its later history by anti-Catholic polemical exaggerations, and by occasionally uncontrolled gestures of accommodation to cultural trends, with which its thinking needed to remain on terms. Could not the Protestant concern for pureness, and the Catholic concern for fulness join in organic union, and would not such a union be fertile for a real and true resurrection of Christ's Church, in all its truth and unity, out of the grave of errors and divisions which has held it for centuries?

The answer to these questions depends on one precise condition,

---

[1] J. Daniélou, *Histoire et mystère*, Paris 1956, p. 117.
[2] Y. M. J. Congar, O.P., 'Il Concilio, la Chiesa e. . . . "gli altri"', in *Il Concilio Ecumenico*, Milan 1960, p. 118.

What do we mean by the 'centre' of theology, and even before theology, of the message and the faith? It would be easy to resolve the answers of both Confessions into one name—Christ. But at bottom that answer would be evasive, the reality is more complex. Do we mean Christ who lived, was crucified, rose from the dead, and ascended into heaven, who lives at the right hand of the Father, or do we mean Christ who prolongs his existence in the form of the Church, and who has a solid being yesterday and today, in the dogmatic, hierarchical and sacramental structure of Catholicism?

On this point there is unanimity between those who hold the theory of integrism and those who are for integration, even if at first sight their positions seem diverse. Here are statements from two of the highest official and responsible spokesmen for Catholic ecumenism, Cardinal Bea and Father Boyer. The first says of the immutability of Catholic Dogma:

> No Catholic of education will believe that the Council can or would change even a single dogma. The Supreme Pontiff and the Council have a duty inherent in their ecclesiastical authority, to preserve whole and entire the doctrine passed to them by tradition, and no love for the separated brethren can induce us to lay even the lightest hand on the sacred deposit of the faith. Every effort in the interests of peace to whittle down or to reduce the doctrine would be disobedience to the order received from the Lord.[1]

The second:

> Many things may be changed, but only in marginal matters. The Council will certainly not build another Church. In particular, dogmas will all remain to be believed firmly, and their meaning will not alter. If these create an insurmountable obstacle today, they will do so to-morrow, too. It is therefore possible to invite Protestants and Orthodox

---

[1] Card. A. Bea, 'Il Concilio sulla via dei protestanti: consensi e difficoltà,' *La Civiltà Cattolica*, 16 Sept., 1961, p. 568 (cf. also the following article in the number of 7 Oct., 1961: 'Il Concilio sulla via dei protestanti: i suoi possibili contributi'). Other statements by the Cardinal made to the great Press Agencies follow the same line; one at a press-conference at New York, according to which no concession is possible in the field of doctrine (*EPS*,17 June, 1960, p. 4), that given at a Conference at Bern, Zürich, Basel according to which, in affirming that what the Church has reckoned as the truth of faith can never be modified, he quoted the Gospel text, 'Heaven and earth shall pass away, but my words shall never pass away' (*La Vie Protestante*, 29 Sept., 1961). Cf. also what *L'Osservatore Romano*, 24 Nov., 1961 had to say of a further conference held at Zürich, in which, referring to the doctrine of the Church as the Mystical Body of Christ, the Cardinal said that 'a whole series of questions will be posed in that light' to remove 'every ground' of preoccupation on the Protestant side. And to confirm and explain his thesis, he quoted the words of the Cardinal Secretary of the Holy Office: 'Once having recognised that truth on which the Church cannot permit compromise, those sons who will make their return to the Church will find the Mother ready for any cordiality which is in her power in the field of liturgy, tradition and discipline.'

to enter into the Roman Church from now on. . . . If it is thought that the sanctification that is asked for them will bring them into the Roman Church, it would be fair that this were said to them. Otherwise one encourages them to dream of a future Church different from the Catholic Church of today, and that is something that does not help them to overcome their distaste for any essential and permanent elements in our Church.[1]

Of reformism then, one might speak, but not of reform. To use terms familiar in Protestant circles, we may speak of revival, but not of reform. We could think of Bernard of Clairvaux or of Francis of Assisi, though today there are no spiritual personalities of that stature, and the normal ecclesiastical bureaucracy is not of the stuff to take their place or their exceptional function, but we must categorically exclude any reform of the sort to which Luther and Calvin called the universal Church of their days. Thus there might be a return in grand style to the Counter-Reformation of Trent, without its reactionary and polemic motivation, rather perhaps all in the light of an ambitious motive of universalism, but none of this would entail the necessity of any sort of change in dogma. In Protestantism there might be reform, for in it there is no security or guarantee of stable and lasting truth and in it the principle of the correction of dogma is accepted, and therefore, of the two (so those who follow Father Boyer's Integrist theory say), it is Protestantism that must change.

What are the theological reasons for this dogmatic immobility?

On the other side there are very well-informed and very well-disposed theologians fully prepared to accept criticism and press for reform in the workings-out of Catholic principles in persons and in history, but never in respect of the principles themselves. No finger must be laid on the institution, at any of the essential points of its dogmatic, juridical or sacramental structure.[2] One can outline

---

[1] C. Boyer, S.J., art. cit., Unitas XVI (1961), pp. 202f., 255. The same author writes in the article 'The Pope of Unity' which appeared in L'Osservatore Romano, 20 Jan., 1962: 'That doctrine which asks Catholics to bind ever tighter the ties of their unity by mutual love and individual submission to the Hierarchical order, is the very doctrine which indicates to Christians separated from the Apostolic Chair the only way possible for the realisation of Christian unity. All this must be said clearly, for the Magisterium has the mission of announcing the doctrine in all its gospel simplicity: est, est; non, non. Our separated brethren who are interested in ecumenism, desire to know the Catholic Church as it is, and we render them a precious service when we save them from the illusion of believing that the Catholic conception of the Church and of unity, and dogmas in general, can ever one day be abandoned or change their significance.'

[2] Significant in this respect are the lucid statements of Cardinal G. B. Montini (now Pope Paul VI) reported in La Civiltà Cattolica, 7 April. 1962, pp, 78f.

the reasoning behind this pattern. Fundamentally, it must not be forgotten that for the last two centuries, and especially in the last few decades, Protestantism 'has undergone an evolution of no small importance' in that it has shown an ecumenical appreciation of traditional elements that had been misunderstood, or overlooked, in its opening phases and in its successive history. The Protestant Church of today knows itself, and must be known outside itself as a 'reformation of the Reformation'.[1] If it holds rigidly to its own positions, claiming that Catholicism only must change, does it not run the risk of becoming another kind of immobile Catholicism, and a poor one at that—as post-Tridentine Catholicism has largely been —and so of rejecting 'a vaster Reformation'? 'Would a Protestant invitation to reform the Church, passive, and unaccompanied by any confession of fault or of error (even on behalf of the Reformers), or any intention to do well or better, be in any way more Christian than an appeal by an inactive Catholicism to re-enter the unity of the Church?'[2] The Protestant Church, if it is to be true to its own essential principles, is for its part, called to the 'reformation of the Reformation', carrying it to its furthest legitimate consequences. This means going out to meet the Catholics 'in brotherly love', and effecing 'a reform of the Protestant Church through the realisation of legitimate Catholic desires', such as would have as its counter, 'a Catholic reform of the Church through the realisation of legitimate Protestant desires'. 'Then the return to unity will not be a simple "return" of Protestants, nor an "exodus" of Catholics, but an *encounter* of brothers from both sides.'[3] Thus both sides would mutually converge—a thing that would not be impossible on the Catholic side, in so far as *quidquid enim verum a quocumque dictur, a sancto dicitur Spiritu*[4] (whatever truth is said by whatever person, is said by the Holy Spirit). Catholicism can embrace in its great arms even non-Catholic truth (non-Catholic, that is, in the sense of not yet being inside the Catholic framework, not non-Catholic in its substance), such as might be discovered even in Luther, even in Barth, as much as in pagan philosophers, 'each and every truth being considered its own particular property'.[5]

The ecumenical method has the effect of setting in relief the positive aspects of the various dissenting religious Confessions, not so that the

---

[1] H. Küng, *op. cit.*, p. 140.   [2] *Op. cit.*, pp. 140f.   [3] *Op. cit.*, pp. 144, 145.
[4] Ambrosiaster, *In I Cor.* 12, 3: *PL* 17, 245, quoted by H. Küng, *Rechtfertigung*, p. 124.
[5] *Op. cit.*, p. 123.

negative aspects should be forgotten or underestimated, but so as to give their full weight to the positive elements, and to incline them where they can converge towards the point of their natural and essential fulness, which can only be the Roman Church. What makes them converge upon this point is partly being liberated from the errors which have been the causes or the effects of separation, and partly restoring to the authentic ecclesiastical truths and realities all their potentialities, fulness and wholeness, and setting them in the place that divine institution has made their natural one, in which alone they can be seen in all their wealth, and can develop all their inherent force. . . . The dissenters, when they enter into the fulness of life and truth, are not called upon to abandon anything of authentic Christianity that is theirs, but to fulfil it. . . . The Catholic Church does its part of the work of convergence when it evaluates in its own life and doctrine the aspects and the points that are especially fitted to express a common doctrinal basis. . . . There is no immediate invitation to union with the Catholic Church. It is not yet the moment to lay this on their consciences, for these must be respected. . . . Total integration is the result, not the method with which one prepares for the result. The return will be the ecumenism of tomorrow. That of today is the action calculated to prepare for it.[1]

What are the theological justifications of this dogmatic syncretism, and the law which governs it?

[1] A. Bellini, *op. cit.*, pp. 143, 145, 147f., 153f.

4

The Historical Problem

1. *Complexio oppositorum*

BETWEEN the end of the first and the beginning of the second centuries, on that hair-line of division between the apostolic and the sub-apostolic generations, it is possible to detect a spiritual phenomenon of incalculable historical importance. Indeed recent studies tend to push it even further into the past, and find its origin in writings more or less dubious, which were later introduced into the canon of the New Testament, and in a sense form its margin. In fact, there is a paradoxical phrase of Käsemann circulating among scholars, to the effect that the New Testament canon is the basis both of the division and of the unity of the Church,[1] However, between the end of the first and the beginning of the second centuries, there was a vast literature in circulation, some of it apostolic in origin, and some not, and in this, alongside motifs recognizably Christian at first glance, there are to be found, dangerously and embarrassingly close to them, motifs deriving from incipient Gnosticism, from the popular philosophy of the era, from mystery religions, from astrology, and from Judaism. It is the phenomenon of the advent into the ecclesiastical field of that syncretistic tendency so prevalent in the Mediterranean Basin in imperial times. Especially in the case of the motifs of Jewish origin, one meets a complete absence of any clear and firm theological understanding of the transition from the Jewish to the

---

[1] E. Käsemann, 'Begründet der neutestamentliche Kanon die Einheit der Kirche?' *Evangelische Theologie* 11 (1951-2), pp. 13f., new in *Exegetische Versuche und Besinnungen*, Göttingen 1960, I, p. 214. The article gave rise to animated discussion in the field of exegesis and systematic theology: W. Marxsen, *Der 'Frühkatholizismus' im Neuen Testament*, Neukirchen Kreis Moers 1958; R. Bultmann, *Theology of the New Testament*, II, p. 142; W. Fuerst, 'Ist das Neue Testament doch katholisch? (Zu den Anfragen H. Schliers)', *Verkündigung und Forschung* 1958-9, pp. 57f.; C. H. Ratschow, 'Zur Frage der Begrüdung des neutestamentlichen Kanons aus der Sicht des systematischen Theologen', *Neue Zeitschrift für systematische Theologie* 2 (1960), pp. 150f.; W. Marxsen, 'Das Problem der Neutestamentlichen Kanons aus der Sicht des Exegeten', *ibid.*, 2 (1960), pp. 173f.; 'Kontingenz der Offenbarung oder (und?) Kontingenz des Kanons?', *ibid.*, 2 (1960), pp. 355f.; K. Aland, *The Problem of the New Testament Canon*, London 1962.

Christian dispensation, or of the implications and significance of the idea of fulfilment. The fixing of the Canon would come later, and it has been pointed out that the writings of the second half of the second century, though removed further in point of time from the apostolic age, and though themselves not without the imprint of systems that had preceded or surrounded them and engaged them in polemics, nevertheless made a fundamental impact more markedly Christian than had the writers of an age nearer in time to the apostles.[1]

It is in the characteristics of the generation that preceded the closing of the Canon that we can isolate the historical and theological germ from which grew the structure of Catholicism with its two thousand years of history, as well as of modern Catholic ecumenism. It is a phenomenon of *complexio oppositorum*, into which totality is gathered. A Catholic theologian has said typically: 'A Protestant theologian is never so wrong as when he says this or that is *not* Catholic doctrine.'[2]

The incipient Catholicism of the end of the first century seems to have misunderstood, just as the Catholicism of the beginning of the second half of our century does not seem to understand, the meaning of two Gospel parables: the parable of the vine and the branches, and the parable of the old bottles and the new wine.

In the Johannine parable the condition of the branch's bearing fruit is, on the one hand, remaining in the vine, but on the other, being cleansed and pruned. The operation of pruning is valid both for the individual believer, and for the Church as a whole as it advances in history. Catholicism does not understand the parable in this light; it sees in the vine Christ materialized in history, i.e., the Church; it sees the pruning operation—if it goes beyond certain well-defined limits in the way of ethics, discipline and liturgy—as just the folly of some impossible husbandman quite at sea with his shears, who cuts the trunk together with the branches instead of the branches. It incorporates into the truth of the gospel the various contributions offered by history and makes them its own, in the belief that the blend of tradition and gospel christianizes these contributions. Thus it understands the operation of pruning as impiety against the work and the mandate of Christ, and confines it to the process of keeping the institutional structure up to date and

---

[1] K. Barth, *Die kirchliche Dogmatik*, Zollikon–Zürich 1947⁵, I/I, pp. 101f. [*CD*, 1936, pp. 111f.]; H. Diem, *Das Problem des Schriftkanons*, Zollikon–Zürich 1952; O. Cullmann, *La tradition*, Neuchâtel–Paris 1953, pp. 41f. [ET in *The Early Church*, 1956, pp. 89f.].
[2] H. Küng, *op. cit.*, p. 123.

vigorous. But in Jesus' words, the branches do not become the vine, and all that is not the vine is subject to the pruning knife. 'I am the Vine, ye are the branches' (John 15.5). Father Congar relates how he once saw 'a picture depicting the Catholic Church under the form of a robust tree with centuries of life behind it. In every century of its life the tree produced some magnificent and fruitful branches, great missionary movements, religious foundations, out-standing theologians and saints. But at the same time, every century had branches that split off. These had names, those of the great heretics, Arius, Sabellius . . ., but also Photius, Luther, Calvin. Cut from the tree, these branches fell into the flames, where demons worked their pleasure on them.'[1] Congar remarks in an irenic spirit that 'this piece of success-apologetics' does not correspond to reality, since the separated Christian Churches 'also' have positive elements. It might be asked pertinently from the other side if these Churches would ever have arisen and been separated, and have maintained their separate existence today, had the pruning process been applied right from the start with proper skill and without indulgence by the Latin Church, cutting out and not allowing motifs that were not evangelical to grow to inordinate size, and so obtaining fruits more obviously Christian.

The synoptic parable teaches that putting new wine in old bottles 'bursts the bottles', and as a result 'the wine is lost together with the bottles'; 'new wine must be put in new bottles' (Mark 2.22). Keeping the old bottle of Judaism gave rise to Judeo-Christianity, denounced so roundly by St Paul as a substantial travesty of the gospel. The Judeo-Christians gathered all the elements of the Chris-tian message and put them together with the elements of their Judaism. As a result their position was no longer Jewish, but it was also not Christian. Faced with this synthesis of Law and Gospel, Moses and Christ, Sinai and Golgotha, works and faith, circumcision and baptism, one's own righteousness and justifying grace, Paul, the apostle not of the Jews but of the Gentiles, who nevertheless in every one of his epistles, did not hesitate to underline the Jewish basis of the gospel, was never tired of declaring 'When you seek to be justi-fied by way of law, your relation with Christ is completely severed: you have fallen out of the domain of God's grace' (Gal. 5.4). By the new theory of integration, which means seeking to keep the old traditional bottles of Catholicism and pouring into them the wine of

---

[1] Y. M. J. Congar, *art. cit.*, in *Il Concilio Ecumenico*, p. 99.

biblicism (i.e., all the 'values', all the 'positive', 'legitimate' elements of the gospel message), and so ever extending and widening within the ecumenical context of our day that fatal *and*, which has shaped Catholicism in the various phases of its development (i.e., blending the doctrine of Scripture with the doctrine of tradition, that of Revelation with that of Natural Theology, that of Christ with that of Mary, that of Grace with that of Works and Merits, the doctrine of Faith with that of free judgment and reason, the doctrine of the resurrection from the dead with that of the immortality of the soul, the doctrine of the *collegium* of the Church with that of the Primacy of the Popes, the doctrine of the Laity with that of the Priesthood)— Catholicism in all this is attempting an operation of extreme risk to its structure. The span of one generation affords too limited a vision on which to forecast what the distant future will mean for this kind of procedure. But we cannot pretend that the operation is not just as dangerous for the gospel also, which could lose its savour, that is, its meaning as truth, its power of liberation, its paradoxical and incomparable uniqueness over against all human religions, ethics and doctrines.

It would indeed be absurd to qualify, *sic et simpliciter*, Catholicism as just this mixture of heterogeneous elements. Catholicism does not forget that a criterion of truth and a criterion of ecumenical encounter is necessary. On the contrary, the massive insistence of Catholicism on the matter of a criterion in solemnly pronounced formulae of the Hierarchy, and in well-established dogmatic defini-tions, has often convinced Catholic theologians themselves and neutral observers, that of the two sides to the dialogue, the only one that held rigidly and unequivocally directly to a criterion of truth, even if only from a formal point of view without any discussion of its merits, was Catholicism. Protestantism, on the other hand, seemed the realm, more or less free, or more or less chaotic—according to one's point of view—where subjective notions reigned varying with the age and with the Church or the sect, the product of the tempera-ment of the individuals themselves, as they were swayed by the laws of the so-called 'free examination' (a matter which deserves settling once and for all in an ecumenical study).[1]

Catholicism is a grandiose synthesis of syncretism and authority. It has become a *complexio oppositorum*, in which gospel elements exist alongside non-gospel elements in a confusion that at times

[1] Cf. V. Subilia, 'Il libero esame', *Protestantesimo* 10 (1955), pp. 97f.

prevents their recognition, and the whole is ruled by a rigid hierarchical discipline. What is the explanation of the phenomenon? It is this. Catholicism has made the norm of the Church the Church itself, without there being over the Church any authoritative point of reference to determine in the ultimate instance what is truth. This is the element in modern ecumenism which makes us despair. Here is the ultimate question to resolve, and to approach it we must return to a point alluded to at the outset of our study.

2. The Gnostic Myth of the total Man

The factors that have produced this seeming impasse are, we believe, to be sought far back in history, even before the protest of the sixteenth century occurred and gave rise to the Catholic-Protestant confrontation. We must seek them in the most distant Christian times, on the frontier between the apostolic and the sub-apostolic generations, and in that Hellenistic world in which the Christian message was first heard and propagated. What interpretations must have been given to that message in that world to which allusion was made above in reference to the *complexio oppositorum*, where religions blossomed in such variety and luxury of colour? In that world, for example, of the initiates of the mystery religions, where rites of transfiguration, even of divinization, were practised, in the course of which the initiate took on immortality and incorruptibility and became in fact a participator in divinity itself? This was the case especially with the Gnostics among whose complicated speculations was the cult of the myth of Anthropos, that primordial redeeming Man, a being with a body of huge proportions, with his head in the heavens, and his members scattered in the world of shadowy matter, whose passion was to reconstruct the ἕνωσις, the unity of his body, by collecting its myriad fragments that were dispersed throughout the universe, in order that their totality might be re-established in the highest realm of light, and that the πλήρωμα should be restored between the head and the members, in the fulness of a single spiritual substance in which redeemer and redeemed were joined.[1] No one has yet precisely dated the sources of this information,

---

[1] For a treatment that gives a synthesis of the state of studies on the topic, cf. C. Colpe, *Die religionsgeschichtliche Schule—Darstellung und Kritik ihres Bildes vom gnostischen Erlösermythus*, Göttingen 1961. It is not possible to make even the slightest indication here of the very extensive literature in existence. It will be enough to recall some of the items of the *Theologisches Wörterbuch zum Neuen Testament* (G. Kittel—G. Friedrich): J. Jeremias, art. ἄνθρωπος I, pp. 365f.; H. Schlier, art. κεφαλή III, pp. 672f. J. Horst, art. μέλος IV, p. 556f. G. Delling, art. πλήρωμα VI, pp. 297f.

but by and large, we can say that these ideas were in the air at the time of the transmission of the Christian message, even if the documents in which we find them are often much later in date. Now the apostle Paul, like the apostle John, brought the licence of genius to bear on this complex of contemporary ideas, in order to preach Jesus in language comprehensible to their contemporaries. But their hearers interpreted the message, as Bultmann puts it, 'in their own way, i.e., in terms of their objectives and the problems they were concerned with'.[1]

It is the opinion of several scholars that the apostle Paul in particular has in all likelihood availed himself of the Gnostic myth of the head and the members, but has used it as a Greek sculptor of his day would use a chisel, to shape the marble. He was very conscious of the risk that a tap too strong might shatter the marble instead of shaping it, and still with complete mastery he proclaimed the sovereignty of the Head over the members in his epistles. The head certainly has communion with the members, and this communion is not just an ideal one—Paul speaks of it with a realism that somewhat shocks our modern spiritualizing bent—yet Paul, ever mindful of his Israelite heritage, never lost sight of that absolute division that keeps the Head from becoming part of the members, and the members from becoming part of the Head. The Lord gives himself, and yet remains himself, and as a result the Lord and man are not joined in an intimacy that deconsecrates God, and the personal relationship of faith, love, and obedience does not degenerate into a fusion that deifies man, be this materialistic in concept as in Hellenistic myths and at bottom naturalistic and sexual, or spiritualistic as in Gnosticism.

Within the Christian pale, faith has never lost sight of its essential nature by falling prey to such grave deviations. Yet one cannot deny that the content of the message of the apostles has undergone with a rapidity as surprising as it is disturbing a process of radical adaptation on this score. Some scholars even detect the beginning of the process in one of the canonical epistles, where the language, if it does not indeed ever overstep the conceptual boundaries, lends itself to interpretation as if it did. The fact becomes the more comprehensible if the letter has undergone substantial editing by some collaborator of the apostle Paul, perhaps Tychicus, as some critics

[1] R. Bultmann, *Das Urchristentum im Rahmen der antiken Religionen*, Zürich 1949 [*Primitive Christianity in its Contemporary Setting*, London 1956].

have suggested.[1] The epistle is that to the Ephesians. How must some of its statements about the relations between Christ as Head and the Church as body, be interpreted (Eph. 1.23; 2.15–16; 4.15–16; 5.22–32)?

Heinrich Schlier[2] whose knowledge of the epistle is of the best, asserts that in the background of the epistle we glimpse 'the myth of the primordial-heavenly Man who descends to the earth, gathers the souls into his body and reunites them in the *pleroma*'.[3] The imagery of the myth allows the work of redemption done in history by Christ to be understood and explained. From this hypothesis Schlier draws his conclusions. There is no denial that between the Church and Christ there exists a relationship of submission and obedience on the Church's part—'the Church would not be the Church without this relationship of submission before Christ'[4]—but it is however pushed into the background, so as to spotlight 'the idea of the indissoluble union between Christ and the Church. For there is need of head and body to form the heavenly *anthropos*. Without the Head, the Church would not have any supreme heavenly principle, nor any heavenly goal higher than this world. Without a body the Head would have no being on earth, nor any reality.'[5] As it is by this intimate co-ordination between them the Church holds 'the place' of the Head, and 'substitutes for it', inasmuch as 'the way to God and the Head passes through the body of Christ'.[6] The concept is developed in these terms. The Church 'is not the real and proper fulness of God. It is not even the fulness of God incarnate in Christ. But it is the place in which the fulness of Christ has abased itself, and is present, and is the means by which Christ gathers everything and the universe into his fulness.'[7] It is 'in the new world of God and Christ, their new aeon. It is the "space" filled by the presence and by the power of God, its *pleroma*, the place of heavenly fulness.'[8]

It is highly significant that exegesis of this sort should have led Schlier into Catholicism. His theological destiny has been decided by his Gnostic preconceptions learned at the school of the history of

---

[1] Cf. the critical essay by R. Kasser, 'L'autore dell'Epistola agli Efesini', *Protestantesimo* 17 (1962), p. 74ff.

[2] His first study on the subject goes back to 1930: H. Schlier, *Christus und die Kirche im Epheserbrief*, Tübingen 1930.

[3] H. Schlier, *Die Zeit der Kirche—Exegetische Aufsätze und Vorträge*, Freiburg i. Br. 1958, cf. pp. 159–186, the chapter: 'Die Kirche nach dem Brief an die Epheser.'

[4] *Ibid.*   [5] *Ibid.*   [6] *Ibid.*

[7] H. Schlier, *Der Brief an die Epheser*, Düsseldorf 1962³, p. 99.

[8] H. Schlier, *Die Zeit der Kirche, cap. cit.*

religions. Yet a Protestant mind can hardly find pages more stimulating to the understanding of Catholicism than those of Heinrich Schlier, in which he traces the distinctive features of Catholicism to the New Testament. In his exegesis the New Testament appears 'Catholic', and Catholic principles are presented as 'apostolic'.[1] The New Testament and 'not only the Epistle to the Ephesians and the Pastorals, and other documents of primitive Christianity in its later period, which open a door to incipient Catholicism',[2] but the New Testament of Paulinism and of the great Epistles need no longer seem an 'embarrassment' to the Church of Rome. Taken out of the monopolistic hold of the Reformation, and fairly and squarely considered ontologically, it can be seen as the theological basis of the idea of the *Una Sancta*.[3] The simple question to be put is: Is this a right exegesis?

It is only possible to find a New Testament basis for Catholicism —Schlier is a case in point—on one condition, and that is by using a system of interpretation for the New Testament that permits an absolute identity being supposed between the content of the apostolic message and the Gnostic concepts which the primitive Christian generation used, and used always carefully and critically with undoubted polemic intent, as an instrument to transmit Christ's message to their contemporaries. How could such an identification be taken seriously? Would it be legitimate to identify the content of the Christian message with the hints of psychoanalytical, or existentialist, or Marxist language that characterize the attempts of men of the twentieth century to convey to our contemporaries a message which transcends the linguistic instruments used to express it? Could such instruments ever reach the bottom of the message itself, which is the person and the work of him to whom the message alludes? This is a distinction which can and must be made, without however falling into the opposite danger—a danger that at times proves too much for the Bultmann school—of throwing out the content of the message along with the language tool used in the attempt to transmit it.

But the legitimacy of interpreting the relations between Christ the Head and the Church the body in this Gnostic light, is strongly contested not merely by those theologians who hold the point

[1] *Op. cit.*, p. 308.
[2] W. Fuerst, *Kirche oder Gnosis? Heinrich Schliers Absage an den Protestantismus*, Munich 1961, p. 23 (*Theologische Existenz Heute* N.F., Heft 94).
[3] *Ibid.*

incapable of proof and play down even a merely formal influence of Gnosticism on Paul's ecclesiological thought,[1] but even by those theologians who recognize and emphasize such an influence. Käsemann, for example, goes as far to affirm that 'in Paul, when the motif of the Body of Christ occurs, the Church is defined in terms of Christology' but vice versa, in the epistle to the Ephesians 'Christology is interpreted almost exclusively from an ecclesiological point of view', so that 'soteriology and eschatology are systematically conceived as aspects of ecclesiology'.[2] Yet he states forcefully that, even if we regard this as a phenomenon of the history of religion, and find statements ontological in form, we must not interpret the statements themselves ontologically, in so far as the Christ-Church relationship is constantly presented, in both Pauline and deutero-Pauline writings, in the shape of the obedience of the second to the first, who remains always the Lord, fully autonomous, in relation to the second, nor do we ever find any trespassing over the boundaries between Head and body, nor Head and body ever seeming to constitute one single, grand, supernatural entity.[3]

It is not that this is another line of *a priori* reasoning that has no basis in exegesis, running exactly counter to Schlier and the Catholic theologians, and emphasizing the aspect of submission to Christ while rejecting basically that of union with him. Both aspects are present in the New Testament, we repeat, both. Slacken the dialectical tension that holds them together, and communion with Christ takes its shape from Hellenistic mysticism, and not from the New Testament, with the result that any ecumenical conversation on the subject is compromised at the outset.

Catholic theology does not deny this double relationship, but it sends perilous tremors across their mutual balance when it speaks of it now in language Christian in its inspiration, and now in concepts of Hellenistic origin. We find phrases to give us qualms in the pages of Catholic theologians and the official pronouncements of the *magisterium*. We encounter expressions like 'the physiological bond that unites the body to the Head', 'the physical union of the body of Christians with the dead and risen body of Christ', by means of which they, the Christians, who 'receive into their bodies in the

---

[1] Cf. the useful survey of J. R. Nelson, *The Realm of Redemption—Studies in the Doctrine of the Nature of the Church in Contemporary Protestant Theology*, London 1956[3], pp. 67f.
[2] E. Käsemann, 'Das Interpretationsproblem des Epheserbrief,' *Theologische Literaturzeitung* 86 (1961), col. 3.   [3] *Art. cit.*, col. 5.

sacramental rite the body of Christ, "are", all together, one sole body, viz., that body which despite its essential individuality, assumes into itself all the bodies of those whom he joins to himself'.[1] Or one hears of the inseparability of body and Spirit spoken of as if it were an ecclesiological law essential to the 'mystery of the total Christ', implying an 'organic integration' between Christ and the Church'.[2] Or again, of 'a perfect, natural community between the head and the members'.[3] Despite distinctions drawn and reserves expressed (and there is no lack of them), one cannot escape the serious dogmatic significance of these sentences, which can in no way be made to harmonize with the central truths of the Bible message.[4]

Yet Catholic theology can make these statements with a good conscience, for it can give an air of legitimacy to its dogmatic procedure at this critical juncture, by citing very ancient Christian traditions, so enabling its doctors to read the New Testament in a particular light that takes no critical account of the historical and dogmatic points wherein these traditions deviate from the apostolic message.[5] One may thus keep up the pretence of a perfect harmony between the Church's teaching and the Gospel, even if as a result the gospel loses its power to liberate and renew.

3. The Mystique of Unity

Just outside the confines of the New Testament, there is a writer who seems to have lost sight of this distinction, and of the boundary between Head and body, and so he assumes, quite unconsciously,

[1] P. Benoit, O.P., 'Corps, tête et plérôme dans les Epîtres de la captivité', *Revue biblique* 63 (1956), pp. 27, 30, 14.

[2] G. Martelet, 'Le mystère du corps et de l'Esprit dans le Christ ressuscité et dans l'Eglise', *Verbum Caro* XII (1958), pp. 49f. The author has tried to apply to the Church the notion of 'spiritual body', which Pauline thought reserves for application to the condition of the redeemed after the return of Christ. The editors of the Review (the Community of Taizé) assess the Catholic contribution as 'an ecclesiology hopeful for an ecumenical solution thanks to its deeply Christological inspiration' (p. 3). But different is the judgment of P. Bonnard, 'L'Eglise corps du Christ dans le paulinisme', *Revue de théologie et de philosophie* 8 (1958), p. 280.

[3] Medebielle, art. 'Eglise, corps du Christ', *Dictionnaire de la Bible—Supplément*, vol. II, Paris 1936, col. 662. Pius XII in the Encyclical *'Mystici Corporis'* in dealing with the relations between the Head and the Body and with the Church as *alter Christus* used a similar phrase: 'they being of the same nature' (I/II, b). And quoting the *'Satis Cognitum'* of Leo XIII: 'As Christ, Head and exemplar of the Church "is not the whole Christ if one only thinks of the human, visible nature in him, or only of his divine, invisible nature . . . but is one with two natures, and in two natures, so is his mystic body".'

[4] W. Graf, *Ja und Nein—Ein Konfessionsgespräch*, Munich 1950, p. 35.

[5] Cf. E. Mersch, S.J., *Le corps mystique du Christ—Etudes de théologie historique*, Brussels–Paris 1951³, I–Ecriture, Tradition grecque, II–Tradition occidentale.

the mythical meaning of the imagery. This is a writer who would have known apostolic circles, a writer whom ancient patristic evidence assigns to the period between the end of the first and the beginning of the second centuries, who suffered martyrdom perhaps in the Flavian Amphitheatre (i.e., the Colosseum), about AD 110—Ignatius of Antioch. In his letter *To the Trallians*, 11.2, he writes:

> The Head cannot be generated without the members, in that God is unity, and has promised unity.[1]

What lies hidden behind this strange phrase, penned, we must not forget, with a polemical motive precisely against the docetism of the Gnostics? Ignatius wished to set against the Gnostic timeless, spiritual realm, the Christian reality of history, but literary exigencies understandably compelled him to go about it by superimposing Christian and Gnostic ideas upon each other. Inevitably, there was interplay between them. It would be indeed difficult to deny that here not only in the language but in the content too, a gnostic leaven seeps out from the typical word ἕνωσις and the underlying idea of 'gathering the fragments of the divine substance' into a perfect unity.[2] The effect of this influence is to transform the Pauline concept of Church. Its unity (in contradistinction to what had been found in the apostolic communities and to what is evidenced in the Pauline epistles, I Cor. 1.10ff., etc.) is no more conceived in simple terms of relationships with Christ. Instead it becomes something guaranteed ontologically, it loses its dialectic character, which derives from the paradox of belonging both to this present world and to the world to come, and it seems to acquire a certain solidarity, never more to be split by schism, controversy or sect.[3] It is participation in divinity (Ephes. 4.2), i.e., the fulfillment of ἕνωσις with Christ that renders

---

[1] The Greek text says: οὐ δύναται οὖν κεφαλὴ χωρὶς γεννηθῆναι ἄνευ μελῶν, τοῦ θεοῦ ἕνωσιν ἐπαγγελλομένου, ὅ ἐστιν αὐτός.
Cf. *Corona Patrum Salesiana*: Series Graeca, XIV—*I Padri Apostolici*, Parte II, Turin 1942, p. 95.

[2] T. Preiss, 'La mystique de l'imitation du Christ et de l'unité chez Ignace d'Antioche', *Revue d'histoire et de philosophie religieuses* 18 (1938), pp. 197–242, republished in the volume *La Vie en Christ*, Neuchâtel–Paris, 1951, pp. 7–45, cf. p. 43. The influence upon Ignatius' thought of his religious environment has been shown in many studies, of which we cite only: H. Schlier, *Religionsgeschichtliche Untersuchungen zu den Ignatiusbriefen*, Giessen 1929; H. B. Bartsch, *Gnostisches Gut und Gemeindetradition bei Ignatius von Antiochien*, Gütersloh 1940. We have a good bibliography in J. Quasten, *Initiation aux Pères de l'Eglise*, Paris 1955, I, pp. 86f.

[3] Cf. on this head the observation of R. Bultmann, 'Ignatius und Paulus', in *Studia Paulina in honorem J. De Zwaan*, Haarlem 1953, pp. 37f.; Id.—*Theology of the New Testament*, II, pp. 191f.

the members of the body from then on immune to any risk of division, both individually and collectively. Ignatius' insistence on union with the bishop is a direct consequence of this originally Gnostic conception of unity, and presages those developments in Catholic ecclesiology that were to follow so fatefully. It is not for nothing that the earliest document known in which the phrase 'Catholic Church' appears is a letter of Ignatius (*Smyrn.* 8.2). Union with the bishop, who holds the place of God, and with the presbyters who hold that of the synedrion of the apostles, is τύπον καὶ διδαχὴν ἀφθαρσίας (type and teaching—evidence—of incorruptibility) (*Magn.* 6.1–2). Just as in the New Testament nothing could be done without Christ, so now nothing can be done without the bishop who represents and incarnates him (*Philad.* 7.2). The bishop must be considered as the Lord himself (*Ephes.* 6.1). That which the bishop approves is automatically approved by God, so that the whole of ecclesiastical practice comes to be put beyond the range of all criticism, and vested with a sacred aura of guaranteed authenticity and validity (*Smyrn.* 8.2). Submission to bishop and presbyters is the same as submission to the grace of God, to the law and to the authority of Jesus Christ himself (*Magn.* 2.1; *Trall.* 2.1; 13.2; *Ephes.* 5.3). Sin itself seems visualized as separation from the Church, repentance as return to the Church (*Smyrn.* 9.1). Christ's incorruptibility thus reverts upon the Church (*Ephes.* 17.1); the unity between the heavenly divine Head and the still earthly members of the Church is now realized in this ominous synthesis made between one aspect of Christian eschatology, and a central element of Gnostic myth. As Preiss has said in his unsurpassed study of Ignatius, his theory of the unity and the authority of the Church 'derives directly from this mystic theory of unity'. The hierarchy on earth is 'an imitation, a reflection, of the hierarchy in heaven'.[1] Thus there was introduced into the Church, there to become a system, 'something that could never have happened in the thought of Paul, and in general in that of the New Testament', viz., 'the *confounding* pure and simple of an external way of organisation with a divine system, the elevation of the *res juris humani* to the rank of *res juris divini*'.[2] When divine and human, transcendent and historical, spiritual and carnal (*Magn.* 13.2) are thus united, what is ultimately at stake is the very idea of God. The dominant notion of the Ignatian God is unity—'the unity that is God himself' (*Trall.* 11.2): Christ has destroyed the wall of partition

[1] T. Preiss, *op. cit.*, p. 36.   [2] *Ibid*, p. 37.

between the low imprisoning world of matter and shadow, the manifold and the fragmentary world, and the highest world of spirit and light, the incorruptible and the immutable world, so re-establishing their unity. Bartsch has cleverly called the idea of God the Trojan horse in which Gnosticism made its fatal entry into the Christian message.[1] It is this combination of the elements of Gnostic mythology and historic Christianity that forms the oriental contribution to the formation of Catholicism. Catholicism is seen to be in its origin what it increasingly shows itself to be in its development—a transformation of the concept of Church, and specially of the concept of body of Christ—the concept that Albert Schweitzer quite understandably saw to be the deepest enigma in the whole of mystic literature.[2] In the future we shall have to study deeper than has so far been done what were the consequences of this shaping of Christian concepts in Gnostic moulds for the transformation of the idea of Church, as we follow its development also in the champions of orthodoxy.[3]

4. *Roman Juridicism*

The western contribution—or, more exactly that one of many factors which was to shape others also—can be traced to another writer whose destiny it was to live on the frontier between the apostolic and sub-apostolic generation, but of whom we know very little—Clement of Rome. His name has already been mentioned in connection with the question of the laity. Here we confine ourselves to observing that the image of the body with head and members is found in the first epistle of Clement to the Corinthians 37.5; 38.1.[4] The writer's intention is an exortation to submission to Christ and to brotherly service to one's neighbour, but the reference is explicitly to the military discipline of the Empire. He refers simply to the

---

[1] H. B. Bartsch, *op. cit.*, pp. 33, 76f., 166f., etc.; art. 'Ignatius von Antiochien', *RGG³* III, cols. 665f.; cf. C. Maurer, *Ignatius von Antiochien und das Johannesevangelium*, Zürich 1949, p. 66.

[2] A. Schweitzer, *Die Mystik des Apostels Paulus*, Tübingen 1954², p. 117.

[3] One should study from this angle e.g., the great antagonist of Arius, Athanasius, and his theology of 'divinisation', which could be summed up in this typical statement: 'The Son of God became man that we might become God in him. Ours is the body of a common man, but we receive the body of the Logos himself and we are made divine', *Contra Arianos* 2. 47. Athanasius' works are in the *Patrologia Graeca* of Migne, vols. 25–28. Cf. *Sources Chrétiennes: Athanase d'Alexandrie—Contre les Païens et Sur l'incarnation du Verbe*, Paris 1946. Also the study by L. Bouyer, *L'Incarnation et l'Eglise—Corps du Christ dans la théologie de saint Athanase*, Paris 1943.

[4] *Corona Patrum Salesiana:* Series Graeca, VII, *I Padri Apostolici*, Turin 1940, I, pp. 154f.

image of the social organism, amply illustrated in the literature of the period;[1] there is no sign of any idea of the incorporation of Christ in the Church. However, another element enters, and one that contributed not a little to imparting a sacred aura to the Church in its hierarchy. Clement speaks of the Christian ministry on the basis of the Old Testament Law (*I Cor.* 40, 41, 43). The expressions refer to the Jewish dispensation, but the immediate context, even if in a confused and indirect manner, suggests the parallel of the Christian dispensation, naming bishops and deacons, and also 'the lay man', who must abide by the tenets for the laity. To set them thus side by side, as we indicated in the earlier reference, betrays a confusion about the relations of the two systems and their full theological implications, for the Christian ministry thus features as a new edition of the Jewish sacerdotal ministry, and is not allowed to assume its proper and original character, which derives from the fact that Christ has fulfilled the sacerdotal requirements of the Old Covenant. This persistence of ideas associated with Jewish legalism becomes more serious in view of the note of insistence in Clement on learning to be submissive and obedient before those who are referred to (in terms and nuances that smack of a political way of thought) as heads, guides, those who bear rule in the Church (*I Cor.* 1. 3; 2.1; 21.6; 57.1–2, etc.).[2] Here we begin to note the first traces of the process whereby the Church came to form part of the texture and spirit of its political and juridical environment, with all the troublesome consequences that this was destined to have.[3] It was not for nothing that the context of this process was Rome, for this same mental process must have contributed much to that transformation of the gospel in the same environment into a juridical shape (*Juridifizierung*), that has been the object of many studies.[4] However, that element that we have called the oriental contribution, although it has been less studied from an ecclesiological angle, offers more interesting prospects for research, and is theologically the more significant.

---

[1] Cf. M. Spanneut, *Le stoïcisme et les pères de l'Eglise de Clément de Rome à Clément d'Alexandrie*, Paris 1957; W. C. van Unnik, 'Is I. Clem. 20 purely Stoic?', *Vigiliae Christianae* IV (1950), pp. 181f.

[2] C. Eggenberger, *Die Quellen der politischen Ethik des 1. Klemensbriefes*, Zürich 1951; A. A. T. Ehrhardt, *Politische Metaphysik von Solon bis Augustin*, Tübingen 1959, II, pp. 55f.

[3] A. A. T. Ehrhardt, *op. cit.*, II, p. 58.

[4] The bearing of juridical thinking on the Church of Rome is admirably shown by J. Klein, *Skandalon—Um das Wesen des Katholizismus*, Tübingen 1958.

5. Totus Christus

It may seem strange to speak of Catholicism, which is an eminently Latin and Western phenomenon, as having an oriental aspect. Here we do not descend to the detailed stages of the process, in which the mysterious ways of Manichaean Gnosticism were particularly involved. We only say that the vigour of the strain issued in the grandiose Augustinian conception of *Totus Christus*, upon which we have already touched and to which we find ourselves returning. The old complaint of Julian of Eclanum that Augustine remained always a Manichee, and was responsible for introducing Manichaeism into the Church's theology, might perhaps be worth a second glance, provided we eliminate the Pelagianism that inspired it, and extend it beyond the anthropological and ethical plane to that of ecclesiology.[1] Ernesto Buonaiuti tried to locate the point of transition between what he called 'the anti-Manichee' and the 'neo-Manichee' Augustine.[2] One would need to follow very closely this transition in the doctrine of the Church, and particularly in the doctrine of the Church as the body of Christ. Certainly the Augustine idea of the *Corpus permixtum* is closely and typically related to the 'basic viewpoints of Manichaeism', and Augustine's whole concept of *Corpus* 'is not Roman, nor juridical, but oriental'.[3] It is our conviction that it would be a useful service to ecumenism to follow this clue and

[1] This line of investigation does not seem to have been dealt with sufficiently systematically, apart from the worthy dissertation (lithograph, never printed) of E. Franz, cited above, p. 25. The classical Histories of Dogma do not consider the point. Cf. e.g. R. Seeberg, *Lehrbuch der Dogmengeschichte*, Erlangen–Leipzig 1923³, II, pp. 445, 464, 482; F. Loofs, *Leitfaden zum Studium der Dogmengeschichte*, Halle 1953⁵, II, pp. 294f., 330f. In justification of this omission it must be said that some Manichaean sources, useful for the study, are of recent discovery (cf. C. Colpe, art. 'Manichäismus', *RGG*³ IV, cols. 714f. H. C. Puech, 'Le manichéisme', in *Histoire générale des religions* : Indo-Iraniens—Judaisme—Origines chrétiennes—Christianismes orientaux, Paris 1945, pp. 85f.; same author, *Le Manichéisme*, Paris 1949; H. Jonas, *Gnosis und spätantiker Geist*, Göttingen 1954², I, pp. 284f.; *Texte zum Manichäismus*, selected and ed. by A. Adam, Berlin 1954; G. Widengren, *Mani und Manichäismus*, Stuttgart 1961) and that the study of ecclesiology in connection with Christology is also a recent ecumenical interest—subsequent to the third World Conference on Faith and Order, Lund 1952.

[2] E. Buonaiuti, *Storia del Cristianesimo*, Milan 1942, I, p. 369. We have not been able to consult the article of W. H. C. Frend, 'The Gnostic-Manichaean Tradition in Roman North-Africa', *Journal of Ecclesiastical History* 4 (1953), pp. 13–26 which does not overlook the relationship between the legacy of Gnostic and Manichaean ideas, and the theology of Augustine.

[3] A. Adam, 'Der Manichäische Ursprung der Lehre von den zwei Reichen bei Augustin', *Theologische Literaturzeitung* 77 (1952), col. 390. Cf. the same author's brief but profound treatment of Augustinian ecclesiology: art. 'Kirche, III—Dogmengeschichtlich', *RGG*³ III, col. 1306.

throw light on the problem of the conception of the *Totus Christus* by tracing it to its source.

It has been said that before Augustine, even in Cyprian, the Church was thought of as the communion of believers with Christ.[1] The change in the concept of Church is alleged to have made its first appearance in Augustine, who, to use the famous phraseology of Harnack, gave it a 'religious' value, in that he saw it as the source of authority.[2] We believe that we have if not established at least indicated the fact that the germ of the change, far from being so late in history, is to be found as far back as the remotest Christian times, indeed in the very margins of the New Testament. Such a thesis does not lend support to any claim of legitimacy for the change. Antiquity is not synonymous with authenticity. The axiom that antiquity means truth is not a Christian axiom, but one derived from the Saturnian myth of the lost age of gold. However, even if the process can be traced back to certain phrases used by the authors of the New Testament, which were however developed in a sense quite different from the message of the New Testament, there is no doubt that the process issues in real and proper theology in him who 'dominated the story of Catholic piety and dogma from the beginning of the fifth century as far as the Reformation'.[3] The Augustinian idea of the Church has obtained permanent citizenship in Catholicism.

At the beginning of this study we tried to collect some typical expressions of this concept. One could multiply them over and over again from passages which are just endless variations of the theme, with some ominous notations that are too insistent and widespread to be passed off simply as rhetorical exaggerations without theological significance. In the legacy of dogma that Augustine has left us, we find alongside seed-thoughts of unquestionable and highly fertile Christian origin traces of others, both Manichaean and Neoplatonist. It would thus be folly to lump all Augustine's ecclesiology into just one of these last two categories. It is obvious that in the doctrine of the *Totus Christus* Augustine distinguishes the Head from the body. In exhorting the hearing of Christ, he warns that one should hear

the head as the head, and the body as the body. Persons are not divided, but there is a distinction of dignity. For it is the head that saves, the

[1] A. Adam, 'Das Fortwirken des Manichäismus bei Augustin', *Zeitschrift für Kirchengeschichte* 69 (1958), p. 12.
[2] A. Harnack, *Lehrbuch der Dogmengeschichte*, Freiburg i. Br. 1904[4], III, p. 76f.
[3] *Op. cit.*, III, p. 3.

body that is saved. Let the head show mercy, let the body beseech it. The head is for the purging, the body for the confessing of sins.[1]

But what is the use of this reservation indubitably Christian in content, if the sovereignty of the Head over the body is disastrously lost to view, buried under statements that ring very differently and cancel out the previous ones? For example, there is a metaphor in that canonical New Testament epistle whose phraseology is the source of later ecclesiological misinterpretations (in Eph. 5.22-33). This metaphor has its precedents in Old Testament literature and in extra-biblical religions. The relations between Christ and the Church are presented under the analogy of the relationships between man and wife. And in this respect the old words of Genesis are cited: 'The man shall leave his father and mother. and shall cleave unto his wife, and the two shall become one flesh' (Gen. 2.24; Eph. 5.31). This becoming, or being 'one flesh', as applied to Christ and the Church, is obviously on the same level as innumerable biblical expressions which also express the relationship between the Lord and the faithful under a varied imagery, the rock, the corner-stone, the vine, the door, the bread, in none of which cases could it be said without the most obvious absurdity, that God was of the same nature as the earthly elements that make up a mineral, or are used in building, in agriculture, in furnishing or in catering. The reality to which the imagery refers is one of real relationship, yet if the images are identified with the reality, they cease to be images; nor is the reality to be found in the things of the imagery, nor do the images completely represent it.[2] What was Augustine's ideological concern, and what were his dogmatic motives when he forced this metaphor, and instead of keeping to the universe of relationships, shifted dangerously into a universe which smacks of ontology? In other words, why does he handle his terms and his concepts not in the Old and New Testament sense, but in a sense that deflects thought towards non-biblical religions? In fact Augustine says:

If he himself said: Now no longer twain, but one flesh, what is there strange in speaking of one flesh, one tongue, and of the same words as if they belong to one flesh, to head and body? Let us hear him as if

[1] 'Caput tamquam caput, et corpus tamquam corpus. Non diuiduntur personae, sed distinguitur dignitas; quia caput saluat, saluatur corpus. Caput exhibeat misericordiam, corpus defleat miseriam. Caput est ad purganda, corpus ad confitenda peccata', *In Psalmum XXXVII: Corpus Christianorum: Series Latina* XXXVIII, p. 387.
[2] Cf. the useful survey of the great variety of imagery, in P. S. Minear, *Images of the Church in the New Testament*, Philadelphia 1960.

he were only one. . . . He for his part speaks as one. . . . When you hear the voices of the body, you would not separate the head; neither, when you hear the voices of the head, would you separate the body; because they are now not twain, but one flesh.[1]

Therefore he was made head of the Church, and has both head and members. Seek out his members who now groan throughout all the world . . . and now we sing in hope, all gathered into one. For having put on Christ, we are Christ with our head. . . . Because we are his members and his body; with our head we are one man.[2]

Christ and the Church are one, that is one sole man, perfect in the form of his fulness.[3]

And that man is everywhere diffused, whose head is on high, whose members are beneath.[4]

Thus one man stretches as far as the end of time.[5]

We are himself.[6]

We are sons, we are then the Son.[7]

Who will have a head, who has not a body? Is not the Son this whole, head and body?[8]

There is only one direction in which to look for an explanation of this phenomenon in the context of the culture and the religion of the time. Catholic thought sees no difference between the doctrine of the *Totus Christus* and the apostolic message.[9] But it must be said

---

[1] 'Si ergo ipse dixit: *Iam non duo, sed una est caro*, quid mirum si una caro, una lingua, eadem uerba, tamquam unius carnis, capitis et corporis? Sic audiamus tamquam unum. . . . Ille autem tamquam unus loquitur. . . . Neque cum corporis uoces audieritis, separetis caput; neque cum capitis uoces audieritis, separetis corpus; quia iam non duo, sed una caro', *In Psalmum XXXVII: ibid.*

[2] 'Factus est ergo caput ecclesiae, habet et corpus et membra. Quaere membra ipsius, modo gemunt per uniuersum orbem terrarum. . . . Et modo ergo cantemus in spe, omnes in unum collecti. Christum enim induti Christus sumus cum capite nostro; . . . quia membra eius et corpus eius sumus, cum capite nostro unus homo sumus', *In Psalmum C*, 3: *ibid.* XXXIX, p. 1408.

[3] 'Christus et ecclesia utrumque unus, unus quidam uir perfectus in forma plenitudinis suae', *In Psalmum CI*, 2: *ibid.* XL, p. 1427.

[4] 'Et homo ille ubique diffusus, cuius caput sursum est, membra deorsum', *In Psalmum XLII*, 1: *ibid.* XXXVIII, p. 474.

[5] 'Unus homo usque in finem saeculi extenditur', *In Psalmum LXXXV*, 5: *ibid.* XXXIX, p. 1180.

[6] 'Nos ipse sumus', *In Iohannis Evangelium—Tractatus CXI*, 6: *ibid.* XXXVI, p. 633.

[7] 'Filii sumus, filius sumus', *In Psalmum CXXII*, 5: *ibid.* XL, p. 1818.

[8] 'Cui erit caput, si non erit corpus? An forte totum hoc Filius, caput et corpus?', *In Iohannis Evangelium—Tractatus XLI*, 8: *ibid.* XXXVI, p. 361.

[9] Cf. E. Mersch, *op. cit.*, II. Cf. also J. Vetter, *Der Heilige Augustin und das Geheimnis des Leibes Christi*, Mainz 1929.

that this conception of the *Totus Christus*, who gathered his members together from their dispersal throughout the universe, and with them forms the One Perfect Man in the form of his Fulness, smacks far too much of Gnostic mythology, to be accepted without uneasiness, and to be let pass without critical inquiry.

The image of the Perfect Man—this must be admitted, or the problem becomes too facile, and we miss its complexity—has already appeared in the New Testament Canon, in Ephesians 4.13.[1] Augustine understands the Perfect Man of Eph. 4.13, not in the sense of the individual, but in the sense of collective personality. This appears from the passages already quoted, and indeed he says so explicitly, in contrast with the argument of his opponents, in a passage of the City of God:

> Lo then, the Perfect Man, the head and the body, which consists of all the members, whose numbers will be completed in the proper time, yet who are daily being added to the one body even as the Church is being built up—the Church to whom it is said '*Ye are the body of Christ and members*'.[2]

Paul's dominant motif in conceiving of the Church as the body of Christ, is not the motif of the body as the totality of the members, the sum of head and body, but the common relationship of the members (different as they may be as regards their racial, social and religious background, and manifold as may be their spiritual gifts and the religious forms and trends that result from their acceptance and cultivation of the gospel) to Christ, who is not different and manifold, but one, the Lord and Head of all, who was crucified and rose again for all, who acts in all by the operation of his Spirit, and who calls all to be of one mind and one spirit, addressing a common calling to all, and pointing all to one single hope.[3]

---

[1] Many versions, including the revised Italian version of G. Luzzi, avoid the difficulty by rendering the phrase in the plural, and so making it individual.

[2] 'Ecce qui est uir perfectus, caput et corpus, quod constat omnibus membris, quae suo tempore complebuntur, cotidie tamen eidem corpori accedunt, dum aedificatur ecclesia, cui dicitur: *Vos autem estis corpus Christi et membra*', *De Civitate Dei* XXII, 18: *ibid*. XLVIII, p. 837. Cf. also *De Trinitate* IV, 7, 11; IV, 9, 12.

[3] Cf. the various meaning of the phrase *In Christo*: W. Schmauch, *In Christus—Eine Untersuchung zur Sprache und Theologie des Apostels Paulus*, Gütersloh 1935; F. Büchsel, '"In Christus" bei Paulus', *Zeitschrift für die neutestamentliche Wissenschaft* 42 (1949), p. 141f.; F. Neugebauer, *In Christus—Eine Untersuchung zum Paulinischen Glaubenverständnis*, Göttingen 1961, p. 97, etc.; M. Bouttier, *En Christ—Etude d'exégèse et de théologie pauliniennes*, Paris 1962. Cf. also L. Cerfaux, *La théologie de l'Eglise suivant saint Paul*, Paris 1948², pp. 159f.; J. A. T. Robinson, *The Body—A Study in Pauline Theology*, London 1952, pp. 55f.; A. Oepke, 'Leib Christi oder Volk Gottes bei Paulus?', *Theologische Literaturzeitung* 79 (1954), pp. 363f;. E. Schweizer, *Lordship and Discipleship* [ET], London 1960, pp. 45ff.

Set alongside the concept of Paul, Augustine's conception of the *Perfect Man*, and the *Whole Christ* (which has even been called 'the factor that determines the whole theology of the mature Augustine')[1] is seen as a deviation that opens the door to irreversible error. Stepping out of Jewish-Christian categories, we find ourselves in categories of substance and space which set 'all the weight of emphasis on collective totality, presenting the parts as mere incompleteness, and hence mere imperfection. The essential strength, i.e. authority, resides only in the totality.'[2]

The verdict of the historian must here be that the use of these categories of thought is explicable only by recourse to the idea of Gnostic and Manichee mythology.

The verdict of the theologian must here be that, in utter contrast to New Testament practice, these categories have been so used that they have mutilated the thought-content they express.

We are here beholding something with incalculably serious and far-reaching consequences. Gnosticism is infiltrating into Christianity and producing damage so deep-seated that the very life-centres of the Christian organism are affected, and it is being changed into quite a different organism. It is a phenomenon strongly reminiscent of the language of modern scientists when they say that atomic radioactivity can be so destructive as perhaps to alter certain characteristics of the human race in future generations. Troeltsch has tried to link Augustine's ecclesiology with the 'nexus of ideas of primitive Catholicism', denying that it is possible to trace any of the theological and juridical premises of later medieval ecclesiology in the thought of the great Bishop of Hippo.[3] But such a presentation relies on a far too subjective schematization of sociological ideas, according to which types and cycles of culture are classified in a way that fails to take proper account of the fact that ideas shape history long before they become systemized in history in the form of recognizable institutions conditioned to the historic situation of their particular epochs.[4] In reality the notion of the *Totus Christus* is the very soul of the Catholic conception of the Church and of Christianity

---

[1] E. Franz, *op. cit.*, p. 258.
[2] A. Adam, *Das Fortwirken . . .*, p. 14.
[3] E. Troeltsch, *Augustin, die christliche Antike und das Mittelalter*, Munich and Berlin 1915 [Ital. trs., Rome 1930, p. 35].
[4] Cf. the criticism of E. Buonaiuti, *S. Agostino*, Rome 1923², p. 64; C. Antoni, *Dallo storicismo alla sociologia*, Florence 1940, p. 70; P. Rossi, *Lo storicismo tedesco contemporaneo*, Turin 1956, pp. 441f.; W. Bodenstein, *Der Entwicklungsgang Tröltsch's*, Gütersloh 1958.

as a whole, and not a few of the essential aspects of this conception, without which it would not be what it is, depend upon a Gnostic ecclesiological idea. Without needlessly repeating the truth that the transformation of the concept of the Church is a complex process, involving innumerable coefficients, we maintain that on the lines indicated in this study it could be established that among these factors, one, and a very decisive one at that, is the Gnostic element.

Horace put in an epigram the paradox of the cultural and political inter-relationship of Greek and Roman civilization:

Graecia capta ferum victorem cepit. (Captive Greece made her fierce captor her captive.) [1]

One might adapt the thought to our ends in these words:

Gnosis capta Ecclesiam cepit. (Captive Gnosticism made the Church her captive.)

All of which means that the roots of the division in the Church can be traced definitely to a non-ecclesiastical factor. A foreign element has entered Christendom and has divided Christianity, just as in the Gospel parable, an enemy enters the field and sows tares amongst the grain. The proper growth of the grain of Christianity has been rendered irredeemably compromised, choked by the rude vitality of the tares of Gnosticism, which the Church thought it had eradicated out of its field through the labours of its polemicists and apologists. Such an assessment allows us to say this: The point chiefly at issue in the Catholic-Protestant dispute, and the point on which hangs all particular issues, and apart from which all discussion of these issues is useless, lies in an element itself quite foreign to the Gospel.

[1] *Ep.* 2, 1, 156.

5

The Ecclesiological Disagreement

WE have traced the origins of our difference in history just sufficiently to have some notion of its real nature. Now we must make a synthesis of our findings on the ecclesiological plane, and so clarify the consequent issues for inter-confessional relations.

To use ideas derived from Gnostic and Manichee sources in interpreting the New Testament concept of the Church as the Body of Christ, even if those ideas are given a content consonant with the Bible message and ecclesiastical tradition, means adopting a method of exegesis for Paul's phrases which Protestantism must pronounce absolutely invalid, inasmuch as the basic law of relationship between head and body is violated and twisted into its complete opposite. This outlook affects the distinction between Head and body. The variegated spiritualizing movements that have influenced and moved alongside the spreading Christian message, have had no difficulty in overlooking this distinction which however may never be overlooked by the apostolic gospel. This distinction becomes vague and indefinite when the body assumes to itself the attributes of the Head—authority, infallibility and sanctity, and this not in a dialectic process of the anticipations of hope and faith, but in a massive take-over by the institution and its hierarchy. The grand New Testament phrases, 'through Christ', 'in Christ', 'with Christ', 'in the sight of Christ' undergo a change from a Christological to an ecclesiological reference, and take on the meaning 'through the Church', 'in the Church', 'with the Church', 'in the sight of the Church'. Köhler is thinking of Augustine himself and citing his typical words:

> Thou goest to the Church, she answers thy questions, not thyself. For the Church *has* truth, thou dost but seek it,

when he remarks that this is how the Church 'becomes *Mistress* over the faith', and the regulator of faith, even to the extent of changing its nature and making it simply 'a series of acts of obedience towards the Church'.[1] There is a shifting movement from Christ to Church, from apostles to bishops, from revelation to dogma, from gospel to tradition; and so there occurs a real and true succession for the passage of powers, authorities and truth. So it is but natural that the attitude of discipleship, submission, obedience that is due to Christ, be applied to the Church, and that Christ's mediatory function pass to the Church, and that he who is *Dominus et Magister* be represented by the Church, *Domina et Magistra* and that the one name that is given to men whereby they may be saved, be attributed not only to the Lord, but to his legitimate representative on earth, *Sanctissimus Dominus noster Papa*.[2] In all this the Catholic sees no offence against Christ, no usurping of the glory due to him, no will to power, no authoritarian imperialism on the part of the Church and his hierarchy, but only what is meant for the Christian by communion with Christ and his never-failing presence. St Augustine commented thus on the gospel promise:

> Since the whole Christ is his head and his body, then let us hear the voices of the body as we hear those of the head. For he was unwilling that there should be a distinction in speaking, because he was unwilling to speak separately, saying: *Lo, I am with you always even to the consummation of the ages.* If he is with us, he speaks in us, he speaks of us, he speaks through us, because we too speak in him, and we speak in truth, because we speak in him. For when we wish to speak in ourselves and out of ourselves, we remain in untruth.[3]

No substantial, personal, change is involved, nor in the nature of the case can be:

> There is no apparent change of person, since the Head is not separated from the body.[4]

[1] W. Köhler, *Dogmengeschichte als Geschichte des christlichen Selbstbewusstsein*, Zürich and Leipzig 1943[2], pp. 242f.
[2] As is known, this is the official style of address used in documents and acts of the Pontiff. E.g. the first Encyclical of John XXIII, often cited here '*Ad Petri Cathedram*' has the title: *Sanctissimi Domini Nostri Ioannis Divina Providentia Papae XXIII Litterae Encyclicae*. The announcement of papal audiences in the official Journal of the Holy See bears the introductory formula: 'The Holiness of our Lord has received. . . .'
[3] Quia ergo totus Christus caput est et corpus eius . . ., sic audiamus uoces capitis, ut audiamus et uoces corporis. Noluit enim loqui separatim, quia noluit esse separatus, dicens: *Ecce ego uobiscum sum usque ad consummationem saeculi*. Si nobiscum est, loquitur in nobis, loquitur de nobis, loquitur per nos, quia et nos loquimur in illo; et ideo uerum loquimur quia in illo loquimur. Nam quando in nobis et ex nobis loqui uoluerimus, in mendacio remanebimus', *In Psalmum LVI*, 1: *Corpus Christianorum*: Series Latina XXXIX, pp. 694f.
[4] 'Non uidetur mutasse personam; quia non separatur caput a corpore', *In Psalmum XC, Sermo* II, 1: *ibid*. XXXIX, p. 1266. C. Journet, *L'Eglise du Verbe incarné* II, p. 123

At the Ascension Christ in no way abandoned the earth. He remained 'in the form of the Church'.[1]

What is there then to do but assume an attitude of reverent obedience that asks no questions? To raise an objection, frame a criticism, draw oneself away from this authority, means not passing judgment on an authority rooted in humanity and history, but discrediting the indisputable word of Christ that this authority has laid down. The divine presence is to be located, not in some transcendent realm where a faith that knows not the Incarnation might seek it, nor yet in an Incarnation that happened one distant day, never to be repeated, and now is only something to be remembered, but it is to be found as a continuing and developing fact in time of which Jesus is the beginning. The whole of the history and life of the Church is just one endless repetition and unfolding of the 'initial instant' that started off the process.[2] The divine has entered into time, there to make its lasting abode, with every institutional guarantee for its inviolate preservation and its certain recognition. The Church as such enjoys 'a privilege of loyalty'[3] and is in possession of its credentials and its grounds, visible and rational for being believed.

The year 1959 saw the publication of a book by Jean Guitton, *L'Eglise et l'Evangile*,[4] whose title (with terms reversed) recalls the famous work of Loisy. Some years before, Guitton had brought to the attention of the erudite of the modern world a work on the problem of Jesus. Subsequently he felt the necessity to discover if the 'relationship of equivalence (almost identity) between *Jesus* and *the Church* is authentic'.[5] Then, noting how in the present-day ecumenical climate 'the question of Jesus reunites—the question of the Church divides,'[6] he has written *L'Eglise et l'Evangile*. The book has been especially well received in Catholic quarters[7] considering that the author is not a specialist. It works out the application of a saying of Jesus in John's Gospel in a way not unfamiliar in

---

cites a similar phrase of Cardinal Giovanni di Turrecremata, *Summa de Ecclesia, Lib.* I, *cap.* XLIII, Venice 1560, p. 50: 'unus homo, una persona'. The work of this Cardinal (1388–1468) is considered the first systematic treatment of the doctrine of the Church.
[1] P. Rousselot-J. Huby, 'Christus', *Manuel d'historie des religions*, p. 734, cited by C. Journet, *op. cit.*, II, p. 93.
[2] M. Villain, *Introduction à l'Oecuménisme*, p. 254.
[3] Y. M. J. Congar, O.P., *Vraie et fausse réforme*, p. 457.
[4] J. Guitton, *L'Eglise et l'Evangile*, Paris 1959 [*The Church and the Gospel*, London 1961].
[5] *Op. cit.*, p. 8.   [6] *Op. cit.*, p. 10.
[7] The verdict of Father Villain, *op. cit.*, pp. 251f.

Catholic literature. In one of the farewell discourses in the Fourth Gospel which precede the account of the arrest in Gethsemane, the trial before the Sanhedrin and then before Pilate and the Crucifixion, Jesus says: 'I am the Way, the Truth and the Life' (John 14.6). Guitton makes the elaboration of this the theme of the whole book. The application, characteristically and impressively, is this: The *Way* is the ecclesiastical authority, the *Truth* is ecclesiastical dogma, the *Life* is the ecclesiastical sacrament.[1] And the significant and ominous conclusion is this: 'Jesus and the Church are simply one being.'[2]

Specialists, especially those more alive to Protestant criticisms, would no doubt use expressions more guarded, and qualify the extent of this identification, which, as we have seen, does indeed root in the most ancient parts of the Catholic tradition.[3] However the implication of such premises are clear. None can go to the Father except by the Church, and going to the Father which is in Heaven is accomplished by going to the Father which is upon the throne of Peter and in every confessional. Unthinkable then is any reform of this Church which is the Way, the Truth and the Life, the guardian and guarantor of divinity. To lay a finger on its structure is to lay indeed a finger on divinity itself. There might be a reform *in* the Church, but not *of* the Church.[4] The Church is no more 'the Synagogue, full of evil will, unworthy, rejecting its election, and faithless'.[5] The Church has the assurance of the assistance of the risen Lord; in the Church the power of the Holy Spirit is at work. This assistance and this power, once *given*, cannot be taken away. Christ has 'built his Church upon the rock, he has given it a message, an organisation and a structure, against all of which Hell cannot prevail. . . . The irreformable constants that God has given through Christ must not be attacked. . . . What God through Christ, in the

---

[1] Cf. J. Bosc–J. Guitton–J. Daniélou, *Le dialogue catholique-protestant*, Paris–Geneva 1960, pp. 58f.   [2] J. Guitton, *op. cit.*, p. 443.
[3] Cf. Y. M. J. Congar, O.P., 'Dogme christologique et Ecclésiologie—Vérité et limites d'un parallèle', in *Das Konzil von Chalkedon—Geschichte und Gegenwart*, ed. by A. Grillmeier, S. J. and H. Bacht, S.J., Würzburg 1959, III, p. 239, 268. On the other hand Congar himself cites (p. 262) very forced expressions of other Catholic specialists, such as those in the classic work of E. Mersch, S.J., *La théologie du Corps Mystique*, 2 vols., Paris–Brussells 1944 or that of J. H. Nicolas in *Revue Thomiste* 46 (1946), p. 430, which we quote: 'Si l'Eglise est vraiment et pleinement humaine, elle est aussi, comme son chef dont elle est le prolongement et la visible expression, vraiment et pleinement divine.'
[4] R. Verardo, 'Riforma "nella" Chiesa e riforma "della" Chiesa. Cattolicesimo e Protestantesimo', in *Sacra Doctrina* N.S. VI (1961), p. 317, Quaderno 23, *Il volto del protestantesimo europeo.*
[5] H. Küng, *The Council and Reunion*, pp. 43f.

Holy Spirit, has instituted and constituted in the Church, partakes of the indestructible perfection of the holiness of God, and has no need of reform.'[1]

In other words, we are witnessing in Catholicism a translation into terms of ecclesiology of the classical *locus* of Christology, the doctrine of the three offices of Christ, Prophet, Priest and King.[2] 'The threefold office of Christ, Prophet, Priest and King prefigured in the Old Testament, has its continuation in the New, in the Church where Christ himself lives on mystically as priest, teacher and pastor, for the continuation and completion of his saving work. . . . It is from the nature of the Church as Christ mysteriously continuing on earth his life . . . that the Church's triple office derives.'[3] As the Encyclical '*Mystici Corporis*' taught (in a passage partially quoted earlier, at the outset of our study):

> . . . It is necessary to accustom ourselves to recognise Christ himself in the Church.
>
> It is in fact Christ who lives in the Church, and by means of her teaches, governs and communicates holiness

in such a way that through the members of the hierarchy,

> in virtue of the very mandate of the Redeemer, the gifts of Teacher, King and Priest become everlasting.[4]

1. *Magisterium*

First, let us consider the Church exercising its *magisterium*.

The gospel according to Luke (10.16) records in the context of the mission of the Seventy, a saying of Jesus that seems to be an echo of a rabbinic dictum to the effect that the envoy was to be received as he that sent him:[5]

He that hears you, hears me.

[1] *Op. cit.*, p. 76.
[2] It is of note that in the history of dogma the first systematic treatment of this doctrine in the area of Christology was Calvin followed by the traditional Reformed dogmatics: H. Heppe, *Die Dogmatik der evangelisch-reformierten Kirche-Dargestellt und aus den Quellen belegt*, revised and ed. by E. Bizer, Neukirchen Kreis Moers 1935, pp. 356f.; W. A. Visser t Hooft, *La royauté de Jesus-Christ*, Geneva 1948, p. 12: E. Brunner, *Dogmatics*, II, *The Christian Doctrine of Creation and Redemption* [ET], London 1952, p. 273; W. Niesel, *Die Theologie Calvins*, Munich 1957[2], p. 117; O. Weber, *Grundlagen der Dogmatik*, II, Neukirchen Kreis Moers 1962, p. 198.
[3] K. Algermissen, *Konfessionskunde*, Hanover 1930 [Ital. trs. entitled: *La Chiesa e le Chiese*, Brescia 1942, p. 22].
[4] *AAS* XXXV (1943), p. 217.
[5] H. L. Strack–P. Billerbeck, *Kommentar zum Neuen Testament aus Talmud und Midrasch*, Munich 1922, I, p. 590, II, p. 167; R. Bultmann, *The History of the Synoptic Tradition* [ET], Oxford 1963, p. 143. Cf. John 13.20.

According to the Catholic idea, the voice of Christ continues to sound through the centuries in the voice of the Church personified in the voice of its ministers. It is a conception that a Christian can justify, and it is not an exclusively Catholic doctrine, but has its counterpart in the Protestant doctrine of Scripture and Preaching. However in the Catholic context we are faced with a process of assimilation, not to say downright identification, between that 'me' and that 'you', which renders any sort of critical distinction out of the question. The voice of the Church in its *magisterium* is 'the organ through which he who is Master of all makes his voice heard'.[1] The promise of the divine presence becomes so embodied in the Church that it has ceased to be a promise. It has passed from the hands of God into the hands of chosen men, approved and blessed of God. It has become a reality, a fixed reality, endowed with guarantees and assurances to demonstrate its divine-human character. The Church's own existence can no more be separated from it. The conjunction of the Head and the members of his body is now a phenomenon conceived organically, and the Christological-ecclesiological organism that results can no longer suffer dissolution; indeed any sickness it suffers can be only passing and epidermic. Where the Church is, there is Christ, and where the voice of the Church sounds, there sounds the voice of Christ. The Church is the extension of Christ's incarnation in his ministry of Prophet and Teacher. It is his fulness, his perennial visible representative, his presence in history through every age. This sacred *magisterium* is 'the immediate and universal norm of truth',[2] and finds its typical expression and its chief epitomy in the Pontiff when he speaks *ex cathedra*, and exercises his function of pastor and doctor over all Christians, in order to ensure that a doctrine in matter of faith or morals be observed by the universal Church.[3] A Catholic theologian says that the Pope 'is, in a certain sense, Christ making himself visible to the whole of the Church'.[4] But the whole of the teaching ministry of the Church has a share in

---

[1] Pius XII, Address of 1950, contained in *Discorsi e Radiomessaggi* XII, p. 297, quoted *L'Osservatore Romano*, 20 Nov., 1960. The Pontiff was alluding to his own office as 'Vicar of Christ', 'his Representative on earth'. Speaking on Luke 10.16, a verse often quoted by Catholics, Luther comments: 'They fill their mouths with this text to support their teaching, but Christ in speaking to his disciples as they prepare to preach the gospel uses the phrase in such a way that it must refer to the gospel. They however leaving the gospel aside, use Christ's words as authority for their fables', *De captivitate Babylonica ecclesiae: WA* VI, p. 536, 20.

[2] Pius XII, Encyclical *'Humani Generis'*: Denzinger, 3013.

[3] (First) Vatican Council: Denzinger, 1839.

[4] M. Schmaus, *Katholische Dogmatik*, Munich 1940[2], I, p. 35.

this investiture of magisterial powers, and, because of this divine privilege is outside the range of all possible error or dogmatic fault. Hence it can consider itself immune from all criticism—not of course as regards its human aspect, for here it has always taken up a position in opposition to Donatist and Catharic presumptions, but in its essential and non-contingent aspect. 'By the will of Christ, infallibility belongs as an inalienable charisma, both to the Pope, when as the supreme Teacher of the Church, he issues a decision in the matter of faith or morals that is binding upon the entire Catholic community, and to the whole body of bishops in their entirety when in concert with the Pope. It does not matter if the College of Bishops exercises its teaching authority in the solemn manner of a Council, or in the ordinary and normal way (preaching, pastoral letters, authorization of catechisms, oversight of religious instruction, etc.). The essential fundamental reason for the infallibility enjoyed by the Pope and the Episcopate in conjunction with him lies in the fact that the Church is the mystical body of Christ. Jesus is its Head, and the Holy Spirit whom he sent, its heart and soul. The Church then in its totality is as incapable of error in the truth of its faith, as Christ himself was.'[1]

If this unbreakable union between Head and body be the grounds for asserting that in points of doctrine error on the part of the teaching hierarchy is as unthinkable as it would be in Christ himself, then, as a Protestant critic observes, 'all appeal to an authority higher than the *magisterium* is impossible, since in the last analysis, it would be setting something above Christ'.[2] Thus all idea of reference to the word of the Gospel which testifies to Christ's own word is lost, because the Church sees itself as its own point of reference. Here is proof of the fundamental, and not merely relative, sterility of the whole of Catholic biblicism, and of the dogmatic shortsightedness of those Protestant theologians who give to it meanings that it cannot ever have for a Catholic. For in Catholicism the Gospel can never be received as the Word of the Lord spoken *to* the Church for the instruction of the Church about salvation, so that any errors in the Church may be confronted with the truth of God, but only as the Word spoken by the Lord *in* the Church, and *through* the Church, a word entrusted to the keeping of the Church, of which the

---

[1] *Op. cit., ibid.* Cf. B. Bartmann, *Lehrbuch der Dogmatik*, Freiburg i. Br. 1932[8]; L. Ott, *Grundriss der Dogmatik*, Freiburg i Br.

[2] P. E. Persson, *Romerskt och evangeliskt*, Lund (German trs., *Evangelisch und Römisch-katholisch—Kernfragen der heutigen Diskussion*, Göttingen 1961, p. 48).

Church (and mark well—this means the Church of Rome and that alone) possesses exclusively the key of interpretation. Thus in the last resort the Gospel is the self-expression of the Church. It was the Church that preceded the writing of the apostles' testimony, the Church that saw to provision of a canon of scripture, and anointed it with the oil of authenticity, the Church that transmits and expounds in its true sense to every generation that Christian message that is not to be found exhaustively and completely in the written books, but also in unwritten traditions which the apostles received from either Christ's own lips, or by dictation from the Holy Spirit, and which form sources of revelation of the same value as scripture.[1] The oft-quoted phrase of Augustine is apposite:

> I would not believe the gospel were I not moved thereto by the authority of the Catholic Church,[2]

and the lesser known one of the Catholic party at the Lausanne disputation of 1536:

> The Church is both prior to and more potent than Scripture. This means that the Church is before Scripture and of more authority than Scripture. For the Church is the body of Jesus Christ.[3]

It is not for nothing that in Catholicism the function of exegesis is to establish the correctness of dogma as expounded by the *magisterium*. This leads to a reversal of roles between exegesis and dogmatics. It is not that dogmatics is founded on exegesis, but exegesis is at the service of dogmatics. The pattern of dogmatic treatment is usually this. *First* the dogma is set out. Then it is declared a matter of faith. And only *then* is a search made in scripture and tradition for explicit and implicit proofs of its divine origin. Pius XII in the Encyclical '*Humani Generis*' has put in very clear language what is meant by a return to the sources of revelation in the Roman sense; the task of the theologian is to

> show how the teachings of the living *magisterium* are to be found either explicitly or implicitly in holy scripture or in divine tradition.

---

[1] Council of Trent, Session IV, 8 April, 1546. Cf. Denzinger, 783; (First) Vatican Council Session III, 24 April, 1870. Cf. *ibid.*, 1787; M. Schmaus, *op. cit.*, I, pp. 98f.

[2] 'Ego evangelio non crederem nisi me commoveret Ecclesiae catholicae auctoritas', *Contra Epistulam Fundamenti* 5: *Corpus Scriptorum Ecclesiasticorum Latinorum* XXV 1, Vienna 1887f.

[3] 'Et ecclesia est prior scriptura et potior. C'est a dire que l'eglise est devant et de plus d'auctorité que l'escripture. Car l'eglise est le corp de Jesuchrist', *Les Actes de la Dispute de Lausanne 1536, publiés intégralement d'après le manuscrit de Berne par* A. Piaget Neuchâtel 1928, p. 43.

It is not that we must expose the doctrine of the Holy Fathers and the Sacred Magisterium to the critical gaze of Holy Scripture, but rather one must expound scripture

> according to the mind of the Church, which has been made by Christ the Lord, guardian and interpreter of the whole deposit of revealed truth.[1]

Once more we have that overlaying of Christ by the Church, that doctrine that asserts that

> the mystical body of Christ and the Roman Catholic Church are one identical thing.[2]

From this point of view we can see how dogma (here presented in its dual aspect of 'immediate revelation from God', and the Church's proclamation of 'an article of faith') can be conceived as an 'extension' of the Incarnation, and more generally how the *magisterium* appears as 'the place of meeting between men and the revelation and word of God', and the Church in its teaching authority as 'the immediate and direct source both of faith and of science as it concerns faith'.[3]

Indicative of this elevation of the *magisterium* over scripture is the characteristic contrast made between scripture, called the dead word, and the *magisterium*, called the living word. This contrast is occasionally supported even by scriptural quotations. The distinction that the apostle Paul makes, in opposing the Old Covenant written on tables of stone to the New Covenant written on the tables of the hearts of flesh, and the letter that slays to the Spirit that makes alive (II Cor. 3), is used with breath-taking novelty and not a little sheer fantasy to illustrate the contrast between the inert letter of scripture and the living voice of the *magisterium*. This latter

> has in itself something that the bible as a dead letter does not and cannot possess, and which is its highest prerogative—the living spirit of revelation, the vitality of revealed thought, the *instinctus fidei*, the φρόνημα ἐκκλησιαστικόν, the *sensus Ecclesiae*, that lies behind every written and unwritten word. The spirit of revelation lives not in dead documents, but in the beating hearts of the faithful, called into being and

---

[1] Denzinger, 3014-3015. Cf. M. Schmaus, *op. cit.*, I, p. 127.
[2] Denzinger, 3019: '... corpus Christi mysticum et Ecclesiam Catholicam Romanam unum idemque esse'.
[3] M. Schmaus, *op. cit.*, I, pp. 54f., 72f. Cf. W. Schweitzer, *Schrift und Dogma in der Oekumene*, Gütersloh 1953, pp. 32f., 45; H. Diem, *Theologie als kirchliche Wissenschaft*, Munich 1955, I, *Exegese und Historie*, pp. 140f., II, *Dogmatik*, pp. 40f.; O. Weber, *op. cit.*, Neukirchen Kreis Moers, 1955, I, p. 356.

directed by the apostolic *magisterium* under the illumination of the Holy Spirit.[1]

We must try to understand this contrast and its reasons. The matter might be expressed for Protestants by use of categories that point up the antithesis of dialectic between man's word and God's word, and by resorting to the Barthian doctrine of the Word of God in the threefold system of the revealed, the written and the preached Word.[2] However, the Catholic lacks an essential reservation, that of 'where and when it seems good to God'. For him the where is necessarily and exclusively the Church of Rome, from the Vatican down to the last and least of remote parishes, and the when is every time that the *magisterium* speaks in the exercise of its proper functions; with the effect that the word of men in the Church is ex-officio the Word of God, and so the terms of the equation are completely reversed.

It would not be difficult to detect in the Roman concept of the *charisma veritatis* a threefold Gnostic idea at work. In the first place the notion that truth is known only to the hierarchy introduces into the Church the esoteric idea of there being 'initiates who possess the *gnosis*, and non-initiates who do not possess it, but can receive it from the hierarchy'.[3] Thus the gospel notion of truth is substituted by one which seems not unconnected with Gnostic ideas.

Secondly, there is the idea of the 'living voice of the *magisterium*' and the idea of truth committed by Christ directly to the apostles and passed on by word of mouth without ever being fixed in written form, constituting thus the secret key for interpreting the written traditions in the true sense intended by the Master. Here we cannot but think of that tradition so favoured by the Gnostics, that set the greatest store on that period between the resurrection and ascension of Jesus, which cannot be historically verified and in which he is alleged not only to have communicated to certain favoured disciples the secret knowledge necessary for the understanding of the words he had spoken during his public ministry, but also to have given them a series of special revelations reserved for the 'perfect'.[4]

[1] K. Adam, *Das Wesen des Katholizismus* [Engl. trs., *The Spirit of Catholicism*, London 1934, pp. 169f.].
[2] K. Barth, *Die kirchliche Dogmatik* I/1—*Die Lehre vom Wort Gottes*, Zollikon–Zürich 1947[5], p. 89 [*CD*, 1936, p. 136].
[3] The remark is that of a Russian theologian, S. Boulgakoff, *L'orthodoxie*, Paris 1932, p. 79.
[4] D. van den Eynde, O.F.M., 'Tradizione e Magistero', in *Problemi e orientamenti di Teologia dommatica*, Milan 1957, I, pp. 237f., calling attention to the words of J. Ranft (*Der Ursprung des katholischen Traditionsprinzip*, Würzburg 1931) minimises the influence

In the third place one might note a Gnostic, as well as Jewish, influence, in the way of interpreting the apostolic succession as a succession both of doctrine and of persons from the apostles down, a chain of transmission through history, intended to guarantee the apostolicity both of the content and the origins of the message and of its interpretation. This seems to have been a device, used by both the Gnostic and the Christian sides, to counter each other's propaganda attacks, from Irenaeus, perhaps even from Hegesippus on.[1] The concept is closely bound up with that of oral tradition, and it is to be recalled that the most ancient document known to us in which we first find the phrases 'apostolic tradition' and 'succession' is not a document of the Church, but a Gnostic one of Valentinian tendencies, the Epistle of Ptolomy to 'sister' Flora.[2]

However it is more important to establish the fact that this kind of extension into ecclesiology of the office of Christ the Prophet which produces an objectivization of truth in an ecclesiological form, is also reminiscent of the spatial and substantial way in which the Gnostic *pleroma* is conceived. As a result of the process that has unified the Head and the body, the truth of Christ has passed to the Church as a deposit to be conserved and taught to men without any further possibility of error, inasmuch as Christ himself speaks with her and in her. The equation is formulated: Christ is truth, the church is truth. The Church possesses the truth objectively and inalienably, and so there cannot exist any Christian truth outside the sphere of Catholic truth in its totality, even though it can and does in effect gather into its own body rational truths that are not

of non-christian religions on the Catholic conception of tradition, describing the resemblances as 'slight and distant'. But recent discoveries of Christian Gnostic documents have thrown more precise light on the Gnostic conception of esoteric revelation and secret doctrines, to which appeal might be made where Scripture cannot be made to apply to situations too alien to it, either by the allegorical or other methods. For example, the documents of Codex Jung. Cf. H. C. Puech–G. Quispel, 'Les écrits gnostiques du Codex Jung', *Vigiliae Christianae* VIII (1954), pp. 1–51; H. C. Puech–G. Quispel–W. C. van Unnik, *The Jung Codex—A Newly Recovered Gnostic Papyrus*, London 1955; M. Malinine–H. C. Puech–G. Quispel, *Évangelium Veritatis—Codex Jung*, Zürich 1956; J. Leipoldt, 'Das "Evangelium der Wahrheit"', *Theologische Literaturzeitung* 82 (1957), pp. 825f.; E. Hennecke, *Neutestamentliche Apokryphen*, I, *Evangelien*, Tübingen 1959³, pp. 160f. The Gnostic origin of unwritten apostolic traditions has been shown by O. Cullmann, 'The Tradition' in his *The Early Church*, London 1956.

[1] Irenaeus of Lyons, *Adversus Haereses*, Bk III. Cf. the passages: III 2.1, 2.2, 2.3 to 4.1, and the article on the subject: V. Subilia, 'Attualità di Ireneo—Alle radici del Cattolicesimo e dell'Ortodossia', *Protestantesimo* 15 (1960), pp. 138f. For Hegesippus cf. E. Buonaiuti, 'Marcione ed Egesippo,' *Religio* 12 (1936), p. 410; H. von Campenhausen, 'Lehrerreihen und Bischofsreihen im 2 Jahrhundert' in *In memoriam Ernst Lohmeyer*, Stuttgart 1951, pp. 240f.

[2] Ptolomy, *Letter to Flora* (edited G. Quispel—*Sources chrétiennes* 24, Paris 1949, VII, 9, p. 69).

Christian. No salvation outside the Church, because no truth; indeed, because no Christ. Outside the fulness (the *pleroma*!) of Catholicism, within which all the scattered particles of light and truth continue to bifurcate *ad infinitum*, there can be only particles of darkness and error. Hence adherence to truth, and profession of truth, mean simply to enter into the sphere of the Catholic Church and submit to its *magisterium*. Not to submit, not to adhere means simply shutting one's eyes to the clear light of truth, and declaring in favour of darkness and error. Truth is then identified with unity, with a consequent devaluation of truth in the interests of unity. Augustine uses the context of the idea of the total Christ to assert that nothing that schismatics or heretics possess outside the Church, either symbol of faith, or church sacraments, or liturgies, can avail for salvation.[1] The statement, as we have said, derives from the idea of the body of Christ. Yet the author of the idea, the apostle Paul himself, said something very different. Learning while in chains that some were preaching Christ in envy, he did not excommunicate them, but rejoiced in the fact that 'notwithstanding' Christ was preached (Phil. 1.15–8). And this saying is just an echo of a sentence of Jesus recorded by the synoptic Gospels. He answers the disciples who have forbidden someone to cast out demons in his name because the man did not 'follow' them: 'Forbid him not, for there is no man which shall do a miracle in my name, that can lightly speak evil of me' (Mark 9.38–9).[2] The difference is that Augustine has assimilated Christ and the Church, while the New Testament knows no such assimilation.

It is not easy to come to grips with this discrepancy.

If we try to describe the phenomenon of Catholicism in categories of space and substance, such as Gnostic myth used, we risk not merely failing to be comprehensible to modern minds because we use unfamiliar categories in our explanation, but also betraying instead of explaining the idea, and consequently exposing our flank to Catholic criticism.[3] We must find other means of reaching the point of distinction.

---

[1] *De baptismo contra Donatistas* IV 17, 24, quoted from C. Journet, *op. cit.*, II, p. 1091.

[2] Some commentators have supposed that Paul is the one figured as the doer of mighty works outside the circle of the Twelve. Cf. E. Klostermann, *Das Markusevangelium*, Tübingen 1950[4], p. 95. It may however be that the *logion* in its phrasing bears the mark of the situation of the nascent Church. Cf. E. Lohmeyer, *Das Evangelium des Markus*, Göttingen 1953, p. 195. In any case it is richly instructive.

[3] The Encyclical '*Mystici Corporis*', after speaking of the 'self-same nature' of Head and Body, and of participation in the 'divine nature', takes proper precautions and

Certainly every Christian Confession is ready to subscribe to the axiom if it means: *Outside Christ no salvation*.[1] The use of the phrase in this sense certainly does not mean a Christ disincarnate, and removed from historic reality, but rather Christ believed, obeyed, preached by the Church, who makes himself known, and is known, through the Church. The Reformers use language in this sense at times that to an uninstructed eye might seem identical with that of the Romans. Enough to think of Luther's phrases in the Great Catechism, where the Church is described in the language of Cyprian as the mother who brings forth every Christian, and nourishes him on the divine word:

> Where nothing is taught of Christ, the Holy Spirit is not present either, who constitutes, summons and unifies the communion of Christians, outside of which none can come to Christ the Lord.[2]

Or, the phrases of the first chapter of the fourth book of the *Christian Institutes*, where Calvin, having declared that

> There is no other way to enter into life unless this mother conceive us in her womb, give us birth, nourish us at her breast, and lastly, unless she keep us under her care and guidance

because 'away from her bosom one cannot hope for any forgiveness of sins or any salvation', he then sets in bold relief the necessity and the place of the preaching of the Gospel. God 'hath established Pastors and Doctors by whose mouth he teaches us', and we must hear them 'as if he spake himself'.

Those who limit themselves to private bible reading 'receive the due wage of such divorce, in that they get entangled in errors and fantasies, which lead to their confounding'.[3] The whole process is very carefully described. God chooses himself certain men, and appoints them

condemns 'those who do not sufficiently pay regard to the metaphor, and do not make the absolutely necessary distinction between the particular and specific meanings of physical, moral and mystical bodies, and hence give a perverted explanation of this union. Thus they unite and confuse in one single physical personality the divine Redeemer and the members of the Church, and attributing divine things to men, make Jesus Christ subject to error and humour weaknesses.'

[1] K. Barth, *op. cit.*, IV/1—*Die Lehre von der Versöhnung*, Zürich 1960, p. 769. Cf. I/2, pp. 232f. [*CD*, 1956, p. 688; cf. I/2, p. 213].

[2] *Die Bekenntnisschriften der Evangelisch-Lutherischen Kirche*, Göttingen 1956³, p. 655. The statements of Cyprian of Carthage, 'habere non potest Deum patrem qui ecclesiam non habet matrem' and 'salus extra ecclesiam non est' are found in *De unitate ecclesiae* 6 (cf. *Epist.* 74.7) and in *Epist.* 73.21: *Corpus Scriptorum Ecclesiasticorum Latinorum* III, 1–3.

[3] J. Calvin, *Institution de la religion chrestienne* IV 1.1, 4, 5.

as his lieutenants, not indeed to yield to them his honour and superiority, but merely to do his work by means of them, just as a workman uses the assistance of tools.[1]

Calvin shows great lucidity and insight in referring to contemporary discussions about the ministry in the Church, and distinguishes on the one hand the tendency (of the Catholics) to 'magnify' the dignity of the Christian ministry inordinately, turning the service of Christ into its precise opposite, in 'stealing from God his honour and drawing it upon oneself'—and on the other hand the (Anabaptist) tendency promoted by a fear of usurping the Holy Spirit's function, that leads to the attempt to abolish all ministry.[2]

Today there is once more a full realization in Protestantism of ecclesiological problems, even if they are no longer cast in the same form, and even if some sectors of Protestantism still use the old Anabaptist and Pietistic terms (shorn however of their original substance, fervour and historical significance) in considering their community aspect.

Now all these expressions indicate clearly that in every respect salvation is in Christ who is come, is crucified, is risen and is to come, and not in the Church. One does not 'believe in' the Church, one is not baptized into the name of the Church, one is not saved by the virtue of the Church, the Church has not been crucified for us, nor risen again for us (I Cor. 1.13–5; 3.10–1). The Church is a tool that God uses to bring men to himself, but tools remain tools and cannot outstep their limitations. God is greater than his tools. He does not allow himself to be confused with his instruments. He may even discard them when they grow rusty and unserviceable, and make himself new ones. Four centuries of controversy and the resultant inter-confessional divisions reveal clearly that these truths are not superficial. And here is the point of division. Quite simple, yet decisive, and grave to the ultimate degree.

What is compromised in the Catholic conception is God's very freedom. We may start on the very edge of the generation of the apostles with Ignatius of Antioch, who used apostolic admonitions in a very different context, declaring:

Those who are of God and of Jesus Christ are with the bishop. . . . If any follow a schismatic, he will not inherit the kingdom of God. If any walk in another opinion, he will have no part in the passion of Christ (*Philad.* 3. 2–3).

[1] *Op. cit.*, IV 3.1.   [2] *Op. cit.*, IV 1.6; IV 7.25.

We may take John XXIII who in his apostolic letter '*Quotiescumque nobis*' addressed to Cardinal Tien-Chen-Sin, Archbishop of Pekin, on 29th June, 1961 wrote:

> There is no service rendered properly and acceptably to God and none can come to him, except through Jesus Christ. It is not possible to be united with Christ except in the Church and through the Church, which is his mystic body. It is not indeed possible to belong to the Church, except through the bishops, the successors of the apostles, united with the Supreme Pastor, the successor of Peter.[1]

What is so perplexing in all the course of Catholic tradition is this too high exaltation of the ecclesiastical instruments till they seem to usurp the place of him who wields them, this too fluid continuity, this too easy, too unrestricted—one is tempted to say too irreverent— passage from the Lord to his human mediators, this too rigid, too logical sequence, which drains the essential dialectical tension from the relationships of God and man, imprisons the truth of God in a legalist straight-jacket and objectivizes God in the Church, in the *magisterium* and in dogma, and encloses him (as in a capsule) inside the sacred institution, its system and its function.

Such presuppositions naturally lead the Church to invert its proper condition of discipleship into that of teacher. Inevitably the permanently valid warning of Jesus falls on deaf ears:

> But be ye not called master, for one is your master, and ye are all brethren. And do not call any on the earth your father, for one alone is your father, him who is in heaven. And be ye not called guides, for one only is your guide, even Christ (Matt. 23. 8–10).

The seriousness of the situation is revealed in the fact that our difficulty does not show itself on the level of ethics or psychology, for in this area Catholicism indeed possesses a rigorous code of mortification and the disciplined restraint of feelings, which applies from the Roman Pontiff down to the humblest monk in a monastery cloister with his rule of obedience. Human nature being what it is, it may be that the situation is reflected in interior states of mind, just as it reflects in the Church's outward show. The objective observer, whether Christian or not, all too often experiences an inescapable sense of disquietude, and of disharmony with the gospel. But the gravity does not lie here, these are but the outward symptoms of

---

[1] Quoted *L'Osservatore Romano*, 10 May, 1962 in the scheme for the dogmatic Constitution on the Church, outlined by Cardinal Alfredo Ottaviani, President of the Theological Commission and examined by the Central Commission of the Second Vatican Council. The Latin text will be found in *AAS* LIII, 1961, p. 466.

the fundamental issue. This is an ecclesiological, not a personal affair. It is shaped not by the negligence born of infidelity, but by the understanding born of dogma. The Church of Rome sees herself as mother, mistress and guide, because she sees in herself the living Christ, incarnate that moment in the history of men. How impossible then to avoid the risk of losing sight of the fact that Christ alone has had the anointing of truth, and that the Church

> is the daughter, born of the word, not the word's mother,

as Luther well knew.[1] Or that the whole Church is eternally the

> *ecclesia discens*, the learning Church, that learns from its Head and from the spirit of truth. It is in its entirety under the ultimate authority of the divinely revealed truth,

as the Orthodox know.[2] The tremendous peril is thus revealed, not as a mere latent temptation, but in the very systematic structure of the institution. It is the peril of a Church that listens to itself and is without a Master.

This point of view makes it quite clear how inconceivable is any alternative sort of Christianity outside the circle of that *magisterium* that regards itself as the exclusive keeper of Christian wisdom and truth, in the face of all the follies and human errors that lie in the trends and the times. Long ago, Fra Paolo Sarpi tells us, Leo X dismissed the 'business' of Martin Luther as a mere friar's quarrel, not 'worth a thought', as 'nothing very important', which 'if not made a fuss of, few would take seriously', and 'it would run its course and fade away'.[3] From then up to the declarations of John XXIII to the effect that the 'separated brethren' must not expect the Council to be a 'speculative assembly',[4] since 'it would be as impossible as useless to initiate discussions that could only lead to nothing',[5]

---

[1] 'Est filia, nata ex verbo, non est mater verbi', M. Luther, *Vorlesungen über 1. Mose : WA* XLII, p. 334, 12. Cf. the studies of K. G. Steck, 'Ecclesia—creatura verbi', in J. Beckmann–K. G. Steck–F. Viering, *Von Einheit und Wesen der Kirche—Fragen am Vorabend des ökumenischen Konzils*, Göttingen 1960, pp. 40f.; and *Kirche des Wortes oder Kirche des Lehramts?*, Zürich 1962.

[2] G. Florovsky, 'Le corps du Christ vivant. Une interprétation orthodoxe de l'Eglise', in *La Sainte Eglise Universelle—Confrontation oecuménique*, Neuchâtel–Paris 1948, p. 53.

[3] Fra Paolo Sarpi, *Opere*, III, *Istoria del Concilio Tridentino*, ed. by G. Gambarin, Bari 1953, I, p. 16.

[4] John XXIII *'Progredientes leniter'*—Address delivered 20 June, 1961 to the Fathers of the Central Commission: *AAS* LIII (1961), p. 502. The Latin text reads: '*Concilium speculativus coetus non est*, sed potius corpus quoddam viventi vividaque natura, quod oculis conspicit, lacertis universum terrarum orbem amplectitur.' Italics as in text.

[5] H. Küng, *op. cit.*, p. 5, attributes these phrases to John XXIII on the strength of *Informations catholiques internationales* 1959, 59/5 [not in Engl. trs.]. We have not succeeded in tracing them in *AAS*. The sense of impatience with those who still want to

Rome has never taken seriously the dogmatic issues posed by the Reformation and has never indeed realized their ultimate gravity. For Rome there is nothing to discuss; there could not be. The 'separated brethren' cannot but be struck with admiration at the spectacle of the Council and its 'salutary fruits'. Faced with 'such a revival of Catholic faith, such a new flowering of love, such an enhancement of Christian moral standards', they cannot but feel 'a vivid and overpowering desire for a sincere and practical unity in one single fold, under one single shepherd'.[1] Rome does not permit discussion of the Church's *magisterium*; it is considered an unthinkable, scandalous, thing. From their point of view it would mean discussing, i.e., casting doubt upon, Christ himself, and this would imply abandoning oneself to rationalistic relativism. Human life, human works, human customs, one may discuss and go on to modify. But such discussions and modifications are fruitful only if one does not touch the one untouchable thing, 'the source of true life, which is Christ living in his Church and acting through its agency, by means of its infallible *magisterium*'.[2] Through the words of recent writers Rome has come to the point of admitting the existence of 'very grave disorders and abuses which had invaded the Church at the time of the Renaissance . . . distressing conditions in the ecclesiastical life of the period, the flagrant scandals of the worldly lives of the Popes, cardinals, and bishops as well as the lower clergy.'[3] Having shifted

stay and discuss theological questions considered as settled, had been even more marked in the broadcast announcement of 23 Dec., 1949 by Pius XII at the opening of the Holy Year: 'Oh that this Holy Year might hail also the great long-awaited return to the one true Church of those many believers in Jesus Christ now for various motives separated from it! With groanings that cannot be uttered, the Spirit who is in the hearts of good men, today raises in a cry of the very prayer of the Lord: *"that they may be one"*. Rightly distressed at the audacity of the advance of the solid front of militant atheism, the question long asked now becomes a call: Why still separation?, Why still schism?, How long till a union of concord between all the forces of the spirit and of love?', *AAS* XXXXII, 1950, p. 126.

Also the present Pope, when Archbishop of Milan, in a pastoral letter of 22 Feb., 1962, showed explicitly his impatience at the suggestion of any theological discussion over Protestants and Orthodox. 'May the Council loose us from the shackles of the sorrowful memories of a past when discussions on points of historical exegesis, of honour and of prestige sapped the dynamism which must be assumed at the proper moment if the great problem is to be solved' (*La Civiltà Cattolica*, 7 April, 1962, p. 81; *L'Osservatore Romano*, 14 March, 1962).

[1] John XXIII, Encyclical '*Paenitentiam agere*' of 1 July, 1962, published in *L'Osservatore Romano* of 6 July, 1962. The Encyclical contains two notes hardly auspicious for relations with the 'separated brethren'. Allusion is made to the 'comforting teaching of the Council of Trent, that faithful echo of Catholic doctrine'. Mention is also made of 'a solemn novena' 'to invoke upon the Fathers of the Council a shower of heavenly illumination and divine graces' and adds that 'all who take part in the novena will receive the grant of Plenary Indulgence, to be enjoyed according to the usual conditions'.

[2] R. Verardo, O.P., *art. cit.*, p. 342.   [3] *Art. cit.*, p. 327.

the problem onto the level of ethics and discipline, she sees the Reformation justifiably caused by this momentary laxity. Yet she is convinced that 'all that is needed for the elimination of the pagan poison that has entered from without into the life of the Church, is a return to the intensity of Christian living'.[1] Once the Counter-Reformation had brought Catholicism again to the seriousness of ethical and disciplined behaviour, the continued existence of the Reformation becomes 'an absolutely inexplicable fact'.[2] It can be explained, that is, on any level except the dogmatic, by making innumerable suppositions, denigratory or malicious, about Luther's psychological state. Thus, from Cochläus[3] to Weijenborg[4] by way of Denifle[5] and Grisar,[6] there has been a series of erudite variations oblivious of any sense of proportion imposed by history, on the theme that the Reformation is to be laid at the door of Luther's defective morals, attributable to various physiological or family factors, which made him incapable of enduring the severities of monastic life, and drove him to propound the doctrine of justification without works. This, despite all correctives, continues to circulate subtly as the small coinage of propaganda, especially in Catholic countries, where there is no direct knowledge of Protestantism, and no possibility of checking facts. Or the explanation follows the line of rehabilitating Luther, as in German Catholicism—a line regretted by some who stand well in the favour of the hierarchy,[7] and which

---

[1] *Art. cit.*, p. 328.   [2] *Art. cit.*, p. 327.

[3] For this and the following series of interpretations cf.: R. Stauffer, 'Les recherches sur Luther dans le catholicisme: leur évolution du début du siècle à nos jours', *Eglise et Théologie* 24 (1961), pp. 1ff.; V. Vinay, 'Nuovo orientamento dell'indagine cattolica su Lutero?', *Protestantesimo* 17 (1962), pp. 158f. The work of J. Cochlaeus, *Commentaria de actis et scriptis Martini Lutheri*, dates from 1549.

[4] R. Weijenborg, O.F.M., 'Un caso di esegesi esistenzialista presso Lutero', in *Il Protestantesimo ieri e oggi*, ed. by A. Piolanti, Rome 1958, pp. 66f. The author, a specialist in Protestant theology at the Pontificio Ateneo Antoniano of Rome, maintains the thesis that Luther's vocation to the monastic life was only an act of self-deceit to escape his duty of repaying his father 'the expenses of the University education' (p. 68), and that 'Luther's reformation of doctrine was the outworking of this fraud' (p. 84). He deduces from this that the way to make Protestants return to the 'true Church of Christ' is to convince them that they have been victims of a man who is to be ranked 'among cogenital, more or less psychopathic, tricksters' (p. 84). Cf. V. Subilia, 'Il Protestantesimo nel giudizio del Cattolicesimo', *Protestantesimo* 15 (1960), pp. 210f.

[5] H. Denifle, O.P., *Luther und Luthertum in den ersten Entwicklung quellenmässig dargestellt*, I-II, Mainz, 1904-9.

[6] H. Grisar, S.J., *Luther*, I-II-III, Freiburg i. Br. 1911-12.

[7] P. Parente, 'Necessità del Magistero', report presented to the 'Settimana dei Concili and published in *L'Osservatore Romano*, 16 Nov., 1960: 'I know that the predominant tendency today is to rehabilitate even Luther. But a study in depth of his stormy career and of his mind so restive of all law, even of that of logic, can only lead to a very severe verdict. By his ideology and by his actions, Luther has undermined the

has even provoked disciplinary measures.[1] On this thesis, the Catholicism of the sixteenth century did not possess the proper Catholic fulness.[2] Yet a close look shows that even here the dogmatic issue is evaded: Luther suffered from his Occamite upbringing—a system 'radically not Catholic'[3]—and so, lacking the adequate knowledge a study of Thomas Aquinas would have brought, he could not understand the soul of Catholicism. Thus he was a theological Don Quixote, and fought not real Catholic dogma, but the windmill of an imaginary and distorted Catholicism, a Catholicism that was not really Catholic.[4] Hence he was led to confuse his planes. Not recognizing the real Church and her dogma,[5] he directed his attack against the divine-human reality of the Church, which he should never have assailed. 'Unity, absolute unity, is the essence of the Church.'[6] But Luther destroyed that precious, irreplaceable blessing of unity, all because he was the victim of illusion and misunderstanding. He missed the reality of the Church.[7] Here also, despite the change of key, and despite the deeper objectivity with which the study is made, the criterion remains as ever 'submission to the Church'.[8] The *magisterium* is as ever, today as in the sixteenth century, the 'judge who has no judge'.[9] It no longer matters *what* is said, but *who* says it—'the capital question for the Church is not that of the purity of the gospel, but that of the correctness of office'.[10]

In the new ecumenical atmosphere of today, this creates a sense of impatience. Surely the Protest is now without point? Has not Catholic truth survived intact despite that painful yet unsuccessful

essential structure of the Church of Christ which is a God–man organism in which human and divine are in harmony. . . .'

[1] R. Stauffer, *art. cit.*, p. 49.
[2] J. Lortz, *Die Reformation als religiöse Anliegen heute*, Trier 1948, pp. 99f.
[3] J. Lortz, *Die Reformation in Deutschland*, Frieburg i. Br. 1941², I, p. 173.
[4] *Op. cit.*, I, pp. 176, 436.
[5] J. Hessen, *Luther in Katholischer Sicht*, Bonn 1949².
[6] J. Lortz, *Die Reformation in Deutschland*, II, p. 307.
[7] *Op. cit.*, I, p. 394.
[8] W. von Loewenich, *Der moderne Katholizismus*, Witten 1952², p. 339. Von Loewenich observes that in these Catholic studies that tend to rehabilitate Luther (he alludes to Lortz) there is 'something shifting, something too elastic, that prevents us from comprehending anything clearly and soberly, something that refuses to call white white, and black black, that leaves the not-over-critical mentality in a state more dangerously confused than the works of Denifle and Grisar' (pp. 340f.). Some Protestant critics have valued positively the work of A. Brandenburg, *Gericht und Evangelium—Zur Worttheologie in Luthers ersten Psalmvorlesung*, Paderborn 1960. Cf. F. Lau, 'Luthers Worttheologie in katholischer Sicht', in *Luther-Jahrbuch 1961*, Berlin 1961, pp. 110f.; V.Vinay *art. cit.*
[9] *'Iudex sine judice'*, *Epitoma responsionis ad Martinum Luther per Fratrem Silvestrum de Prierio*, 1520: *WA* VI, pp. 334, 26.
[10] P. E. Persson, *op. cit.*, p. 41.

attack by the Reformation? Has not Catholicism responded from
the time of Trent on, to the call for purification and reform? Is not
the Council to impart still more vigour to its system and restore it to
its genuine fulness and essential Catholicity?[1] If the victims of this
great misunderstanding of history persist, and harden in, their
attitude, they only show their rather pathological abnormality; it is
clear there is an irrational blockage in their thinking, the relic of an
age-long set pattern of thought and of insuperable ignorance; and
so it seems only natural and proper for Catholic circles to use again,
with regard to a Protestantism now better informed[2] and better
disposed[3] than it was, the advice which originated with Monsignor
Gerolamo Ragazzoni, bishop of Nazianzo and coadjutor of Fama-
gosta, who addressing the ninth and final session of the Council of
Trent (Dec. 3 and 4, 1563) first pointed out that all had now been
done to ensure that 'they' (the Protestants) should come to the
knowledge of the truth and hear the voice of the Lord (even to the
point of holding the Council in a city that stood on the very threshold
of their home—*in Germaniae faucibus*), and then said:

> We have been some time preparing the medicine needed for health,
> but if one intends to be rid of the sickness, it must now be taken, and
> spread through the veins into all the body.[4]

The medicine which the rebellious and capricious children (now
the 'separated brethren') must make up their minds to take in order

---

[1] H. Küng, *op. cit.*, pp. 116, 275.

[2] On 16 Oct., 1518, M. Luther appealed 'from the Pope ill informed to the Pope better
informed'. Cf. G. Miegge, *Lutero*, Torre Pellice 1946, p. 266.

[3] On 7 March, 1962 John XXIII delivered a discourse in Santa Sabina which was
reported in summary in *L'Osservatore Romano* of 10 March, 1962, wherein he voiced
the following ideas: first, he pointed out that while in previous centuries the invitations
given by Rome to the separated brethren did not meet with 'the hoped-for response',
'now instead the Holy Father recognises—and must give glory and thanks to God for
it—that from those quarters which had always treated the Catholic Church and the Holy
See with hostility and slights, comes a flow of good words and courtesies. For him it
signifies that the grace of the Lord goes on its way passing upon souls: further, as they
advance in affection, all realise, when they discover us in this world so blessed by so many
heavenly graces, that it is pointless to lose themselves further in tortuous ways that lead
to confusion and universal ruin.'

[4] The text of the speech is found in *Canones et Decreta Sacrosanti Oecumenici Concilii
Tridentini*, Turin 1913, pp. 273f. The passage cited from the speech itself was cited by
John XXIII, who called it 'words of charity and wisdom' in an address given 9 March,
1962 to the members of the Secretariat for the Promotion of Christian Unity, in reply
to an address of homage given by Cardinal A. Bea. Cf. *L'Osservatore Romano*, 9 March,
1962 and *La Civiltà Cattolica*, 7 April, 1962, p. 71. The quotation was repeated in the
account published in *L'Osservatore Romano* of 22–3 June, 1962 on the conclusion of the
work of the Central Commission of the Council, when discussions were held on the
following themes: Church Unity—Devotion to the Mother of God—Prayers and
concern for the Return of the separated brethren.

to prevent a worsening of their sickness, is submission to the inviolable rule and norm of the Roman *magisterium*. Their sickness is now chronic, and instead of abating, or at least remaining arrested, shows signs of worsening. History, backed by a battery of evidence, has for long taught that abandoning the source of truth, Christ incarnate in his Church in the history of men, leads to worse excesses. This and this only is the key by which Rome interprets all modern history from the sixteenth to the twentieth centuries. The history of modern times is just the disastrous byproduct of the Protestant apostasy. The history of the critical spirit and the scientific method, the history of political emancipation and economic and social liberties, is just the history of the Anti-church. And at the bottom of the Antichurch movement is Protestantism with its heedless attack upon the *magisterium*, that indubitable representative upon earth of the truth.

This attack was delivered in successive waves, which Küng thus designates: 'after Lutheranism and Calvinism, Jansenism, Gallicanism, Absolute Despotism, Illuminism, Febronianism; then, as it were, the beginning of a new age, the French Revolution, Secularism, the Napoleonic Wars, and then Material Atheism, Liberalism and Socialism'.[1] It may be summed up: In the space of 400 years, the abandonment of the Church has led to the abandonment first of Christ, and then of God himself.[2] In the end, Protestantism is portrayed as one contingent step on the road that leads to Atheism; to that existential Nihilism evidenced today in such widespread and alarming fashion, which is just the counterpart of a loss of understanding of the meaning of life; to that interior shattering of thought that reveals itself in the individual in the miseries of neuroses, and on the international plane in the conflict of cultures; to that disintegration of man himself (illustrated with such sharp insight, and so drastically, in modern art), which seems to have now passed into the very structure of civilization itself, with life fragmented into specialized departments, and the universal idea well nigh lost.

But the modern age is now drawing its last breaths of life. Civilization has reached an impasse; it has come to one of those points that Alpine jargon calls 'sixth grade plus'; with the rock covered with *Verglas* and exposed to falls of ice, further advance is impossible and a deviation essential. Knowledge of this mortal crisis into which history is come, and of the desperate necessity of taking emergency action, demands the opening of a new road, quite different from the

[1] H. Küng, *op. cit.*, p. 120.   [2] *Op. cit.*, p. 121.

one followed in the last few centuries. This may be done by eliminating the original cause of the present situation, by gathering up such
positive elements as it may have produced, and somehow or other
by a mass enlistment of humans to embody these elements. Since it
was a detachment from the norm of all truth that led to these
catastrophic consequences, the premise of the work of recovery
must be the elimination of the movement that produced the detachment. That is the order of the day which humanity is living through.
The alternatives cannot be Catholicism or Protestantism, but Catholicism or Atheism.[1] The hope of catholicizing the Reformation,
however, brings the shape of a new age over the horizon. There is
need to outline in advance the laws that are to govern it, so as to
prevent a repetition of the chaos of arbitrariness. Hence the serious
appeal to Protestantism to integrate with Catholicism and collaborate
in the recovery of that world, which Pilate-like washes its hands and
says: What is truth? Modern man has need of a norm if he is to find
himself again. He has become the victim of myths that drive him
into isolation or illusion, or, bereft of every myth, he is shut out from
hope, and so from himself. The Marxist analysis of the phenomenon
of man as no longer himself can be made to serve as a means of
understanding the necessity of Catholicism. Catholicism puts itself
forward as 'the eternal synthesis' capable of blending the divergent
currents of civilisation,[2] the 'symbolic point of support', the 'refuge
immediately secure' that offers man a place where to lay his head,
the lode-star for thought and life.[3] That Rome should direct the
conscience is considered the only means to secure for the new
humanism now in preparation purpose and safety. And this can only
come about by an up-to-date use of the methods of Thomists and
Dominicans in making all culture Catholic, be it Protestant or lay,
by absorbing and assimilating it.

At the bottom of these notions is undoubtedly the grandiose idea
of the *ordinatio ad unum* of the universe, of *christianitas*, of the
corpus christianum, a unit 'under a single head, in temporal affairs

---

[1] This concept affects individual psychology, particularly in Catholic countries. If a
man leaves Catholicism for one reason or another, his mental structure makes it very
difficult for him to conceive of any Christian alternative to Catholicism itself. For him,
to abandon Catholicism usually means to abandon Christianity. Even when he has
adopted an anti-christian attitude, his unconscious dogmatic presuppositions remain
Catholic. It is not only the priest in Catholicism that preserves a *character indelebilis*.
[2] M. F. Sciacca, 'Les deux traditions de la civilisation européenne et leur unité
substantielle', in *Problèmes de civilisation européenne*, Strasbourg 1956, p. 78.
[3] R. Guardini, *La fine dell'epoca moderna*, Brescia 1960, pp. 45, 122.

the emperor, in spiritual the Pontiff. Both powers are but two aspects of one single double-faced being, two sides of a single body. The Church is unique, and embraces all, spirit and body, religion and politics. For practical purposes only is there a division of functions, some exercised by one class of men, the clergy, others by another, the laity.'[1] Rome has never been able to escape a nostalgia for the medieval myth of civilization theocratically unified, wherein orthodoxy was considered 'the presupposition of political unity'.[2] Two forces were at play in the myth, the constant pressure of the Christian challenge, which however never could get beyond the mere preaching and promise of it; and active attempts to realize it, although history never allowed it to be more than a figment of the mind. But we are not dealing just with an attempt at a restoration. We are beholding an attempt at aligning different civilizations, such as might be compared with that unity of the Hellenistic world in which the original Christian message was spread.[3] Among peoples of different political systems and different historical traditions, techniques of production, transport and communication are spreading on a world scale, and this 'tends to produce an outward uniformity on the surface of life (architecture, housing, dress, means of transport, etc.), much more rapidly than any uniformity in standards of living, and in cultures'.[4] It is proposed to grasp the occasion offered by history and try to make out of this superficial unity of the human race (glossing over, as it does, a perilous void within) a new humanism on a universal scale, such as would be enriched by singleness of soul, and capable of breathing a single spiritual life both into peoples of longstanding Christian tradition, and also into peoples whose traditions had been of other religions, and who were but newly emerged from the state of tutelage and subjection of the colonial age. Could the old idea of the *respublica christiana* be thus extended, against all hope, it would mean at one and the same time that the Church would be healed of its scandalous and 'now obsolete' divisions, and the world of its tragic tensions.

Enough has surely been said above to make it superfluous to ask further whether the principles behind this can stand in the light of

---

[1] F. Chabod, *Storia dell'idea d'Europa*, Bari 1961, p. 28.

[2] A. Passerin d'Entrèves, *La dottrina dello Stato*, Turin 1962, p. 192.

[3] Card. J. Frings, 'Il Concilio di fronte al pensiero moderno', in *Concilio Ecumenico Vaticano II*, Geneva n.d. (1962), p. 153.

[4] D. de Rougemont, 'Principes et méthodes du dialogue entre les cultures', *Le dialogue des cultures—Colloque de Genève, 15-17 Sept., 1961*, Neuchâtel 1962, p. 5. Cf. J. L. Hromadka, *Von der Reformation zum Morgen*, Leipzig 1959, pp. 309-349f.

the gospel, and whether the canons of interpreting past and present history which it inspires correspond with reality.

2. *Priesthood*

We have endeavoured to set out the Catholic conception of Christ as he continues his ministry of Prophet in the Church. This treatment will enable us to deal with the other two points more in outline. First we must seek to understand and explain the conception of Christ as he continues in the Church his ministry of Priest.

At the heart of the concept is the idea that the work of Christ cannot be limited to the short years of his earthly ministry. Every generation has to be put in contact with him. This means that Christ must be made present to men. This perpetual presence takes place in the persons of his ministers. The priest is an *alter Christus* (a second Christ).[1] Consecration, i.e., the sacrament of ordination, confers on the priest 'the power to act in virtue of, and in the person of, Christ himself'.[2] This representation is to be understood in the most complete sense of the term *re-praesentatio*, the visible, present manifestation of Christ, and divides itself into two aspects, depicted in the symbolism of worship by the different moments when the priest faces now towards the people, now towards the altar.

> The priest represents the Divine Redeemer, and since Jesus Christ is the Head of that body of which Christians are members, he represents God among the people.[3]

On the other hand he represents 'the people before God', playing both roles.[4]

Thus he assumes the figure and function of mediator. He exercises a mediation of the ascendent type, and one of the descendent. This of necessity identifies him with the believing people whom he represents before God, and at the same time distinguishes him from them, in so far as before the people, he represents God. The people

> representing in no sense the person of the Divine Redeemer, neither being mediators between themselves and God, cannot in any way enjoy sacerdotal powers. . . . To the priests then, must he have recourse, whoever wishes to live in Christ,

because they are the

---

[1] Pius XI, Encyclical '*Ad catholici sacerdotii*', 20 Dec., 1935: *AAS* XXVIII (1936), p. 10.
[2] Pius XII, Encyclical '*Mediator Dei*', 20 Nov., 1947: *AAS* XXXIX (1947), p. 548.
[3] *Ibid.*   [4] *Ibid.*

divine instruments, by means of which one shares the supernatural life with the Mystical Body of Jesus Christ.[1]

How is this mediation applied? First, through the power of the keys, that is the power to represent Christ as Judge and Saviour. This is a power of the Judiciary, power wherein the faculty of loosing and retaining sins, i.e., absolving or condemning sinners, is made subordinate to 'the objectivity of a judgment, after due previous knowledge of the state of guilt'[2] determined through the confessional.

> Though the absolution of the priest is the dispensing of a blessing given by another, yet the priest's ministry is not simply that of announcing the gospel or declaring that sins are forgiven. There is also the form of an act of a judge, whereby sentence is pronounced by the priest, as though by a judge.[3]

This power can be exercised because

> Our Lord Jesus Christ, when he ascended from earth to heaven, left behind priests as his vicars, to be as it were presidents or judges, to whom should be referred all the mortal charges under which Christ's faithful might fall, and who should pronounce sentence for the remission or retention of sins in the name of the power of the keys.[4]

Once more we have before us a transfer of powers from the Head to the members. Whereas in the Gospel language of binding and loosing, there is a dialectical relationship in which Christ is bound to his representatives in his love, and loosed from them in the freedom of his judgment, here he is only bound to them in a unilateral tie which fixes and makes concrete his pardon and his judgment by identifying them exclusively with those of his representatives. His *potestas* is handed over, it becomes the *potestas* of his representatives.[5]

---

[1] *Ibid.*

[2] I. Tibaldo, I.M.C., 'La confessione e le indulgenze', in *Il Protestantesimo ieri e oggi*, p. 1130. Cf. A. Mayer, O.S.B., 'Storia e teologia della penitenza', in *Problemi e orientamenti di teologia dommatica*, II, p. 881.

[3] 'Quamvis autem absolutio sacerdotis alieni beneficii sit dispensatio, tamen non est solum nudum ministerium vel annuntiandi Evangelium vel declarandi remissa esse peccata: sed ad instar actus iudicialis quo ab ipso velut a iudice sententia pronuntiatur', Denzinger, 902, 919 (Concilio Tridentino, Sess. XIV, Doctrina de sacramento poenitentiae).

[4] 'Dominus noster Jesus Christus, e terris ascensurus ad coelos, sacerdotes sui ipsius vicarios reliquit, tamquam praesides et iudices, ad quos omnia mortalia crimina deferantur, in quae Christi fideles ceciderint, qui pro potestate clavium remissionis aut retentionis peccatorum sententiam pronuntient', Denzinger, 899.

[5] For this *potestas* in Reformation theology, cf.: J. Calvin, *Instruction et Confession de Foi, dont on use en l'Eglise de Genève*, a small work published in 1537 (in Latin in 1538), in *Calvini Opera Selecta*, Munich 1926, I, pp. 427f.; E. Roth, *Die Privatbeichte und die Schlüsselgewalt*, Gütersloh 1952; K. G. Steck, *Recht und Grenzen kirchlicher Vollmacht*, Munich 1956; etc.

K

Secondly, this mediation shows itself in the power more appropriately called sacerdotal, investing as it does the priest with the power to 'consecrate, offer and administer the body and blood' of Christ,[1] i.e., to ensure the presence to the end of time of Christ's sacrifice in its bloodless, though real and true form, and apply its benefits to the living and the dead.

Every time indeed, that the priest repeats that which the Divine Redeemer did at the last supper, the sacrifice is really consummated. . . .

The eucharistic sacrifice essentially consists in the bloodless immolation of the divine victim, an immolation that is mystically manifested in the separation of the sacred species, and their oblation to the Eternal Father.

. . . the minister of the altar acts in the person of Christ, as the Head who makes the offering in the name of all the members.[2]

The Church of Rome teaches that the effect of this sacerdotal act of consecration, *ex opere operato*, is that in the divine sacrifice of the altar, under the species of bread and wine, Christ is contained—*continetur*—'truly, really, and substantially', 'true God and man', body and blood, soul and body, the total Christ, who 'has once offered himself on the altar of the cross'.[3]

Since the Eucharist, in distinction from other sacraments, 'not only produces grace, but also contains the author of grace permanently in it', it is to be adored,[4] 'as is clear from the very ritual of the August Sacrifice, where the sacred ministers are enjoined to adore the Most Holy Sacrament by genuflection and deep obeisances'.[5]

---

[1] Denzinger, 957.

[2] Pius XII, *encycl. cit.* Cf. C. Journet, *La Sainte Messe, ou la permanence du sacrifice de la loi nouvelle*, Fribourg 1950; J. A. Jungmann, S. J., *Missarum Sollemnia* [Engl. trs., *The Mass of the Roman Rite*, New York 1951–55]; A. Piolanti, *Il mistero eucaristico*, Florence 1955; same author, 'Il sacrificio della Messa nella teologia contemporanea', in *Problemi e orientamenti di teologia dommatica*, II, pp. 831f.; and 'L'Eucaristia', in *I Sacramenti*, ed. by A. Piolanti, Rome 1959, pp. 433f.

[3] *Professio fidei Durando de Osca et sociis eius Waldensibus praescripta*, 1208: Denzinger, 424; Conc. Lateranense IV, 1215, Oecumenicum XII (contra Albigenses, Ioachim, Waldenses, etc.): *ibid.*, 430; Council of Constance, 1414–18: *ibid.*, 626; Council of Florence, 1438–45: *ibid.*, 698; Council of Trent, 1545–63: *ibid.*, 874, 883, 885, 886, 940.

[4] Pius XII, *encycl. cit.* Cf. Denzinger, 876: '. . . in Eucharistia ipse sanctitatis auctor . . . est'.

[5] Pius XII, *encycl. cit.* The Pope quoted two sentences from a passage of Augustine: *In Psalmum XCVIII*, 9, here quoted more fully: 'Et quia in ipsa carne hic ambulavit, et ipsam carnem nobis manducandam ad salutem dedit; nemo autem illam carnem manducat, nisi prius adoraverit; . . . non solum non peccemus adorando, sed peccemus non adorando.'

Augustine recalls the comment of the disciples to some of the paradoxical sayings of Jesus in St John about the bread of life, and about 'eating' his flesh and 'drinking' his

This enables us to understand the developments in Catholic dogmatics:

> *In this way there is an ontological bond between the mystery of the Eucharist and that of the Incarnation, as there is between this last and that of the Trinity.* . . . These mysteries have a considerable likeness and affinity for each other. All three show us the same *Son of God*; the first, *in the bosom of the Eternal Father*, i.e., as he receives his being from the same; the second, in the *bosom of the Virgin*, i.e., as he comes through her into the world; The third *in the bosom of the Church*, i.e., as he lives among men and is made one with them in a universal and abiding presence.[1]

In this way too, we see how some seemingly imprudent assertions are legitimized: such as qualify priests as

> men who have power over God and their own kind, to the point of making God alive in them.[2]

Further, from the idea that the Host of the Mass, reserved in the tabernacle, is Christ himself (*Missae hostia ipse Christus*), there understandably derives the notion of churches as the dwelling places of the Lord, and the exhortation to keep them always open to the street, so that passers-by may there meet the Lord and have from him favour and consolation.

> See to it then, venerable brethren, with your habitual maximum care, that the churches built in the course of centuries by the piety and faith of generations of Christians, to be an eternal hymn of glory to God omnipotent, and to be the dwelling place of our Redeemer as he hides himself under the forms of the Eucharist, may be open as often as possible to that growing number of the faithful that desire to gather at the feet of our Saviour and hear his sweetest of invitations: 'Come unto me, all ye that labour and are heavy laden, and I will give you rest' (Matt. 11. 28). Let the churches be indeed the house of God, in which all who enter to ask a favour, may rejoice at receiving all they ask (cf. the Collect in the Roman Missal for the dedication of a church), and obtain the heavenly consolation.[3]

---

blood (John 6. 48–63), and comments: '. . . dixerunt: *Durus est hic sermo.* Ipsi erant duri, non sermo. Etenim si duri non essent, sed mites essent, dicerent sibi: Non sine causa dicit hoc, nisi quia est ibi aliquod sacramentum latens.' Cf. *Corpus Christianorum*: Series Latina XXXIX, pp. 1385f.

[1] M. J. Scheeben, *Die Mysterien des Christentums*, Freiburg i. Br. 1941.

[2] E. Degano, 'Il sacramento dell'Ordine', in *I Sacramenti*, p. 664, cf. also p. 689 and C. Journet, *op. cit.*, I, p. 13 [I, p. 9]: 'Men invested with divine powers.'

[3] Pius XII, *encycl. cit.* The 'Ordonnances sur la police des Eglises des villages dépendant de la Seigneurie de Genève qui semblent avis être utiles', put out at Geneva in 1547 ordered the churches to be kept shut except at the hours of preaching, 'afin que nul n'y entre hors heure par superstition'. Cf. *Calvin homme d'Eglise—Oeuvres choissie du réformateur et documents sur les Eglises Réformées du XVIe. siècle*, Geneva–Paris 1936, p. 53.

Hence the reaction of the Catholic who enters a Protestant church, knowing this much but little more, and exclaims: 'But there is no God here!' His is a reaction that is reminiscent of the disconcerted amazement felt by that Roman who, in the autumn of 63 BC entered the Holy of Holies of the Temple at Jerusalem, and found it completely empty.

Hence derives the urge to build more and more churches, for it means multiplying the presence of divinity, by localizing it in the greatest possible number of places, and so procuring the *consecratio mundi*. The divine is materially present on every altar where there is offered the sacrifice that has vicarious worth for all the world. According to the Gospel of St John, Jesus has taken the place of the Temple at Jerusalem wherein the *Shekinah* dwelt, the presence and glory of Yahweh. But in the Catholic mind, the Lord being present with 'a real presence' in the host, the once-destroyed Temple of Jerusalem is rebuilt, and since there has been an end of the Jewish, preparatory, dispensation, this time it is rebuilt not in one place only, but on an universal scale. A novel notion of that worship 'in spirit and truth' (John 4.20–3)—which New Testament exegesis will not allow us to confuse in any over-simplification with 'spiritual, interior', formless worship, but rather is the sign of the advent in the person of Jesus of the eschatological age in which there is no more 'any temple' nor any worship 'tied to places'.[1]

Ecclesiastical *potestas* thus asserted over the divine and the human, this monolithic *est*, this bald, unqualified *continetur* reveal to us a tremendous, glaring, objectivization of God, wherein he is administered, put at man's disposal, made visible, touchable, graspable. How grave an error of judgment would it be to attribute the violent revolt of the Reformers against this massive process of objectification simply to the spirit of age, and to a polemical but only contingent attitude now providentially rendered obsolete by the ecumenism abroad today.[2] Here too we touch the foundations of our disagreement. It is no accident that this was the point at which Luther affirmed on the side of the Reformation that no concession was

---

[1] R. Bultmann, *Das Evangelium des Johannes*, Göttingen 1952, pp. 139f.

[2] It should suffice to quote in this respect: M. Luther, 'Articuli christianae doctrinae' of 1537 (Schmalkaldic Articles), which were meant to indicate what could and what could not be accepted on the Reformation side: *Die Bekenntnisschriften der Evangelisch-Lutherischen Kirche*, Göttingen 1956³, pp. 416–19; J. Calvin, *Petit traité de la sainte Cène*, 1541: *Oeuvres*, Paris–Geneva, 1934 II, pp. 130–4; *Heidelberger Katechismus*, 1563: *Bekenntnisschriften und Kirchenordnungen der nach Gottes Wort reformierte Kirche*, Zollikon–Zürich n.d., p. 169.

possible, and remarked that Rome, for its part, always gave the firm impression that the fall of the Mass was the same as the fall of the Papacy, i.e., the fall of the whole Catholic system.[1]

This divergence of view is not limited to the theological field specifically. The two different conceptions of how the divine is present produce two different understandings of history and of the world. In every sector of contemporary life the Church is brusquely confronted with a problem of vast proportions. Reaction to it may take the form of nostalgia for lost values of earlier ages, or of condemnations of the present age as useless as they are void of historical sense. No one has yet been able to reflect sufficiently profoundly or systematically on the phenomenon to sum up the situation clearly. To style it 'post-christian' implies a secret predeliction to conform to the prevalent scepticism. More appropriate, we suggest, would be the label of secularization. We can adopt the helpful definition of Mehl:

> Secularization is the process by which one suddenly detaches oneself from the religious notions, beliefs and institutions which hitherto had ordered one's existence, and locates in one's own self the principle on which to organise oneself. . . . A secularized society then is a society that is constituted on purely lay foundations.[2]

On the Roman side, naturally enough, the beginning and the cause of this process is attributed to the secularizing of monasteries,[3] to the expropriation of Church goods, to the abolition of the distinction between clergy and laity, and the new professional pattern that set

---

[1] *Op. cit.*, p. 416: 'Hic nihil permittendum nec cedendum est'; p. 419: 'Sentiunt quidem optime cadente missa cadere papatum'.

[2] R. Mehl, 'La sécularisation de la cité', in *Le problème de la civilisation chrétienne*, Paris 1951, p. 14. Near enough to this is the definition in the first of the famous theses of H. Gollwitzer, 'Die christliche Kirche und der kommunistische Atheismus', *Evangelische Theologie* 19 (1959), p. 291: 'By communistic atheism one must mean: the exaltation of a rationalism and an immanentism till they become a dogma of a social revolutionary movement. This implies: the movement avails itself of a system of explaining the world, to which system for its part it binds itself to serve. The system allows of only one way of regarding the nature, history and life of man, viz. that which admits only of elements which can be understood rationally, and rationalised: it recognises the existence of only that which is conceivable inside these limits, and all that thus exists is known only on the grounds of its immanental relationships. At the same time it is alleged that this kind of thought about things is absolutely sufficient and better than any other.' Cf. also the commentary by various authors: 'Sécularisation du monde moderne', *La revue réformée* 5 (1954), pp. 1–216; and the brief treatment by M. Stallmann, *Was ist Säkularisierung?*, Tübingen 1960.

[3] Cf. J. Lortz, *Die Reformation in Deutschland*, I, pp. 368f.

sacred and profane on a level, all products of the Protestant Reformation of the sixteenth century. The Reformation is seen as the great attack which unleashed those forces which eventually led to the secularization of the world, the rationalist mentality of Illuminism, the conception of life associated with that form of laicism that Pius XI called '*pestem aetatis nostrae*' (the pest of our times),[1] and to the atheistic materialism of Marx. Detachment from the Church which has in its custody the sacred emblems of humanity, was bound sooner or later to bring its fatal consequences in a godless humanism, defenceless before the spirit of the world. Our age has reached the penultimate stage of the process of the profanation of the sacred. Measures must be taken before it enters the final stage. The moment has come to face up to the scandalous monstrosity of a Europe, not to say a world, overhung by the fearful shadow of the sacred thus eclipsed,[2] and answer it with a programme of systematic 're-sacralizing' such as might subject the profane values to the influence of metaphysical and sacramental ideas deriving from a religious institution which surpasses the transient element of years. Surely any living and authentically Christian force that remains in Protestantism cannot fail to collaborate with this splendid drive to rebaptize the life of the world, even if certain compromises and certain opportunisms in the order of concordats with political and social forces were the price of practical success. In other words, the idea is to follow, in the new age of technology and sociology, the same old road of the days of feudalism, of bourgeoisie, of nationalism and colonialism, and set the seal of the sacred upon the institutions of the *polis*, from those of government itself down to those of the school, the law, the army, hospitals, sport, etc. This means to introduce the presence of priesthood into every sector of the common life, together with all its offices and symbols, and not to tolerate any claim to disbelief, or to Christian dissent, as far as theology is concerned, even if the law should prove more lenient. Nor does there seem any awareness of the tragic impracticality or the deep-seated hypocrisy of the operation. It is not worth while concerning ourselves with the methods suggested to make the Church equal to the situation, since such are purely contingent and principles are not involved. The attempt is certainly not motivated by any desire to

---

[1] Pius XI, Encyclical '*Quas primas*', 11 Dec., 1925: Denzinger, 2197.
[2] It is the title of a not too helpful work by S. S. Acquaviva, *L'eclissi del sacro nella civiltà industriale*, Milan 1961.

maintain a formal or authoritarian position, or to retain customary privileges on the part of a group who do not realize that the regime of privilege is over. It is due to dogmatic convictions which the Church of Rome cannot renounce, since they root in the essence of the principle on which the Church is founded, that of being the Church which objectively represents the person of Christ the Priest, and continues his work as Redeemer of all humanity, and which must remain visibly present in human history and in earthly human institutions in order to exercise this function.

Naturally while the principle still stands, the consequences remain also, and it would be illusory to try to avoid the consequences while retaining the principle, as at different times in the history of Catholic countries lay movements have tried in vain to do. But without here discussing the principle, we might still ask if the problem can be dealt with without reconsidering patterns centuries old. It was the ancient world, just before and contemporary with the rise of Christianity, that introduced the idea of the sacred into the realm of things, by dividing them into sacred and profane. And it has been, has it not, just the Christian gospel—preaching a God who secularized himself, and became history and so capable of misinterpretation, with the consequent risk of profanation, preaching Jesus who sat at profane tables, who attacked the priestly piety, who did not fear to be in contact with dubious environments, who was condemned to a punishment of infamy—it has been the Christian gospel that has taken reality out of the realm of the sacred, cancelled the division between the profane world on the one hand, and a sacred sphere of institutions, places, persons and objects on the other? It has been Christianity, has it not, that has judged the process of history as ambiguous and contradictory, and has introduced the paradox of dialectic into our very relationship with God, until the day in which all things will be made manifest?[1] In all this there is no confounding of holiness and worldliness, faith and sin, nor even a setting of them on the same level. On the contrary, it means that the problem has an unexpected answer. It means that there can be introduced into this world, which goes on misunderstanding and

---

[1] In recent years the question of secularization has also been discussed under this aspect. Cf. F. Gogarten, *Verhängnis und Hoffnung der Neuzeit—Die Säkularisierung als theologisches Problem*, Stuttgart 1953; R. Prenter, 'Das Evangelium der Säkularisierung —Bemerkungen zu F. Gogartens letzten Werken', *Theologischen Zeitschrift* 12 (1956), pp. 604f.; F. Delekat, *Ueber den Begriff der Säkularisation*, Heidelberg 1958; W. Dantine, *Ueber den protestantischen Menschen—Kritik und Erwartung*, Hamburg 1959, pp. 20f.; C. Walther, *Typen des Reich-Gottes Verständnisses*, Munich 1961, pp. 14f.

crucifying Christ, the gospel leaven which will make a ferment in every part of being, religious and mundane, depriving every achievement of its satisfaction and certainty, and setting up an ever new tension between itself and something beyond itself that keeps posing it questions. Today the Christians of the West rebuke those of the East for compliant conformity to the fashion of their world. But might not perhaps the Christians of the East rebuke those of the West for their failure to realize that the world is actually one single reality, and that it is not yet conceivable, either in principle or in historical practice, that life may be schematized in a Christian pattern, wherein world and Church show forth a harmony of good? No civilization can be anointed into Christianity, just as no civilization can be pronounced as outside the pale of redemption, by reason of the political or social system it has adopted. Gospel faith does not permit us to preserve and consecrate any existent value, it drives us to question it, it reveals its need of renewal, and assists in the realizing of this in history.

3. *Authority*

It remains to examine the idea of Christ's continuation of his ministry of *King* in the Church.

Protestant critics have often charged Catholicism with practising a theology of glory, illegitimately anticipating the style of the Kingdom of God. There are grounds for the criticisms, as these same pages will show, but it fails to register, since the Roman looks at things from quite a different point of view. Charles Journet, one of the most notable exponents of the theory of Catholic ecclesiology, carefully points out that under the regime of the Church that is to come there will be no more room for a visible hierarchy. In the present regime, however, i.e.,

> while our human nature remains wounded, and anesthetised by the poison of our first sin, if Christ's mediation is to be fully effective in us, it needs corporeal contact. We must be sensibly touched, first by the Christ who walked in Palestine, and later by his hierarchy.[1]

Here a synthesis is taking place between the theology of the Incarnation and that of the Ascension, and on the strength of it it is argued that there is no present possibility of immediacy. So one might indeed deduce from the Gospel. Catholicism however will not

---

[1] *Op. cit.*, I, p. 23 [cf. I, p. 15]. The whole first volume of Journet's great work [pp. xxxi and 569] is dedicated to a treatment of the theme: The Apostolic Hierarchy.

recognize the possibility of mediation outside the hierarchy, and attributes to the Reformation the positions of the Anti-Reformation, i.e., the possibility of immediacy that the Reformers so bitterly contested in the Spiritualism of the sectaries. Journet regards his argument as based on history and exegesis, yet in reality he is weaving a heavy metaphysical web. Jesus' human nature was 'the organ of divinity', and using it as 'a physical instrument of divine power' he was able to act by physical contact, or even from a distance, in working cures, for example. But Jesus' human nature, being corporeal, was limited; to make his influence felt beyond these limits, he had to extend the means of this 'contact action' through space and time, and make use of men endued with his *potestas*, in order to reach the men of every generation 'in the manner natural to him', that is sensibly.[1]

> *The age of the Spirit does not annul the law of Salvation through bodily contact with Christ*, and that which had been given to us, has not been taken from us: 'Lo, I am with you always, even to the end of the world'. *But the immediate contact with Christ's sentient body is replaced by the mediated contact with his 'spiritual body'*, which dwells in heaven under its own proper visible form, and is inaccessible to us except under the veil of mediated visible forms.[2]

> He will therefore continue to touch us in his action, but under the outward visible form of the hierarchy, just as in the greatest of the Sacraments he will continue to touch us with his substance, only under the visible forms of bread and wine. This is the reason that explains immediately and directly the institution of the Christian hierarchy.[3]

Christ's spiritual body, i.e., the Church in its hierarchy, shares then the *potestas* which is inherent in the royal sovereignty of its Head. What is meant is a *potestas gubernandi*, a real and proper power of government, which involves 'as all other powers of government, the threefold authority of *promulgating laws*, of *passing judgment* on their application and observance, and finally of determining the *penalties* of such as transgress them'.[4] It is the Head's present intention to rule his Church by means of orders which find their expression and concrete form in the directives made by the hierarchy. In this way the obedience *of* the Church to the Lord is transmuted to obedience *to* the Church which manifests the Lord's authority.

---

[1] *Op. cit.*, I, pp. 9–13 [I, pp. 7–10].
[2] *Op. cit.*, I, p. 519; italics in text [I, p. 403; no italics].
[3] *Op. cit.*, I, p. 15 [I, p. 10].　　　　[4] R. Bartmann, *op. cit.*, II, p. 416.

Even the renewal of the Church, spoken of in today's ecumenical climate, can only take the form of

> an *obedience*, genuine, loyal, sincere and free, to the ecclesiastical hierarchy, who must pasture the sheep, and in whose voice is heard the voice of the Lord himself.[1]

Return to Christ, centre of unity, that phrase of the Ecumenical Movement, means in Catholic language, the return to his representative on earth, i.e., return to submission to the supreme hierarchy of the Church of Rome, that bond and guarantee of unity.[2]

In private as in public life, individuals must bow to the authority of the Church, diligently observe and obey its laws, seek its honour, guarantee its privileges.[3] The widespread emphasis today on laity could well be 'a temptation to withdraw from the influence and guidance of the hierarchy and the clergy'. However, this movement must be made one of 'awakening the Catholic laity to the duty of extending the orbit of the apostolic light of the hierarchy'.[4] The laity must be trained for this scope, and 'spiritual training in depth is acceptance of the discipline of the hierarchy'.[5] A systematic programme should see that trusted subjects of the hierarchy are placed in every key post of responsibility, at every level of the life of society, so as to ensure the effective extension of the Lord's Kingdom, which means establishing the authority of the hierarchy in whom the Kingdom finds its historic expression. The unquestioning acceptance of the 'pastoral and administrative rule' of the Church of Rome means recognizing 'Christ in the visible acts of his Church', and submitting to the 'salvific action which he performs by means of these visible church actions'. That is, it is a *here and now* entering into the Kingdom of God. The Church of Rome is in fact 'the earthly dwelling place' of the Kingdom of God.[6] This assimilation of Church and Kingdom which foreshortens the gap between ecclesiology and eschatology, and endows, by assumption or appropriation, ecclesiology with a conceptual and psychological framework that belongs

---

[1] H. Küng, *op. cit.*, p. 80.
[2] '... unitate, cuius principium, radix et origo indefectibilis est beati Petri Apostolorum principis, eiusque in Cathedra Romana successorum suprema auctoritas'. Cf. Denzinger, 1686, 1960, 1976.
[3] Leo XIII, Encyclical '*Immortalitate Dei*', 1 Nov., 1885: Denzinger, 1881–5.
[4] Pastoral Letter of the Italian Episcopate on Laicism: *L'Osservatore Romano*, 15 April, 1960; *Il Quotidiano*, 14 April, 1960.
[5] Comment on the scheme of the Council's Preparatory Commission on the Apostolic Mission: *L'Osservatore Romano*, 1 April, 1962.
[6] *Le sens du Concile—Lettre pastorale de l'épiscopat hollandais*, Bruges, 1961, pp. 21f.

by right to the eschatological expectancy of the Kingdom, is, once more, ultimately to be traced to Augustine formulae.

Now the Church is the Kingdom of Christ, and the Kingdom of Heaven.[1]

The Bishop of Hippo is referring to the passage in Revelation 20, and is interpreting the millennium—'they reigned with Christ a thousand years'—in the sense that the kingship is exercised by 'prelates . . . through whom the Church is now governed' and, quoting Rom. 14.9, in which it is said that Christ is 'Lord of both the dead and the living', he explains this lordship of Christ ecclesiologically, saying specifically that the sphere of the Church's jurisdiction extends over living and dead.[2]

The Church that exercises this jurisdiction, this *potestas regendi*, in its three realms of the Church Militant, the Church in Purgatory, and the Church Triumphant, is

a society perfect after its kind, and endowed with all juridical and social elements.[3]

Conceived as *societas perfecta*, it follows that the Church is so organically constituted as to be sovereign and immutable, and that the ecclesiastical power that guides it is, by divine right, distinct and independent of all other power.[4] Just because it is claimed that this *potestas* has been directly instituted by God in Christ, and is the mainspring of his government in history, and just because this claim is just another form of that objectification of the divine that we have seen in the other claims we have already reviewed, it is not possible for the Church of Rome to institute inside itself any critical differentiation between the juridico-political elements of its structure, and the religious elements, divine in their origin, upon which it declares itself to be based. Consequently, vis à vis all outside itself, its interests as an institution are transfigured into divine rights. To defend the Church's rights is to defend God's rights; to assail the Church's rights is to assail those of God.

Christ's kingliness, when exercised by the hierarchical governors of the Church, must also have its visible expression and appropriate

---

[1] 'Et nunc ecclesia regnum Christi est regnumque caelorum', Augustine, *De Civitate Dei* XX, 9, in: *Corpus Christianorum*: Series Latina XLVIII, p. 716.
[2] 'Praepositi . . . per quos nunc ecclesia gubernatur', *ibid.*, pp. 717f.
[3] Pius XII, Encyclical *'Mystici Corporis'*.
[4] Denzinger, 1698, 1719, 1869, 2053. Cf. A. Latreille–A. Siegfried, *Les forces religieuses et la vie politique—Le Catholicisme et le Protestantisme*, Paris 1951, p. 30.

symbolic accompaniments. Ceremonial pomp and ornament are not to be set down to a decadence induced by a worldliness that has carried a fossilized antiquity over into the modern age. Rather the Catholic explanation is that they express outwardly the imperative of what dogma presupposes. They are the reflections on earth of Christ's sovereignty, not indeed indispensable, but fully indicative of the 'absoluteness of the liberty of the spiritual over all that is political'.[1]

The greatest manifestation of Christ's authority, the visible and corporeal point where his kingliness is at present concentrated, is in the person of the Pontiff.

> *Super hanc petram aedificabo Ecclesiam meam. . . : et tibi dabo claves regni caelorum*: On this rock will I build my Church . . . and I will give thee the keys of the kingdom of heaven (Matt. 16. 18–9). What is the meaning of these keys, personally entrusted to Simon bar-Jona, to Peter, if it is not the indication that the universal government of the Church was entrusted to him ?[2]

The first Vatican Council laid it down that the Roman Pontiff has a power of jurisdiction that is immediate (i.e., it derives directly from Christ and not from the Church), and that in respect of him, both pastors and faithful are required to submit and to obey, not merely in matters of faith and morals, but also in matters of the discipline and regime of the Church, which can have only one chief Pastor.[3] His to feed, lead, govern the whole Church; his to summon, prorogue, dissolve Councils; to appoint, translate, judge and punish bishops; to administer the Church's treasury, i.e., the treasury of the merits of Christ and the Saints, granting them to the living in the form of absolution, to the dead in that of suffrage; his to decide in the final instance on the processes of beatification and canonization, through which certain of the dead may be admitted to the honours of the altar; and he is the supreme judge of the faithful, from whom there is no higher appeal, and who is himself not subject to judgment by any man.[4]

> But there is an authority which is not human, even if it is given to a man and is exercised through men, but rather divine, given by divine

---

[1] C. Journet, *op. cit.*, I, p. 609 [I, p. 469].

[2] John XXIII, address delivered 22 Feb., 1962 on the occasion of the feast of St Peter's Chair: published in *L'Osservatore Romano*, 23 Feb., 1962.

[3] Denzinger, p. 1827.

[4] *Op. cit., passim* (Index systematicus III a–i); *Codex Iuris Canonici*, cans. 218f., 329, 2132, 2140.

lips to Peter who was called the rock, and established to him and his successors after him. . . .[1]

This authority is not subject to diminution or compromise, even in the event of a Pope who was 'wicked, and hence a limb of Satan', 'a son of perdition', like Judas Iscariot, who lived in a manner contrary to the law and spirit of Christ. If he has been once duly elected in accordance with the proper regulations, he remains indeposable and untouchable, continuing in possession of all the authority with which he has been objectively invested, and of that doctrinal infallibility in matters of faith and morals that derive from it.[2]

Equally unthinkable would it be to distinguish between Christ and the Pope, as if after the Ascension Christ had handed over the government of the Church into the hands of his Vicar, charging him to act in his place. The Church is no monster of a body with two heads, Christ and Christ's Vicar, Peter, in the persons of his successors. The body of Christ has but one head, and he continues to rule and govern his Church, visibly and audibly, in the person and in the actions of the Pope. There follows the inescapable logical consequence that he who obeys the Pope obeys Christ, and he who refuses obedience to the Pope, by that very act refuses obedience to Christ. It is neither possible nor conceivable that one should submit to the heavenly Head of the Church without yielding an uncomplaining and unreserved submission to him in whose person Christ dwells at present on earth. Those who are unwilling to enter in such submission show by their fatal refusal that they do not belong to the flock of Christ, since Christ had declared that 'there shall be one flock, one shepherd' (John 10.16). The ancient Fathers of the Church used to say '*Ubi Christus, ibi Ecclesia*' (Where Christ is, there is the Church), but it would be quite consistent to render the aphorism as '*Ubi Papa, ibi Ecclesia*'.

From the famous Bull, '*Unam Sanctam*', wherein Boniface VIII solemnly declared on 18th November, 1302:

---

[1] 'Est autem haec auctoritas, etsi data sit homini et exerceatur, per hominem, non humana, sed potius divina, ore divino Petro data sibique suisque successoribus in ipso, quem confessus fuit petra, firmata. . .', Denzinger, 469, 1830.

[2] 'Malus et per consequens membrum diaboli', 'filius perditionis' are phrases from the condemnation of the propositions of John Wyclif and John Hus: cf. Denzinger, 588, 638, 646, 648, 650, 652, 674; also the treatment given by C. Journet, *op. cit.*, I, pp. 547f. [I, pp. 441f.]. Denzinger omits to cite the decisions of the Council of Constance (1414–1418) (Oecumenicum XVI) and of the Council of Basel (1431–49), which contain the argument for the supremacy of the Council over the Pope.

Hence submission to the Roman Pontiff, we declare, proclaim, define and pronounce, to be for every human creature utterly necessary for salvation,

to the formularies voted on the same subject by the first Vatican Council on 18th July, 1870:

This is a doctrine of Catholic truth, from which none may deviate without loss to faith and salvation

and on to the affirmations made by Pius XII on 29th June, 1943 in *'Mystici Corporis'*, and by John XXIII on 11th November, 1961 in *'Aeterna Dei'*, there is a constant repetition of this one single motif, which for its part has its immediate basis in that which Heiler has called the *Papaltheologie* of Thomas Aquinas, and its distant origin in the concept we have already noted, of *totus Christus*.[1]

Catholic thought shows a persistent inability to understand the reasons that lie behind the Protestant distinction between Church and Kingdom,[2] and the basis of the objection against the Catholic idea of the authority of the Church in general and of the Pope in particular. The Protestant point of view is put down to a more or less unconscious bad faith, concomitant with a whole series of prejudices of philosophical, political, sociological or economic origin, but quite without any theological justification.[3] Or, it might be, an insuperable misunderstanding of Jesus' words about lordship and service (Matt. 20.25–8), which should be taken with a mere moral bearing, condemning, that is, the abuse of the Church's power, and

[1] 'Porro subesse Romano Pontifici omni humanae creaturae declaramus, dicimus, definimus et pronuntiamus omnino de necessitate salutis.' 'Haec est catholicae veritatis doctrina, a qua deviare salva fide atque salute nemo potest.' Denzinger, 468, 469, 1827; M. Schmaus, *op. cit.*, III/1, p. 488; P. E. Persson, *op. cit.*, pp. 49f.; F. Heiler, *Altkirchliche Autonomie und päpstlicher Zentralismus*, Munich 1941, p. 280.

[2] Cf. F. M. Braun, O.P., *Aspects nouveaux du problème de l'Eglise*, Fribourg 1942, p. 165; K. G. Steck, 'Eschatologie und Ekklesiologie in der römisch-katholischen Theologie von Heute', *Materialdienst des Konfessionskundlichen Instituts* 9 (1958), pp. 81f. Among Protestant authors, note: K. L. Schmidt, *Le problème du Christianisme primitif*, Paris 1938, pp. 76f.; *Die Polis in Kirche und Welt—Eine lexikographische und exegetische Studie*, Basel 1939; E. Sommerlath, 'Kirche und Reich Gottes', *Zeitschrift für systematische Theologie* 16 (1939), pp. 562f.; W. A. Visser 't Hooft, *La royauté de Jesus-Christ*, Geneva 1948, pp. 109f., 147f.; T. F. Torrance, *Kingdom and Church—A study in the Theology of the Reformation*, Edinburgh 1955, W. A. Visser 't Hooft, *The Renewal of the Church*, London 1956, pp. 37, 56f.; E. Schlink, *Der kommende Christus und die kirchlichen Traditionen—Beiträge zum Gespräch zwischen den getrennten Kirchen*, Göttingen 1961, pp. 88f., 202f., 272f.

[3] G. Vodopivec, 'La Chiesa e la sua autorità gerarchica', in *Il Protestantesimo ieri e oggi*, Rome 1958, pp. 1202–68. Vodopivec frankly states that he cannot find any explanation for the Protestant attitude and considers it an 'enigma'. He suggests bad faith as a hypothesis as almost *per absurdum*: 'Forse non si vede quello che non si vuol vedere?'

not the use of it; all of which has swept Protestantism through its refusal to entertain juridical categories in the concept of Church, into a spiritualistic ecclesiology, abstract and unsustainable.[1] Or again, it is perhaps just a psychological reaction, charged with complexes born of centuries-long polemic, against the expression of authority as it has been found in history and experience. The question of exegesis is however never seriously taken into account.[2] Generally, there is little idea of the existence of religious grounds for its rejection, and theological ones for its criticism of the Catholic position.[3]

It was no act of wrathful impulse or calculated demagogerie that made Martin Luther on 10th December, 1520 cast into the fire before the Magpie Gate (*Elstertor*) of Wittenberg (where the *Corpus Iuris Canonici* and volumes of scholastic theology were already burning), the papal bull which threatened him with excommunication if he did not retract. His action was accompanied by these serious words:

> Since thou hast cast into confusion the truth of God, may the Lord cast thee this day into the confusion of this fire. Amen.

The next day, as he began his usual lesson, he appealed to his students 'to take their stand in the struggle now begun against the Antichrist, offering them no alternatives except martyrdom or the loss of their souls'. In his mind there was already established 'the certainty that he had begun a struggle against a transcendent anti-christian power'.[4] It was not for nothing that when he comments on the occasion a little more than a month later, he confessed that he had acted 'in trembling and in prayer'.[5]

At the back of the Lutheran concept of the Antichrist there is an entire medieval tradition, dating from the polemic of the Waldensians and the Fraticelli, and including that of the Wycliffites and the

---

[1] B. Bartmann, *op. cit.*, II, p. 418.

[2] O. Karrer, 'Successione apostolica e primato', in *Problemi e orientamenti di teologia dommatica*, I, p. 296.

[3] The sole exception is G. Vodopivec, *art. cit.*, pp. 1250, 1267. Turning a remark of K. Heim into its obverse form he loyally and objectively admits the alternative: 'The great question, and at the bottom the only really theological question is: Did Christ wish to found, and did he found a hierarchical Church according to the evidence of the New Testament, or not? Heim had understood the importance of the question when he said that the whole of Protestantism would lie under the malediction of Christ, if the passage "Tu es Petrus" were to signify the primacy of Peter and the apostolic succession. And we are constrained to admit also the contrary. If the power of the hierarchy is not to be found in scripture, it would certainly be no longer legitimate: it would be sacriligious. Either one thing or the other. There is the basic, tragic, decisive dilemma.'

[4] G. Miegge, *Lutero*, Torre Pellice 1946, p. 487.

[5] Letter 14 Jan., 1521 to Johannes von Staupitz, cited by G. Miegge, *op. cit.*, p. 486: 'Exussi libros Papae et Bullam, primum trepidus et orans, sed nunc laetior quam ullo alio totius vitae meae facto; pestilentiores enim sunt quam credebam.'

Hussites.[1] Luther is quite well aware that he may be classed with that line of thought when he exclaims: '*Valdensis ac Viglephista vocabor*'.[2] But the medieval tradition had without exception been confined to the plane of ethics and discipline, and so had revealed its sterility to create anything new. Luther, however, adopted a position that cut directly to the roots in dogma. If he bursts out into indignant invective:

> O woe to you, O Pope, woe to you, Cardinals, woe to you, Bishops, woe to you, Priests, woe to you, Monks and every ecclesiastical order. Who will warn you to flee the wrath that is to come and already is?[3]

it is because he has arrived at the fearful knowledge that a satanical *mysterium iniquitatis* has begun to work in the church—'*nam mysterium iam operatur iniquitatis*': II Thess. 2.7 (for the mystery of lawlessness doth already work)—and under the mask of an *angelica facies*,

> lays waste the Church, corrupts the faith, establishes sin and destroys the conscience.[4]

What is the origin of this distressing process of the contamination of the sacred? Luther and Calvin follow parallel paths in studying the phenomenon, and keep closely to the line of scripture in the different biblical passages that deal with the theme of Antichrist. By synthesizing the various data, we may arrive at the outlines of a full-scale theology of history.

First we must be quite clear that the Bible, quite contrary to ideas widely held both in ancient and modern times, never permits us to understand by Antichrist the pagan and atheistic world:

> It is not at all an enemy from without, but of his own household, that in Christ's own name, makes war on Christ.[5]

---

[1] H. Preuss, *Die Vorstellungen vom Antichrist im späteren Mittelalter, bei Luther und in der konfessionellen Polemik—Ein Beitrag zur Theologie Luthers und zur Geschichte der christlichen Frömmigkeit*, Leipzig 1906; A. Dempf, *Sacrum Imperium*; F. Heiler, *op. cit.*, p. 314.

[2] 'I shall be called Waldensian and Wycliffite': *Ad librum eximii Magistri Nostri Magistri Ambrosii Catharini, defensoris Silvestris Prieratis acerrimi, Responsio Martini Lutheri—Cum exposita Visione Danielis VIII—De Antichristo*, 1521: *WA* VII, p. 734.

[3] 'O ve tibi, Papa, Ve vobis Cardinalibus, Ve vobis Episcopis, Ve vobis sacerdotibus, Ve vobis Monachis et toti ordini Ecclesiastico. Quis vobis monstrabit fugere a ventura et instante ira?': *ibid.*, p. 740.

[4] 'Vastat Ecclesiam, corrumpit fidem, peccatum statuit et perdit conscientias': *ibid.*, p. 763.

[5] 'N'est-ce point un ennemi de dehors, mais domestique, lequel sous le nom de Christ mesme, fait la guerre à Christ', J. Calvin, *Commentaire sur la IIe. Epistre aux Thessaloniciens: Commentaires sur le Nouveau Testament*, Paris 1855, IV, p. 164 (II Thess. 2.4). Cf. H. Berger, *Calvins Geschichtsauffassung*, Zürich 1955, pp. 73f.

It does not refer to an individual person, nor to any particularly critical period of history, but to a system—Calvin calls it a kingdom—which has its own slow and subtle growth through the ages, and will end only on the day of the second coming of Christ. Its origins go back to the infancy of the Church, when alongside the presence of Christ, the presence of many antichrists had to be recognized (I John 2.10; 4.1–3); alongside Peter the confessor, who was granted to know what flesh and blood did not know, there is Peter the denier who has no sense of the things of God ('Get thee behind me, Satan; thou art a stumbling block unto me', says Jesus, immediately after he has spoken to him the words about the rock: Matt. 16.23), and who can say of Jesus: 'I do not know the man' (Matt. 26.72), and who does not see the truth of the gospel with the completeness of vision he should (Gal. 2.14); alongside the apostles who build up the Church there are the pseudo-apostles who parade themselves as angels of light, and overturn the faith. At the beginning, however, the Kingdom of Christ has still the advantage over these subversive elements. Yet, at a certain moment, it is the antichristian forces that get the upper hand and rule over the Church reducing it to servitude. There results 'a general revolt of the visible Church'.[1]

This does not mean that '*l'astuce du diable*' and '*la malice des hommes*' have completely prevailed in the Church over the promises of God and his fidelity towards her:

First, inasmuch as God miraculously preserves the remnants of his people, however pitifully they be scattered; and secondly, inasmuch as there remain some marks of the Church.[2]

It is obvious that here Christian elements are recognized in Catholicism, but at the same time, one knows that these elements are being used in such a way that despite all claims to the contrary, they end in usurping and not establishing the kingdom of the Lord.[3]

[1] 'Un révoltement général de l'Eglise visible', J. Calvin, *op. cit.*, p. 162.

[2] 'Premièrement, entant que Dieu y conserve miraculeusement les reliques de son peuple, combien qu'elles y soyent povrement dispersées. Secondement, entant qu'il y reste quelques marques de l'Eglise', J. Calvin, *Institution de la religion chrestienne*, IV 2.12. On this point Luther is perhaps more positive: 'We admit that under the Papacy there is much of the Christian heritage . . . we admit that in the Papacy there is the proper Holy Scripture, proper baptism, the proper sacrament of the Altar, the proper key for remission of sin, the proper ministry of preaching, the proper catechism, and the our Father, the Ten Commandments, the articles of faith,' *Von der Wiedertauffe an zween Pfarherrn. Ein brieff Mart. Luther*, 1528: *WA* XXVI, p. 147.

[3] Luther in the same passage completes his thought in these terms: 'We are not then fanatics like the sectaries (*die rotten geister*), to the point of rejecting all that the Pope has under him, for in that way we would reject also Christianity, the Temple of God, which it has received from Christ. But we protest and resent the fact that the Pope is unwilling to leave those goods of Christianity which he has inherited from the apostles alone but

L

The struggle against this tyranny which has established itself in the Church, is made difficult just by this coexistence side by side of contradictory elements, and by the illegitimate use of Christian elements in themselves legitimate enough. To fight our foe we must recognise him as such. Yet the Adversary of Christ never wears antichristian uniform. This tyranny

> raised up against the spiritual kingdom of Christ . . . is such as does not wipe out either the name of Christ or of the church, but rather misuses a semblance of Christ, and lurks under the name of the church as under a mask.[1]

Its technique is to transfer to its own person 'what only belongs to one', to the Lord Jesus Christ, and to steal from God his honour, 'to draw it on itself'[2] thus producing a huge counterfeit of the kingdom of the Lord, by means of methods of persuasion in which he is allowed to be singularly effective:

> In thus despoiling God of his honour, he leaves him nothing except the imaginary title of God; all the power, however, that was his, he makes over and carries away for himself.[3]

As we have already said, the *dénouement* will take place on the day of judgment, since this kingdom is not be be thought of as a merely human power that could be unmasked with human weapons and overthrown by the forces of history. There is a relevant if not-too-wellknown passage of Luther that illustrates this eschatological aspect:

> Thus today the Papists outnumber us and make a finer show, whilst we are not merely evil spoken of, but suffer in various ways as well. We must bear it till the Judgment come, when God will show that we are his Church, while the Papists are the Church of Satan.[4]

instead, he makes his diabolical additions and uses these goods for the destruction, and not for the restoration of the Temple of God, giving precedence to his own commandment and order, and not to that of Christ', *op. cit.*, p. 148. Calvin says that it is always the Temple of God, but that this Temple is 'profané d'infinis sacriléges', 'pollu par une tyrannie plene de sacriléges, en sorte que le plus grand ennemi de Christ y aura son siége et domination', *Commentaires, ibid.*, pp. 163, 164.

[1] 'Dressée contre le régne spirituel de Christ . . . est telle, qu'elle n'abolit point le nom de Christ de son Eglise mais plustost qu'elle est cachée sous l'ombre de Jesus-Christ et sous couleur de son Eglise comme sous une masque', J. Calvin, *Institution*, IV 7.25; *Commentaires, ibid.*, p. 167; III, p. 803 (Eph. 4.15).

[2] 'Ce qui estoit propre à un seul . . . pour le tirer à luy', *Institution*, IV 7.25.

[3] 'En despouillant ainsi Dieu de son honneur, il ne luy laisse rien de reste, que le titre de Dieu par imagination: mais toute la puissance d'iceluy il la transfère et ravit à soy', *Commentaires*, IV, p. 163-4; M. Luther, *op. cit.*: *WA* VII, pp. 746f., 774f.

[4] 'Sic hodie praevalent nobis multitudine et praecedunt nos dignitate Papistae. Nos autem non tantum maledicimur, sed etiam patimur varie. Hoc ferendum est, donec iudicium veniat, quo revelabit Deus, nos suam Ecclesiam esse, Papistas autem esse Ecclesiam Satanae', *Enarratio in I Cap. Genesis per reverendum Patrem dominum D. Mart. Lutherum in Schola Wittembergensi: WA* XLII, p. 334. For Calvin cf. *Commentaires*, IV, p. 166; H. Berger, *op. cit.*, pp. 87f.

To await, certain and convinced, the day of this eschatological revelation, means knowing that God's leaven is already at work, as it has ceaselessly been from the beginning. Such knowledge involves a determination to work, without any reserve and without any false pretences such as Nicodemites have,[1] for the re-establishment of the Church in its '*vray estat*',[2] taking sides openly, that is, for the kingdom of Christ, and opposing the kingdom of Antichrist, wherever we see its signs appear.

A full understanding of this line of thought is possible only by use of the fundamental categories of the *theologia crucis* which Loewenich has pointed out as the key to the understanding of Lutheran thought.[3] Then again, one cannot enter these categories of the *theologia crucis*, without coming to terms with the eschatological tension which underlies all Reformation theology, and which, after long neglect, has found new respect in recent studies as the essential exegetical clue.

The recurrent theme of the *theologia crucis* is the motif of conflicting appearances. The supreme revelation of the power of God which liberates unto salvation, takes place *sub contraria specie*, under the opposite form, in that very instant when Jesus on the cross appears defeated, in contrast with Judas, Pilate, Caiaphas, who seem triumphant. The destiny of the world is centred in the mystery of the cross. The ground of things is not yet revealed in its true essence. Everything could be inverted into its opposite; the situation as seen historically remains ambiguous and contradictory.

Applied to ecclesiology, this means that it is just where the Church seems blessed by success, magnificence, numbers, that one must be vigilant, for it could be that we have there a satanical counterfeiting of Christ's kingliness. Whereas, where the Church meets persecution and contempt, and where it is compelled to act only in the hidden strength of faith, it could be that here we are beholding the power of the Lord which reveals itself in weakness. This point of view is only a commentary on New Testament themes. The New Testament clearly distinguishes the times of God's action; 'each in his order: Christ, the firstfruits, then those that shall be Christ's at his coming'

---

[1] Nicodemus is the name of the secret disciple who came to Jesus by night (John 3.1f.): Calvin takes him as a symbol and calls Nicodemites those who think they can cultivate the gospel only in a spiritual way, avoiding open and responsible commitment.

[2] J. Calvin, *Institution* IV 2.12.

[3] W. von Loewenich, *Luthers Theologia crucis*, Munich 1939[3] (1st ed. 1929).

(I Cor. 15.23). These times and moments of God's action cannot be interchanged. In the interval between the Ascension and the second Advent, Christ's Church shares in his glory only through hope; it remains a Church beneath the Cross, which bears in itself the death of Jesus, which is in torment as far as the end of the world. And this is for a reason well calculated by divine wisdom, 'that the excellence of this power be from God and not from us' (II Cor. 4.7). God knows that his power in men's hands—and especially in the hands of religious men, who may keep up the appearance of the love of God, yet insinuate under it the love of self—runs, in the very nature of the case, the risk of counterfeit. If the Church is indeed the Church of him who was crucified and is risen again, it is bound to assume the attitude of its Lord's passion in this time; i.e., its whole structure and mode of being must bear the hall-mark of the lowliness and the state of the servant in whom God has chosen to reveal his sovereignty and glory. The only road the Church can tread is that already trodden by Christ, for if the Church wishes to share in Christ's day of glory, it must, here and now, put on the condition of the Servant, the *Ebed Yahweh*, and live under the obedience which Jesus accepted in the time of his earthly ministry. If it will not respect the times, if it anticipates its share of a glory which can only be eschatological, it inevitably runs the risk of glorifying itself rather than the Lord, and so of changing its nature from that of Church into that of anti-church, against which the gates of Hell are sure, sooner or later, to prevail. In fact, if the Church clothes itself with the authority, the dignity and the power that belong to its Lord, what happens? This authority, power and dignity, stolen from their Lord, change as by a magic spell, into an authority, power and dignity that are no longer those of Christ, but of his Adversary, the Antichrist. In that case, the power with which the Church will be clad will be 'great, but will not be his power', as Luther says, following the thought of a prophecy of Dan. 8.24, and it will rely on 'another's ability', i.e., on that granted by the Antichrist.[1]

Such being the background of the Reformers' criticism of the Catholic conception of Christ the King present in his Church, and such a conception not having lost anything in four centuries, but rather having been in continuous development, what must we think of the validity or otherwise of the criticism? Naturally, as has been

---

[1] M. Luther, *op. cit.*: *WA* VII, pp. 746f.

said,[1] there is a slant of contingency to it all which it is easy to isolate; temperament enters, and language occasionally gets out of control; the mentality is the product of the conditions and habits of that particular moment of history; there are idiosyncrasies of exegesis that would hardly be accepted in the contests of present-day biblical criticism. So much on the irenic side. But when all is said and done, and the criticism is reduced to its simple theological nucleus, it cannot but be taken seriously. As Calvin said, a Church is false when its proper constitution is reversed into its opposite. Now the effect of this tremendous process of objectivizing and sequestrating the authority of the Lord, which we have tried to trace accurately in these pages and the various stages of our study, is that the Church passes from the state of *Servant* to the rank of *Mistress*. From the moment that the body attributed to itself the authority of the Head, the Church of Christ which had been, and is called to be, the Church of Obedience, began the process of transmutation into the Church (to use a famous phrase) of Self-government.

> Now self-government is one, not to say the greatest, of God's prerogatives. Self-government on a creaturely level can only mean that the creature is usurping this prerogative, acting, that is in open disobedience, to God.

A Church which

> acts thus, which is unwilling to hear of an authority greater than its own, which surrounds its own authority with all the emblems of a higher authority, of an authority that transcends its own churchly authority, with the precise object of evading this transcendent authority which is never to be identified with its own authority—a Church, which then stigmatises with its anathema, and with its disesteem; which declares that separation from the Church follows automatically upon any conceivable obedience rendered to any authority that is not identical with but transcendent to its own authority—a Church which does all this, is a Church which refuses to obey, and sets itself as equal with God. And so it ceases to be a Church, and loses whatever authority of its own it has, however high it exalts it, even if it may appear to possess it in all its fulness. . . . It is then imperative and inevitable to decide for a Church of Obedience against a Church of Self-government.[2]

---

[1] E. Muelhaupt, 'Vergängliches und Unvergängliches an Luthers Papstkritik, *Luther-Jahrbuch* 26, Berlin n.d., pp. 56f. Cf. E. Bizer, *Luther und der Papst*, Munich 1958; U. Pflugk, 'Luther und der Papst', *Luther* 31 (1960), pp. 13of.

[2] K. Barth, *KD* I/2, pp. 639f. [*CD*, 1956, pp. 575f.]; H. Vogel, *Gott in Christo—Ein Erkenntnisgang durch die Grundprobleme der Dogmatik*, Berlin 1952[2], p. 816, using an analogous pattern of thought, speaks of the 'falsification of the Church'. The provisional Report of the Faith and Order Commission presented at St Andrews in 1960, having in view its fourth World Conference at Montreal fixed for 1963, says in speaking of the

One attempt at resolving these irreconcilable positions might follow a line that is at bottom Catholic, rigid, admitting of no dialectic. For one form of objectified authority of Christ and of obedience to him in the Church, another one no less objectified might be substituted. There would be two ecclesiological entities, each shaped historically and juridically, and in place of the Roman Church now judged antichristian, the Evangelical Church would offer itself as candidate on the grounds of being completely renewed in the Christian pattern. As in the sixteenth century, such an argument would more readily commend itself today to the more superficial thinkers, and would be no less misguided a solution for any right understanding of the problem. For when all is said and done, the question is not so simple, nor, let us add, one to be resolved in so Pharisaic a way. Certain people there are—Luther called them *Schwärmer* (fantastic dreamers), and Calvin *esprits escervelez et fantastiques*, (brainless individuals who swing this way and that at the dictates of their own imaginations)—modern sectaries, all too willingly confused on the Catholic part with Protestantism itself, who in their anti-Catholic exasperation paradoxically come round to positions very close to Catholic ones, and seek a renewal of the Church, which consists '*in nostra renovatione et propria iustitia*', as the Formula of Concord puts it, and ends, without their realizing it, in a new kind of legalism and a 'new monasticism'.[1]

But such an interpretation is impossible on the basis of Reformed theology. For reasons that are historical and at the same time theological, the Reformers could not denounce as antichristian the Roman Catholic Church, taken by and large, as against a new Church which was to be declared Christian, for the simple yet eloquent consideration that confessionalism was quite alien to their thought. 'They knew only the *single* Church of Jesus Christ.'[2] Pluralism of Churches

Church in terms of relationships between Head and body:'It must never seek to usurp his place or give itself out to be another Christ.' *One Lord One Baptism*—Report on the Divine Trinity and the Unity of the Church and Report on the Meaning of Baptism, by the Theological Commission on Christ and the Church, London 1960, p. 25. Cf. also K. G. Steck, *Der evangelische Christ und die römische Kirche*, Munich 1952, pp. 36f.

[1] Formula Concordiae: *Die Bekenntnisschriften* . . ., p. 1094.

[2] E. Kinder, *Der evangelische Glaube und die Kirche—Grundzüge des evangelisch-lutherischen Kirchenverständnisses*, Berlin 1958, p. 75. Cf. H. Clavier, *Etudes sur le Calvinisme*, Paris 1936, pp. 52f.; E. Wolf, 'Die Einheit der Kirche im Zeugnis der Reformation', *Evangelische Theologie* 1938, p. 124f.; J. Courvoisier, 'Y a-t-il eu fondation d'une Eglise protestante à Genève au XVIe. siècle?', *Verbum Caro* V (1951), pp. 69f.; F. W. Kantzenbach, *Das Ringen um die Einheit der Kirche im Jahrhundert der Reformation*, Stuttgart 1957; R. Rouse–S. C. Neill, *History of the Ecumenical Movement 1517–1948*, London 1954; O. Weber, 'L'unité de l'Eglise chez Calvin,' *Revue de Théologie et de Philosophie*, 1959, pp. 153f.

is a later, indeed a decadent idea, reflecting an age of entrenched positions.[1] No, the Reformation was in its origins, and in general has always sought to be, and even today wishes to be, *not* something existing for itself. It seeks solely to be a reference point to give Christians their bearings. It is an appeal to the Universal Church to renew itself by finding the Alpha and Omega of its proper being, and the guiding principle of its organization in the rediscovered authority of its Lord, and in a glad, free and trustful resolve to live and to act for love of him, and in the service of him alone, never to be moved by anything that might be set before, beside or outside him alone, such as might indeed use his name, but use it in such a way as to degrade his sovereignty. Such an appeal is based on the knowledge that the Church—all the Church—is fallen into captivity to non-christian powers. From being the Church of the Lord, it has become the Church of men. Such an appeal is based on the hope that the Church may be liberated, literally reformed and reedified, in such a way that no more in the Church shall obedience be offered to God *and* the various Mammons of reason and religion, which in the course of the centuries have managed to occupy a place in it to which they have no claim. Rather will it be offered to God alone.

This is no fanatical hope nurtured by ecclesiastical revolutionaries who expect to solve all problems by a change of structure. It is imbued with a sober, pessimistic realism, which steadies without checking its activity. It knows that the Church is not the Kingdom, but it believes that the Kingdom is coming, and that such an expectancy means that we cannot shelve our responsibility to obey. To know, then, that under the present dispensation of the world, no Church, either today or tomorrow, can ever be the true Church, completely freed from the false Church, does not imply the acceptance

---

[1] There is a passage of Calvin, full of controlled passion, which illustrates the rise of the phenomenon: it is found in the Letter to Cardinal G. Sadoleto, written in August 1539 from exile in Strasbourg: 'Tous les tiens, Seigneur, étaient tellement égarés, que non seulement ils ne pouvaient entendre ce qu'on leur commandait: mais aussi il semblait qu'ils eussent mis en oubli, et leur capitaine, et la bataille, et le serment qu'ils y avaient fait. Et moi pour les retirer d'un tel erreur, n'ai point mis au vent une étrangère enseigne: mais celui tien noble étendard, qu'ils nous est nécessaire de suivre, si nous voulons être enrôlés au nombre de ton peuple. En cet endroit . . . ils m'ont résisté avec grande violence. Et a-t-on commencé grièvement à se mutiner: tant que le combat s'est enflammé, jusques à rompre l'union. Mais de quel côté soit la faute et coulpe: c'est maintenant à toi, Seigneur, de le dire et prononcer. De ma part, j'ai toujours montré en paroles et en faits, quel désir j'avais à union et concorde: toutefois j'entendais celle union de l'Eglise, qui prend son commencement de toi, et finit en toi-même', J. Calvin, *Oeuvres*, Paris–Geneva 1934, II, p. 83.

of the ordering of this latter Church as legitimate, but rather to search for orderings that accord better with the will of the Lord of the Church. There is a danger that hangs heavily over every place where the name of the Lord is pronounced. It is the danger of pronouncing the name in order to serve ourselves by it, instead of serving him. The great issue therefore is to see if this danger remains merely as a temptation under control, or if it succeeds in establishing itself as a system. It is the Protestant judgment that in the history of Christianity, Catholicism represents the legalization of that system.

It would be a serious admission of religious obtuseness and theological incompetency on the Protestant side, and a grave error of judgment on the Catholic one, if this criticism were to be discarded in the interests of a species of ecumenical charity which has no stomach for the frankness and brusqueness of doctrinal controversy, and passes them off as mere intellectualism.[1] We make so bold as to say that charity itself can be satanic, if it clouds the clarity of Christian judgment and ignores the basic issue of right faith—him in whom to believe, whom to obey, and who alone can inspire charity with life. Charity without obedience merely replaces the war of the living with the peace of the dead. A letter of Calvin written (22nd October, 1548) to Edward Seymour, Duke of Somerset, Lord Protector of England, contains a warning which seems to have maintained its freshness of application for certain features of our situation today:

> I quite admit that we must keep moderation, and too great extremes are neither good nor useful. . . . But what is of Satan and Antichrist must never get by under that excuse.[2]

There is a way of recognising the religious values of both sides without letting a theological judgment enter; but this is symptomatic of a spiritual lassitude and a haziness of faith, not of ecumen-

---

[1] According to *EPS*, 30 March, 1962, a Protestant dignitary said, referring to Catholic-Protestant relationships and 'courtesy' visits to the Pope: 'The Ecumenical Movement is full of complexities and problems. The separated Churches must learn to live in love with each other, and to lay aside all that conflicts with love. According to the measure in which this happens, will problems and difficulties on the intellectual plane disappear.' Such a position, proclaiming the primacy of love, is not an isolated one. It means reducing the God of the gospel to an abstraction of the intellect, and certainly cannot justify itself by reference to the teaching of Jesus, and the preaching of Paul and John. It does not help the Church to arrive at discernment of the spirits, but rather at their confusion.

[2] 'Je confesse bien qu'il faut tenir modération, et que trop grande extrémité n'est pas bonne, ne utile. . . . Mais il ne faut point que ce qui est de Satan et de l'Antéchrist passe sous cette couleur-là', J. Calvin, *Lettres anglaises—1548-61*, ed. by A. M. Schmidt, Paris 1959, p. 60.

ism. He ill serves the cause of ecumenism who cultivates a pseudo-ecumenism as void of hope as of pain, which hails indiscriminately the Christianity of one side and the other, without the concern *in primis et ante omnia* for Christ's Lordship in his Church. On this ground one builds not the Church, but ecumenical Babel.

One could not speak in this way about Rome without a very realistic and precise awareness of where Protestantism stands ecclesiastically. For it too has largely become a Church thrown back on itself, lacking authority, after the distortions that have resulted from over two centuries of a not so different response to imperatives issuing from quarters other than those of the Lord of the Church. Catholic and Protestant alike must bear responsibility for that infidelity that has defaced the cause of Christianity in the world, and give the most serious thought to the problem.

Catholic thought constantly regards the Reformation as the act of subjective insubordination on the world's part against the one legitimate authority for its government and guidance. Such an interpretation is only another aspect of that idea of Protestantism as detachment from the true and the sacred, that we have examined in the two preceding sections. Insubordination has spilled over from the religious to the secular plane, bringing chaotic consequences for all to see: Protestantism is split into innumerable 'sects', wherein each interprets the gospel as he likes, without any common criterion: society, once a unit, is split into a multitude of nations and parties. It must be Protestantism, then, that is, essentially and *par excellence*, the type of the Church of Self-government, in which each, instead of obeying the Lord, obeys himself, his own reason, his own conscience, his own irresponsible fantasies; this must surely be the Church that has taught the world the disruptive principle of man as his own sovereign. The tale of Protestantism, just as the tale of the modern age, must then be just the sad story of a subjectivism that is no longer able to recognize any authority beyond the individual. Such a hypothesis, which puts Protestantism and modernity in the same camp, and sees both as part of one single bankrupt cycle, lies thus at the opposite pole to the often criticized sociological analysis of Troeltsch, according to which Protestantism belongs still to the sphere of medieval churchly civilization.[1]

---

[1] E. Troeltsch, *Die Bedeutung des Protestantismus für die Entstehung der modernen Welt*, Munich–Berlin 1906. Cf. H. O. Woelber, *Dogma und Ethos—Christentum und Humanismus von Ritschl bis Troeltsch*, Gütersloh 1950.

Such an interpretation is based on a faulty historical understanding of the sixteenth-century Reformation. This declared:

> This is why our theology is sure. Because it takes us from ourselves, and sets us outside ourselves, so that we struggle no more with our own strength, our own conscience, sense, person or resources, but we fight in the strength of that which is outside ourselves, i.e., by the promise and truth of God which cannot fail.[1]

Such an interpretation is however better founded with regard to later Protestantism, in which some of the ideas that had been so sharply contested by the sixteenth-century Reformation succeeded in gaining a foothold, and indeed in being accepted with cordiality and enthusiasm. From the eighteenth century onwards rationalistic theories from the anti-trinitarians, and mystical and spiritualistic ones from the sectaries came to overlay and entwine themselves with Reformation ideas, and in some cases completely to supplant them. Until the reaction under Barth, and the biblical and ecumenical revival, for two centuries Protestantism was as much travestied in its own eyes as in those of Catholicism. Its motifs became confused with the anthropological and the sociological interests of the Age of Illuminism, so that the external observer saw it as tied too closely to the vicissitudes of laicism in the fields of culture, ethics and education, and to the ascendancy of the bourgeoisie in that of sociology. Of the two poles which Luther had pointed out as the lode-stars of faith, 'free from all in God, servant of all in one's neighbour',[2] in the end only the first was retained and even here the pivot was shifted from God to the religious man. Once the laicism of Illuminism had fallen into difficulties and its notions of subjectivism and liberty been discredited before the violent inrush of the sociological and economic forces of the Industrial Revolution, the Catholic observer might well consider that the cause of Protestantism was now lost, and could now offer only fragmentary truths, incapable of playing any further part in history.

Post-Reformation Protestantism certainly cannot avoid its share of responsibility for the fact that so far no Christian formulae have

---

[1] 'Haec est ratio, cur nostra Theologia certa sit: Quia rapit nos a nobis et ponit nos extra nos, ut non nitamur viribus, conscientia, sensu, persona, operibus nostris, sed eo nitamur, quod est extra nos, Hoc est promissione et veritate Dei, quae fallere non potest', *In epistolam S. Pauli ad Galatas Commentarius ex praelectione D. Martini Lutheri collectus* [1531] 1535 : *WA* XL/1, p. 589.

[2] *Mar. Lutheri Tractatus de Libertate Christiana*—1520, in: *WA* VII, p. 49: 'Christianus homo omnium dominus est liberrimus, nulli subiectus. Christianus homo omnium servus est officiosissimus, omnibus subiectus.'

been found for social problems, and that the solutions offered are but a counterfeit of the Christian love of one's neighbour. Hence that Reformation faith which 'sets us outside ourselves' was reduced to 'a psychological process', that gave place slowly to 'a cult of the believer', which has been one of the factors that have produced the bourgeois myth of personality. Hence today we find ourselves watching helplessly the reduction to slavery 'of the free personality, before the demoniac powers of technical perfection',[1] and we no longer know the power of the gospel to release men from the dictatorship of the world and of things, from earthly superindividual forces. In this sense Paul Tillich has been able to speak most appositely of the end of the Protestant era, tracing a cycle of sociological law that conditions civilization, and calling Protestantism at this moment of history to the necessity of discovering its real self.[2]

In the same way post-Reformation Protestantism, and especially later Protestantism in certain sectors shares the responsibility for this present grandiose gesture on the part of Catholicism. For, here too, it has failed for almost two centuries to maintain the Christian dialogue validly and effectively. Pietism and Revivalism have led it to mirror a sentimental and introvert Christianity, incapable of posing authoritatively the question of God. What nourishes the Catholic's illusory hopes of success in his effort to regain his ascendancy is the degree to which Protestantism has become a Church void of authority, i.e., has ceased to be itself, and has abdicated from its true function[3], by yielding to the pressure of eighteenth- and nineteenth-century ideas that brought with them the ruination and isolation of man in the mass age, confounding the means with the ends of life.

Characteristically, a Catholic writer sees Protestant ecumenism as 'an undoubted retraction of the sixteenth century' even if not openly acknowledged.[4] Ecumenism is not this at all, there is no need to stress the point. Yet at the level of the local churches one finds relics of a sentimental, non-dogmatic ecumenicity, which lends favour to the suggestion.

But the fact remains that Catholicism is making this bid today,

---

[1] W. Dantine, *op. cit.*, pp. 29f.

[2] P. Tillich, *The Protestant Era*, Chicago 1948. Cf. H. H. Walz, *Das protestantische Wagnis*, Stuttgart 1958; R. Prenter, *Protestantismen i vor tid*, Copenhagen (Ger. trs. *Der Protestantismus in unsere Zeit*, Stuttgart 1959).

[3] This is the title of a book which however starts from different premisses, and somewhat unilateral ones: F. Hoffet, *Politique romaine et démission des protestants*, Paris 1962.

[4] L. Cristiani, art. 'Protestantesimo', in: *Enciclopedia Cattolica* X (1953), col. 176.

and not simply as a piece of improvization. Against yesterday's individualized subjectivism, and against tomorrow's social schematization, it sets its own project of a civilization clerically directed. It intends to operate indirectly through lay media, and having experimented in the post-war Europe of today, to extend the attempt on a universal scale. Catholicism does not appreciate what great capacities for recovery are latent in Protestantism through its contact with the gospel, and the genius, native to it, and rooted in its anti-institutionalism, of inventing new ways and patterns for faith to work on history, provided it obeys the will of God for the hour and lives to serve those men, who in their infinite distress are alike without the bread of wheat and the bread of God. These latent capacities have now been at work and growing for at least half a century; if they have not perhaps made themselves yet felt in all sectors, it is because every movement of renewal is balked by human inertia and listlessness. Catholicism is incapable of realizing that Protestantism has its internal sources of inspiration; it tends to confuse Luther with Lessing and Calvin with Rousseau; it is confident it can replace it in guiding civilization, and regain control of the reins even after Kant and Marx; it dreams of putting out a modern revised edition of society shaped by clerics. One is driven to think of the pages of a romantic German Catholic, Friedrich von Hardenberg, known under the pseudonym of Novalis. First he conjures up 'the splendours of the times' when 'Europe was a Christian land', then he laments the decline from that 'universal Christian community', for which the Reformation was responsible, and finally he prophesies:

> From the holy bosom of a worthy council of Europe, Christianity will rise again, and success will crown our efforts to revive religion following a universal divine plan.[1]

Perhaps sufficient attention has not been given on the Protestant side to a succession of pontifical utterances, whose significance indeed can only now be seen in true proportion. In the Encyclical *'Annum Sacrum'* of 25th May, 1899, whose purpose was to consecrate men to the 'Heart' of Jesus, Leo XIII laid it down that the *imperium* of Christ is not exercised only over the *gentes catholici nominis*, but that the *universitas generis humani* is set under the *potestate Christi*.[2] In the Encyclical *'E supremi Apostolatus'* of 4th October, 1903 Pius X gave as the formula for the programme of his pontificate:

---

[1] F. Novalis, *Die Christenheit oder Europa*, 1799.
[2] Quoted from Denzinger, 2196.

Instaurare omnia in Christo. The same line was that followed by Pius XI in the Encyclical '*Quas primas*', of 11th December, 1925, in instituting the feast of Christ the King,[1] and so too was that of successive Pontiffs.

Now in Catholic parlance, the phrase

instaurare omnia in Christo (Eph. 1. 10)

means categorically

instaurare omnia in Papa, in Ecclesia

and so Pius XI explains in so many words in his Encyclical. Setting the human race under the sceptre of Christ is at bottom simply recalling them to obedience towards the Church of Rome.[2] Everything we have stressed in this study provides documentation that the Catholic outlook cannot be otherwise.

Even earlier, in his Encyclical '*Au milieu*' of 1892, addressed to France on the subject of forms of government, Leo XIII had defended the Church of Rome against the charge that its action had a political slant, by saying that the same accusation had been brought against Jesus, and had been the pseudo-judicial grounds of his condemnation—'we have established that his fellow said he was Christ a King' (Luke 23.2). As a matter of psychology and intention, perhaps the accusation might prove unjustified, but from the point of view of dogma, is it not inevitable? Does the dogmatic conception of Christ present as a King in his body in history, which is the Church, admit of other procedure? Does it, in other words, allow us to think of Christ's kingdom as one that does not conform to the laws of this world (John 18.36), and is exempt from the privileges of those in authority? And what are we to make of this conception, first in the light of the gospel, and then in the light of this our present age? For this age has won its franchise from the pretences and complexes of the past, and has set its feet decisively on its own independent path of development. Now that civilization is passing thus sharply from a state of subjection to one of responsibility, the sole course open to the Christian Church is to realise that she needs lose none of her universality, and that even the loss of privileges, political and capitalistic, accepted as inevitable in a society that has ceased to

---

[1] *Ibid.*, 2194f.

[2] Cf. A. de Quervain, *Kirche, Volk, Staat* (*Ethik* II/1), Zollikon–Zürich 1945, pp. 218f.; H. Hermelink, *op. cit.*, pp. 5f.; K. G. Steck, *Politischer Katholizismus als theologisches Problem*, Munich 1951, pp. 18f., 34f.

be that of Constantine, can prove to be a gain for the gospel, if it initiates a process of purification and a return to its original functions of service and testimony.[1] Should not the Christian Churches come together again in a free encounter, acknowledge that in seeking to gain the world they have lost it, abandon the old path of lording it over the charge entrusted to them (II Cor. 1.24; I Peter 5.3), and together trace out the new road of service in obedience to him whom they confess as Lord, and who himself took even the 'form of a servant' (Phil. 2.7)? As Calvin said to Cardinal Sadoleto, in the guise of a prayer of confession to the Lord of the Church:

> Thou knowest, O Lord, and the thing itself bears witness before men, how I have sought no other thing except that by thy word all controversy be resolved, to the end that both parties might in a conjunction of spirit tend to the enlargement and stablishing of thy Kingdom.[2]

* * *

We have reviewed the idea of Christ as present in his Church in the qualities of Prophet, Priest and King. All Catholicism is embraced in that idea. It portrayed itself at the universal Exhibition at Brussels under this very symbol—an altar of bare stone, a chair of red damask, a balustrade. Though some process of internal evolution, or some pressure of external events, were to strip Catholicism of all else, its essence would still remain in this triple symbol.[3]

---

[1] Cf. studies by J. L. Hromadka, 'Was heist Herrschaft Christi heute?', and E. Wolf, 'Was heisst "Königsherrschaft Christi" heute?', contained in the collection *Unter der Herrschaft Christi*, Munich 1961, pp. 56f., 67f.

[2] 'Tu sais bien, Seigneur, et la chose même le témoigne envers les hommes, comme je n'ai cherché autre chose, sinon que par ta parole toute controversie fut apaisée: afin que par une conjonction d'esprit, toutes les deux parties tendissent à l'amplification et établissement de ton Royaume', J. Calvin, *op. cit.*, p. 85.

[3] I am indebted to Pastor Giorgio Tourn for observing and indicating this.

Conclusion

IT MAY be useful to end this work with a brief systematic critique of the conception of the Church as '*alter Christus*' or '*totus Christus*'.

With a confident insistency Catholic theologians have accused Protestantism of lacking a true sense of the Incarnation, of having a truncated and stunted Christology,[1] and of limiting its presentation to the Jesus of history with his three-year Palestinian ministry, the Christ of apostolic preaching, and the Christ of the experience of believers, just because it cannot bring itself to conceive of Christ incarnate in history today, which is the Church.

The criticism that Protestantism has thus a defective sense of mediation is pushed in two different directions, according to the tendencies of the authors. Some state that Protestantism is pre-Christian, in that it has not yet arrived at Christ; others that it is post-Christian in that it has now gone beyond him. In neither case is its Christology considered Christian in the full and substantial use of the term.

The first school decries the presence in Protestant ecclesiology of a prophetic 'logic' and the corresponding absence of an apostolic 'logic'. Father Congar, for example, writes:

> I maintain that Protestants have given Christianity, and especially the Church, a basic function which is the prophetic one of announcement and expectancy, and as such an Old Testament one. They have no idea of the conditions proper to the Church's new dispensation. In a phrase which expresses at once the greatness and the error of their position, they are still with John the Baptist.[2]

For its part the Catholic concept has a full sense of *Verbum caro factum est* (John 1.14) as a lasting reality, already definitely involved in history, from which the gates of Hell, in the form of 'God's enemies' of yesterday, today and tomorrow cannot eradicate it.

[1] 'Eine verkürzte Christologie': T. Sartory, O.S.B., *Die oecumenische Bewegung und die Einheit der Kirche—Ein Beitrag im Dienste einer oecumenischen Ekklesiologie*, Meitingen bei Augsburg 1955.
[2] Y. M. J. Congar, O.P., *Vraie at fausse réforme*, p. 425.

All can be put thus: Salvation is not finished—otherwise there would no longer be any Church as an institution—but *the cause of Salvation* has taken place, and *in such a way as to dwell in bodily form in the world*. This is the situation of the Church—between the Synagogue and the Kingdom, between the Synagogue, which was all announcement and expectancy, with simply the slightest and most transient foreshadowings of reality, and the Kingdom, which shall be the full reality and the perfect gift. The Church is that moment in God's work when reality is not yet fully given us to enjoy, but when the means of obtaining it are present, given and operative corporally in our midst.[1]

The transcendent reality, in short, becomes 'immanent and given in the Church'.[2]

The criticisms of the second school, though they take two varying lines, amount to the same. One of these, e.g., that of Schlier, regards Protestantism as a Church which

has detached itself, both in theory and in practice, from the present state of the Church, from its provisional situation in space and time, from its subsequent development, and from its bodily condition.[3]

In this Church, eschatology has been domesticated, the Kingdom of God is brought into history, so setting up a regime of immediate contact with the divine. Once more here the fundamental principle of the Reformation, the mediation of the Word, is confused with the mystic inner light of the Enthusiasts, or the rationalistic criterion of the free examination of Scripture as, e.g., we find in the thought of Sebastian Castellion.[4]

The other variant could be put like this. In Protestantism the fact of Christ is regarded rather as a kind of theophany, a fugitive apparition of deity, a meteor that appears briefly in the firmament of history, and at once disappears, leaving humanity without any guide to its discussions, in the darkness, upon an earth deserted again by its God after the Ascension, its religion a disincarnate spiritualism, simply a Christianity of memory, of nostalgia for a God who appeared and then disappeared,[5] a belief not in the presence of a God, but in his absence.

Let there however be not just Word, not just announcement, but also let it be reality that is given; let us use a 'logic' that is no more

---

[1] *Op. cit.*, pp. 468f.; italics in the text.   [2] *Op. cit.*, p. 502.
[3] H. Schlier, *Die Zeit der Kirche*, p. 148.
[4] S. Castellion, 'De arte dubitandi et confidendi', in *Per la storia degli eretici italiani del secolo XVI in Europa*, compiled by D. Cantimori and E. Feist, Rome 1937.
[5] C. Journet, *Primauté de Pierre dans la perspective protestante et dans la perspective catholique*, Paris 1953, pp. 22, 25, 48.

pre-, or post-, but fully Christian;[1] let Incarnation be set beside
Transcendence; let there be not an antithetical, but a co-ordinating
relation between them;[2] or even more exactly, let but Yahweh's
transcendent holiness, the Lord's incomparable glory, 'enter into
history, and make there itself a body',[3] so establishing '*a continuous
presence of eternity in time*', and 'ensuring Christ's uninterrupted
presence in space and time'; and there we have the 'mystery of
Catholicity'.[4] Then there is no question of any break, there is
continuity between Christ and the Church.

Enough evidence has been gathered in this study to establish that
in Catholic ecclesiology, the Church is predominantly, if not almost
exclusively, considered in connection with Christology. This would
be a sound principle were it not applied so unilaterally. We submit
that if it be true that ecclesiology cannot be treated apart from
Christology, then this treatment must be set in a trinitarian scheme,
which takes account of all the elements of the gospel. Not even in
the field of ecclesiology may one lose sight of, or even sit lightly to,
the recognition that the God of the Church and of the Christian faith
is and remains the God of the Trinity, Father, Son and Holy Spirit.
If ecclesiology is to be treated adequately, one must constantly bear
in mind the interplay of relationships between the revelation and
work of the Trinitarian God and the reality of the Church. There
are specific relationships between the doctrine of God the Father and
the doctrine of the Church, between the doctrine of Christ and that
of the Church, between that of the Holy Spirit and that of the Church.
These are the relationships that have been overlooked or considered
in a partial spirit in Christian conceptions of the Church and so have
led to the present division in Christianity, and the critical situation
in which it finds itself in the world.

To assert in the ecclesiological field that the God of the Church is
and remains God the Father, means to speak of God as he who in
his self-giving does not cease to be himself, does not cease to be
God; and in his self-giving he does not become an object given
that men may dispose of, he remains Lord of his own self-giving,
free even to take himself back after he has been given; even in the
act of giving himself, and precisely in that act, he does not lose

[1] Y. M. J. Congar, O.P., *op. cit.*, pp. 407, 425, 471.
[2] G. Thils, *Transcendance ou Incarnation? Essai sur la conception du Christianisme*,
Louvain 1950.
[3] Y. M. J. Congar, O.P., *op. cit.*, p. 458.
[4] C. Journet, *op. cit.*, p. 22; *L'Eglise du Verbe Incarné*, II, p. 92.

M

himself, nor dissipate his quality of being God the Lord, nor allow his divine reality to be made mundane. To speak of God the Father is to speak of the God who, though he reveals himself, uses a revelation which does not imply a refusal to be hidden any more; who, though he manifests his glory, does not yield it to another; who, though he attends to the expression and the transmission of his glory through instruments that men may understand, keeps his word from ever becoming a word of men, or from draining away into a formal dogmatic system and into a doctrine of clerics, and can make it unintelligible in the very moment of speaking, or fall silent after he has spoken. To speak of God the Father means to speak of the holy God who, though he comes to dwell in the midst of sinners, does not forget his holiness; who, though he works through the agency of men, does not permit his practice to be confused with an ecclesiastical practice which claims sacred privileges for itself; who, though he becomes history in the midst of history, and in the midst of the individual moments of men's histories, does not suppress his eternity; who, though he communicate himself, so does it as never to annul his mystery; who, though he makes himself weak, never loses his strength; though he humbles himself, he never abdicates from being the Most High; though he takes on the form of an obedient servant, he does not give up his sovereignity, nor suspend his constant command.

All this is so much tautology to tease out all the packed content of our original phrase by way of explaining it: the God of the Church is and remains God the Father, Yahweh; that is, he never ceases to be God the Lord, beside whom there is no other. Were it not so, the doctrine of the Church could never be related to that of the Trinity, and specifically in our instance, with theology, i.e., with the doctrine of God, since the doctrine of God the Father would then be merged in that of God the Son, and we should be faced with a patripassionist theology, with a new modalism, however modern the terms in which it were put. Neglect or suppression—frequent as it is in ecclesiological exposition—of the theological connection between the doctrine of the Church and that of God, and the consequent, almost constant and exclusive, consideration only of the doctrine of Christ and/or that of the Holy Spirit, is a grave defect in ecclesiology, a defect not always noticed, but nevertheless capable of inflicting serious damage on a proper understanding of the doctrine of the Church.

Every ecclesiology based on the assumption that the Church has been once and for all given by God to man, and which therefore takes account only of the Christological element, presupposes a crypto-patripassionism, i.e., a doctrine of God the Son which more or less deliberately overlooks the doctrine of God the Father and centres its attention exclusively on the Incarnation. An ecclesiology based so onesidedly on Christology gives rise to the institutional type of Church, in which the emphasis comes to be set on the Church's constitution by the Jesus of history and to a disproportionate stress on the element of succession as the ground of the divine right of hierarchy and teaching, of priesthood and sacrament. Then the Church conceives of herself as an extension of the Incarnation and elevates herself into an institution where truth is deposited, outside of which there is no salvation. She loses her sense of reference to God, the Lord of election, who remains sovereign master of his liberty. Such a Church thinks the dialectic of revelation has come to an end in her; to all intents, she regards the series of the successive times of God's work as at an end; hence in speaking of the time to come, she asserts her jurisdiction over even it, because her self-regarding logic, the logic of a once for all time giveness, includes the *eschaton* inside the scope of her ecclesiastical laws. If ecclesiology holds to a sense of the horizontal and the historical, and lets go of the sense of the vertical and the eternal, the God of the Church is in danger of being another God, and no more the God of Revelation, the God of the Trinity.

There may be still another ecclesiology of giveness, different and seemingly antithetical. It relates not to the Christological giveness, not to the gift of God made man, but to the gift of the Holy Spirit to man. In such an ecclesiology, relating too exclusively to the Holy Spirit, it is the charismatic elements that are overstressed. Faith appears in the unilateral shape of personal acquisition and the element of interior conviction develops in the direction that ultimately makes it autonomous and arbitrary, without contact with the objective elements on which conviction itself is based. Living on itself, for both individual or group, the result is an internalized experience, which in the last analysis means that what is given is immediacy. A Church without the Spirit is inconceivable, but a Church with only the Spirit is a Church of sectaries, who in a state of exaltation, style themselves as prophets, and in the more normal bourgeois life, follow the dictates of their own religious psychological state, high or low as its tone may be, having lost sight of God, the Lord of election. Instead of a process in which *Deus pro nobis* is ecclesiasticized, we find one wherein *Deus in nobis* is individually internalized. And though this kind of ecclesiology refuses to imprison God in the institution of *Deus pro nobis*, that is, it does not transform him into a heritage of doctrine, sacrament and jurisdiction, which the Church administers, it does however opt for a spiritualistic acquisition of *Deus in nobis*, i.e., it seeks to transform him into an object it can manipulate subjectively. If the one ecclesiology was maximal, this is minimal and in the last analysis leads to the dissolution of all ecclesiology. In place of the Church as *Domina et Magistra*, we find Man *dominus et magister*. In each case, we have a Church which lives by its own authority, be that called the sacred *magisterium* of its hierarchy, or the private judgment of the individual members: it has lost its sense of relating to the God of election, i.e., it has lost its sense of authority, and consequently, of obedience. The God followed by such a Church is no more the God to whom witness is borne by Revelation in its entirety. Despite all the worship, all the prayers, all the activities it offers collectively, and all the spirituality of its individual members, the relationship between ecclesiology and theology is broken, i.e., the relation between the Church and its Lord—the Lord that has called and still calls the Church into being as a Church. The loss of the sense of contact with the Lord God, who in coming to man and coming in man does not cease to be God, works the overthrow not only of ecclesiology, but of the doctrine of the Holy Spirit itself, since that which should be set down to the work of the Holy Spirit is set down to man's reason and man's spirit, to moral conscience and religious feeling. God the Father is lost in God the Spirit, in *Deus in nobis*, and so the God in us ceases to be God. If the doctrine of the Church is predominantly or exclusively set forth in terms of the doctrine of the Holy Spirit alone, it clearly implies a Joachimite doctrine of the Church as representing the advent of the last age, the age of the Holy Spirit, wherein the dispensation of faith is replaced by that of vision and immediate perception, and to which the dispensation of the Father and of the Son are merely preparatory stages and now obsolete. This results in the degrading of Yahweh, the God who gives and does not cease to be God even in the very act of coming to us and coming in us; who does not cease to be the one who gives even in the act of becoming the gift that is given, and the gift of the capacity to receive what is given.

*   *   *

From all of this emerges the realization how partial are the ecclesiologies of Christendom, and how much their elements are in need of reconstruction. If one might adapt the title of a famous work,[1] and call the ecclesiologies of today ecclesiologies in becoming, we would recognize in this their distress, but no less their hope. Such a hope depends for its realization upon a knowledge of the basis of division. It is a commonplace today to hear said, in every corner of the world, that what unites Christians is greater than what divides them, and the inference is that on both sides of the barrier Christians should be wise enough to let the secondary go, and hold fast to the essential. We do not think this is quite true. Against the popular judgment, we affirm that we are divided in essential, not in secondary, matters. Were we divided in non-essentials only, it would be an intolerable sin to persevere in division. But the non-essentials in our division are the reflex action that follows by consequence from the essentials. And the essential, where on all depends, is the *question of God*. On this question turns the truth or falsehood of the Church, and the truth or falsehood of its unity. The norm for examining and solving the problem of right faith in God, and of the true Church and true unity, turns on the problem of the criterion of truth, i.e., of the authority by which the Church must be ruled and guided. For four centuries the discussion has raged; it rages still today in a form even more complex than in the sixteenth century,[2] for this question, and the cognate doctrine of the Holy Spirit who interprets the Word and applies it contemporaneously, form the fundamental problem of dogma, on which all others must attend. The Church today must give all her attention to it, if she wishes to arrive at a deep and lucid understanding of our faith in its ecumenical situation, for she must know that behind the problem of the canon of truth, there is (still once more), the problem of God, the God who cannot be objectified either in Church or in Book.[3]

[1] M. D. Koster, *Ekklesiologie im Werden*, Paderborn 1940.

[2] In addition to the studies indicated in note 1, p. 100, there is a clear exposition of the subject to be found in F. W. Kantzenbach, *Evangelium und Dogma—Die Bewältigung des theologischen Problems der Dogmengeschichte im Protestantismus*, Stuttgart 1959, pp. 251–311.

[3] Cf. E. Käsemann, 'Zum Thema der Nichtobjektivierbarkeit', *Evangelische Theologie* 10 (1953), pp. 455f., now in *Exegetische Versuche und Besinnungen*, I, pp. 214, 221, 231f.

But on the other hand, the fact that behind our divisions lies God's very mystery, removes from them something of their intransigency. Many voices in recent years have lamented the polemical tones of both Catholicism and Protestant theology, and called on both sides to change their outlook and deal more with those themes and aspects of the Christian message that are positive. There are good reasons for the observation, but it must include this consideration: Is there not something providential in such a mutual relationship? What would happen to Protestantism the day it sank to the level of living only for itself, and washing its hands of all responsibility for Catholicism? And what would happen to Catholicism the day on which it also, unchanged, sank to an even deeper self-preoccupation than it has today, and rid itself of the thorn in the flesh (which is what Protestantism has been for four and a half centuries, not only in its existence, but in the criticism it provoked)? There is fecundity in this mutual awareness, this reciprocal fetter, between Protestantism and Catholicism. They cannot, and they must not, free themselves from it. Rather it is to be pondered over in constant prayer, and seen in the light of God's own plans of action. We may ignore these, but God continues to work them out by means of us, and perhaps also by means of those whom we think of as without God, and he works with all the steadfastness of a fidelity that overrides all the inconstancy and infidelity of his Church in the world.

INDEX

INDEX